SPIRITS AND DEMONS
AT WORK:

Alcohol and Other Drugs on the Job

HARRISON M. TRICE AND PAUL M. ROMAN

ILR Paperback No. 11   January 1972

NEW YORK STATE SCHOOL OF INDUSTRIAL
AND LABOR RELATIONS, *A Statutory College*
of the State University, CORNELL UNIVERSITY

Price: $5.00

ORDER FROM

Publications Division

New York State School of Industrial and Labor Relations

Cornell University, Ithaca 14850

Second Printing, July 1973

Library of Congress Catalog Card Number: 72-619517

ISBN 0-87546-034-8

PRINTED IN THE UNITED STATES OF AMERICA

BY THE HOFFMAN PRINTING COMPANY

Contents

To Mr. R. Brinkley Smithers
and the Christopher D. Smithers Foundation
for support and encouragement

Preface

THE published literature on drug abuse in the United States is growing at a rapid rate, with new research and theories appearing in the mass media and professional publications almost daily. The excitement over the various issues involved is without doubt a new bandwagon, attracting increasing numbers of behavioral scientists, members of the medical profession, and a vast array of paraprofessionals eager to become involved in "the action."

Staff and line personnel in work organizations, as well as behavioral scientists not directly involved in drug-oriented research, may find it difficult to sift out the relevant facts from the mass of published materials. Our intention in preparing this volume has been to provide a guide through part of this literature for both work-organization personnel and our behavioral science colleagues.

This book is based mainly on two sources of data: research studies from scholarly journals and monographs which have gone through the "referee" process of screening before publication and our own research studies which have focused on alcohol abuse and work life. While both sets of data and ideas are of considerable academic interest in the sociology of deviance, we have attempted here to place them in practical focus. Thus, while much more research is needed before we can draw unequivocal conclusions, we have offered a program of action for work organizations for the management of alcohol and drug abuse.

As many have commented, the current concerns over illegal drugs have taken needed attention away from the drug most prevalently used in American society, alcohol. We have attempted to keep alcohol our primary focus in this volume, for the abuse of this drug clearly is America's major drug problem.

Much of the material presented here has been developed through the Alcoholism and Occupational Health Program at Cornell University, directed by Professor Trice. The research activities of this program would not have been possible without the ongoing, long-term support and interest of the Christopher D. Smithers Foundation and its president, Mr. R. Brinkley Smithers. Mr. Smithers' concern with alcohol problems

PREFACE

in the work place has provided us with the support, encouragement, and freedom to explore many crucial dimensions of these issues, and it is to him and the Smithers Foundation that this volume is dedicated.

Our work has been additionally facilitated by the Research Division of the New York State School of Industrial and Labor Relations. Acknowledgement is due to its former director Professor Leonard P. Adams and to its current director Professor Donald Cullen. Persons whose skills aided several of the projects include Professors James Belasco and George Ritzer and Mrs. Norma Landen.

We are also grateful to several colleagues who gave generously of their time in critically reviewing the manuscript: Professor Alfred Lindesmith, Indiana University; Professor Harold Mulford, University of Iowa; Dr. Alan A. McLean, Cornell Medical College; and Professors William Wasmuth and Emil Mesics of Cornell University. Encouragement and editorial advice were provided by Professor Wayne Hodges, Mrs. Mary Jo Powell, and Miss Charlotte Gold of the ILR School's Publications Division. Diligent typing and retyping were competently and patiently carried out by Mrs. Ruth Hanville and Mrs. Mary Turner.

A final and perhaps unorthodox acknowledgement is made by the co-authors to each other. The joint efforts of writing, rewriting, editing, and de-editing, carried out over a long distance, have been taxing to our working relationships at times, but we have emerged from the task truly amazed that the results are inseparably the product of a team.

H. M. T.
P. M. R.

Ithaca, N. Y. and New Orleans, La.
January 1972

Introduction

THE use of mood-altering drugs, from alcohol to heroin, has become a major concern to Americans. Discussions of many aspects of the topic pervade both the mass media and scientific and professional publications. Issues of concern are numerous and vary across different social groups: Many youths are concerned with the legalization of marihuana, while physicians are concerned with the short- and long-term effects of drug use on physical and mental health. Social scientists are concerned with the distribution of legal and illegal drug use in the population and with the modes by which social factors may encourage or discourage the use and abuse of drugs; law enforcement agencies, with effective programs to control both drug traffic and drug abuse. Leaders of black and other minority communities are concerned with the damaging effects of drug use and the loss of human resources in subcultures attempting to improve their socio-economic level of living. Finally, social philosophers are concerned with the reasons for, and the ultimate consequences of, a society's obsession with drugs. Looking only at the range and depth of these concerns, we can see that America has a drug problem.

In this book we focus upon one segment of this spectrum of concerns, the relation between the use and abuse of mood-altering substances and the performance of work roles. This topic has been relatively neglected in the numerous controversies surrounding alcohol and other drugs. This relative neglect, however, should not belie the importance of the topic. Obviously, the successful functioning of a society's economic sector is crucial to the overall stability of that society. Furthermore, work constitutes the most central and crucial role of most adult American males and, to an increasing extent, adult American females. Disruption of work-role performance can thus have significant consequences for both overall societal functioning and individual stability.

We have not intended simply to describe the adverse consequences of alcohol and drug abuse for individuals and work organizations. On the positive side, it appears that the very nature of work roles and work organizations provides opportunities for the prevention of the long-term consequences of alcohol and drug abuse in a large segment of the population. We do not contend that the solution of America's drug problem lies in the work world, but rather that the work place may provide a framework for prevention without opening lengthy and painful debates about the morality or appropriateness of drug use.

We will first outline the nature of the problem, bringing to bear as many facts as possible and then, using these facts, we will evaluate the potential effectiveness of various strategies of intervention. This book can be divided into three parts. General background information is provided in the first part, Chapters One, Two, and Three. In Chapter One we attempt to outline in some detail the social aspects of alcohol use and abuse, the extent of these problems in American society, and some of the reasons why work organizations should be concerned with control and intervention. In Chapters Two and Three, a similar overview is provided for the illegal and legal drugs that are topics of social concern. Here we attempt to separate and highlight the facts, contrasting them to hysterical concerns that the activities of work organizations will soon be grossly altered by the impact of drug abuse.

In the second part of the book we turn to more specific bases for work world concern. Chapter Four focuses upon risk factors, the characteristics of job roles which may make alcohol or drug abuse particularly attractive to employees and which provide them with opportunities for such abuse to go unnoticed. In Chapter Five, our focus is upon the impact of alcohol and drug abuse on specific job behaviors, examining the relationship between such deviance and turnover, absenteeism, and accidents. Chapter Six describes typical reactions to alcohol abuse in work organizations and outlines basic barriers to intervention that are built into the supervisor's role as well as into the supervisor-subordinate relationship.

The third part of the book is concerned with the bases for policy-program development. In Chapter Seven we outline the fundamentals of the intervention strategy of constructive confrontation. Given the variability of local situations, we do not attempt to spell out a policy program feasible for all organizations. Instead we outline barriers to program implementation that guide policy formation in adjusting to the characteristics of specific organizations. The remaining chapters in the book explore two general considerations crucial to policy development. Chapter Eight focuses upon the importance of union-management cooperation in policy program development and implementation. Here we describe research on alternative cooperative patterns. In Chapter Nine, we explore various treatment resources that may be used to manage alcohol and drug abusers whose use patterns have exceeded their personal control.

To the extent possible, the arguments presented in this book are based upon data gathered by objective researchers. We feel that the facts deserve a much better hearing than they have received to date. As we outline, fears about drug abuse that are encouraged by the "problem industry" and the mass media may lead to programs and actions in work organizations that are far more disruptive and costly than the actual deviant patterns themselves. While we rely heavily upon facts, we recognize that much remains unknown. We hope that the orientation offered here will play some small part in correcting these shortcomings.

I

Drinking, Deviant Drinking, and Work

ADULT alcohol use is part and parcel of American life. Alcohol is best described as ubiquitous in contemporary America; its use can be observed at practically any location at nearly any time. Americans use alcohol to be sociable, Americans use alcohol on occasions of rejoicing, and, although reluctant to admit it, Americans use alcohol as a means of reducing anxieties and avoiding depression.

With enormous public attention currently focused on illegal drugs, the present costs and potential dangers of alcohol abuse are being overlooked and even neglected. Fear and concern over illegal drugs may make alcohol abuse appear to be a "secondary" problem, but alcohol is a drug, albeit a legal one. Unlike many of the drugs currently holding the limelight in the mass media, alcohol can lead to both physical and psychological dependency. Excessive drinking can destroy role performances and permanently impair physical and psychological functioning. But most significant is the fact that alcohol is by far the most widely used mood-altering drug in American society today.

These statements are not puritanical or prohibitionist in intent. As outlined later in this chapter, alcohol does serve positive functions for both individuals and society. There is no question of the positive value of relaxation in a world that seems increasingly fraught with tensions and frustrations. Alcohol's effects may hold advantages over other drugs: as one set of authors surmised, alcohol would probably be regarded as "the miracle drug" if it were discovered today (MacAndrew and Garfinkel, 1962).

The purpose of this chapter is to examine alcohol use in American society and spell out the relevance of alcohol problems for work organizations. We first examine the basic reason why employers should be concerned with alcohol abuse among their employees: it is a costly problem. We then turn to major barriers in the understanding of alcohol problems: the pervasive popular image of the deviant drinker as a Skid Row bum and the distorted views of alcohol problems often presented by the "alcoholism industry." This discussion is followed by a review of working concepts of drinking, deviant drinking, and alcohol addiction and a brief survey of contemporary American drinking patterns. Finally, we briefly review the socio-psychological factors related to the development of problem drinking.

THE COSTS OF DEVIANT DRINKING TO THE EMPLOYER

Most informed estimates of the extent of alcohol problems in work organizations indicate that between 3 and 4 percent of an average work force will be deviant drinkers at any one time. This figure might seem minute, and a problem of such low prevalence might not appear worthy of a management's attention. When the potential impact of any one deviant drinker is considered, however, the relevance of the problem for organizational functioning mounts rapidly. In other words, the disruptive consequences of deviant drinking may far exceed the cost entailed if 4 percent of the work force were absent or simply sat at their jobs and did practically nothing. The very essence of a work organization is the interdependence of job performances. Deviance by one employee may "reverberate" beyond his work station or desk, sometimes disrupting an entire organization. Thus the prevalence figures alone do not tell the full story.

The work-based costs of problem drinking are of three types: (1) those stemming directly from the employee's work behavior; (2) the impact of the deviant drinker on other employees; and (3) the costs of "doing something" about the deviant drinker once the limits of tolerance are reached.

In Chapter Five we review in depth the patterns of work-related behaviors of deviant drinkers. The two most costly behaviors are absenteeism and performance inefficiency. The problem drinker's absenteeism is disruptive primarily because it is erratic. The occasions of his absenteeism simply cannot be predicted. This absenteeism may greatly disrupt the assigned activities of work groups, particularly where jobs are closely interdependent and a high degree of internal coordination is necessary. Probably a more significant problem is partial absenteeism. This occurs when an employee erratically leaves his work post to obtain a drink, to attempt recovery from the effects of his drinking, or simply to cover up the signs of intoxication and hangover. This obviously disrupts work performance. A third type of absenteeism, which applies mainly to white-collar employees, is "on-the-job" absenteeism. On-the-job absenteeism occurs when the worker appears at the job but, due to drinking or hangover, is in such poor condition he is unable to perform his assigned tasks. On-the-job absenteeism is usually coupled with partial absenteeism.

Alcohol abuse is clearly disruptive to job efficiency. Sometimes the drinking worker is simply unable to carry out his assigned tasks. Perhaps more costly is "covered-up" inefficiency which can lead to production errors and a high degree of waste among blue-collar workers. This waste parallels inefficient decision making among drinking white-collar employees. Here also the cost may be indirect and not evident until "the damage is done." Poor decision making or the failure to make needed decisions is perhaps the most marked cost of white-collar drinking, potentially disrupting large segments of an organization's activities.

The deviant drinker may lower the morale of his co-workers. Absenteeism and the consequent disruption in work flow create inconveniences and even hardships for those who must take up the slack. A sense of "distributive injustice" may come to pervade his fellow workers, i.e. the deviant drinker is receiving the same rewards they are, but he is doing only a small part of his assigned tasks. Consequently, they may adjust their own performances. This attitude takes a particularly heavy toll in settings where production quotas are emphasized. Furthermore, alcohol use or hangover can result in an employee's being oversensitive, obnoxious, boisterous, insulting, and, in some instances, even violent.

Curiously, the greatest "morale toll" created by the deviant drinker is among those who must supervise him. In most instances first-line supervisors simply do not know what to do with the problem drinker. This situation may occur in organizations which lack a systematic policy for dealing with deviant employees or have policies which are ambiguous and are erratically implemented. Even if a policy has been developed and line supervisors have been trained in its implementation, the supervisor may still feel confused about the action he should take. This vacillation is a very common and normal reaction, especially when the supervisor has personal relationships with the deviant drinker (Roman and Trice, 1971b). The very nature of deviant drinking adds to natural tendencies towards vacillation: since most persons drink and many have been intoxicated, "true" deviance becomes difficult to define, i.e. no sharp demarcation exists between deviant and "normal" drinking.

The ambivalent supervisor usually devotes inordinate time and attention to the deviant drinker. These efforts represent a clear-cut cost to the organization; and, as shown in Chapter Six, the supervisory headaches brought on by the deviant drinker can adversely affect other aspects of supervisory responsibility. Furthermore, the morale of co-workers may decline further as they become "fed up" with the supervisor's reluctance to take action.

The deviant drinker's impact on the work flow, his fellow employees, and his supervisor is exacerbated when deviant drinking is tolerated and absorbed for a considerable period before any confrontation occurs. This very common "normalization" process is described further in Chapter Six. Normalization is difficult to avoid in many work situations and results in a sharp accumulation of costs for the work organization.

Estimates of the actual dollar costs of deviant drinking have been attempted by many, usually in a crude fashion. Slogans such as "the two billion dollar hangover" (National Institute of Mental Health, 1968:13) have been used to attract the attention of management personnel and gain their attendance at conferences and workshops on alcoholism, but these obvious "guesstimates" often appear irrelevant and ludicrous to hardnosed executives familiar with accounting exactitude.

A recent study, however, is a systematic and comprehensive attempt to compute the dollar costs of deviant drinking in an objective manner. Winslow and his associates (1966) compared three matched samples of employees: one showing evidence of deviant drinking in relation to job performance; the second presenting such problems as "short- or long-term absenteeism, repeated accidents, manifestations of interpersonal friction or inefficiency on the job, frequent visits to medical department without evidence of problem drinking"; and, finally, a sample of "problem free" employees who were considered "by the personnel department to be free from work problems." The research team collected evidence from four general areas of cost accounting: (1) cost of impaired productivity, (2) cost of interpersonal friction, (3) cost of absenteeism, and (4) cost of health and accident problems.

Costs of an employee's impaired productivity were computed by using his supervisor's ratings on the question of "percent potential utilized." This "percent potential utilized" was subtracted from 100 percent, and the remainder was multiplied by the annual salary, and the result represented the economic loss to the company—stemming only from impaired productivity.

Costs of interpersonal friction were based upon estimates made by administrative personnel concerning grievance procedures, disciplinary actions, and garnishment procedures. They estimated how much clerical and administrative working time was involved in each of these proceedings. Dollar figures were secured by multiplying "the amount of time involved in each person by his daily wage rate."

Costs of absences were secured as follows: "Dollar costs were calculated by multiplying the daily wage rate by the number of days absent with pay (cost for the company) and by multiplying the number of days absent without (cost for the individual employee)." Costs of health and accident problems "were estimated for the processing of compensation claims and hospital-medical-surgical benefit claims by estimating the number of clerical and administrative personnel involved and the amount of time occupied by them when assigned to this particular task." In addition,

> medical clinic visit costs were estimated by dividing the yearly operating costs of the clinic by the total number of clinic visits per year, giving a mean cost per medical clinic visit. Added to this was the estimated time, and its related cost to the company, that an employee would be away from his job while attending the medical clinic.

Keeping in mind that each of the three samples included only 19 employees, the following results are revealing:

> The costs to the company of the *"suspected problem drinking"* sample ($31,402) are very similar to the costs for the *"miscellaneous problem"* sample ($30,824) but are approximately twice the amount of the *"problem-free"* sample ($16,481). The costs to the employees are different for all three samples; the *"suspected problem drinking"* sample ($8,238) showing 16 times, and the *"miscellaneous problem"* sample ($4,051) showing 8 times the costs of the *"problem-free"* sample ($524). Costs to the insurer show the *"suspected problem drinking"* sample ($7,099) 3½ times and the *"miscellaneous problem"* sample ($4,716) 2½ times the costs of the *"problem-free"* ($1,935) (Winslow *et al.* 1966:22).

Thus it appears that problem-drinking employees share with other types of "problem" employees much higher costs not only to the company but to themselves and the insurance carriers involved than do the typical "problem free" employees in the two working populations studied. The significance of these figures is not in the actual dollar costs calculated, but in the fact that the deviant drinker costs the employer nearly *twice* as much as the normal employee in terms of red tape, services, and inadequate job performance.

A recent study reported by the Comptroller General of the United States (1970) also attempted cost-accounting estimates of problem drinking, using a cruder formula than that applied in Winslow's study. This study concluded that the costs of deviant drinking among federal civil service employees should be based on a factor of 25 percent of average annual salary. Assuming that 4 percent of this work force (which totals 2,800,000 persons) are deviant drinkers, the cost to the civil service establishment would be $275,000,000. A second study of

5

alcoholism by the Comptroller General's Office (1971) concluded that the health problem was probably as prevalent among military personnel as among civilians — at least 4 percent. Quite likely, the costs of alcoholism among the estimated 2,609,409 military personnel in 1972 would roughly approximate the cost to the U.S. Civil Service.

Insight into a specific aspect of employer costs is provided by a single-company study of the costs of overtime payments resulting from the absenteeism of problem drinkers (Pritchett, 1967). A formula was constructed comparing the annual mean days of absences by problem drinkers against the annual mean days of absences by other employees. Incorporated into the formula was the estimated percentage of absences for which overtime was paid, hours of work per day, the number of problem drinkers, and a weighted average hourly wage for all employees. "The resulting costs were $1,507 per year for [all] the younger problem drinkers and $16,389 for [all] older problem drinkers, making a total of $17,896. Many other consequences of absenteeism resulting in increased costs to the firm were not estimated" (Pritchett, 1967:13).

These data are consistent with earlier results reported by Observer and Maxwell (1959) who examined absence and accident patterns among 48 middle-age problem drinkers known to the staff of a large organization. Matching the problem drinkers in terms of length of service and other status variables, Observer and Maxwell revealed sickness payments for the drinkers ($108,495) to be three times greater than those for the normals ($36,912).

Babbitt (1967) calculated in minute detail the specific costs of one alcoholic's bender. He estimates the direct cost of alcoholic beverages, loss of wages, court fines and costs, medical care costs, loss of home or furnishings or place of business, accident expenses, loss or sale of personal belongings, sale of other items, and miscellaneous expenses. Assuming a 15-day bender, the author estimates a cost to the deviant drinker of $695. This estimate was actually made for an individual who was a shoe salesman. Should "Joe," the shoe salesman, go on a drinking spree every 14 months for approximately six years, he would spend a total of $3,475, according to Babbitt. Obviously this estimate might well rise for those in higher status positions.

Other writers suggest specific kinds of formulas although they do not attempt a specific dollar figure. For example, in a study of supervisory reactions to problem drinkers, Warkov and Bacon (1965:66) state that their findings "appear to reflect deterioration in personal relationships on the part of the problem drinker with others in his work environment."

Thus regardless of the method used and the dollar amounts revealed, these studies all point out that the deviant drinker costs his employer dollars that might be used elsewhere. Furthermore, no estimating formula can include the costs of errors in production or of foggy decision making, where consequences to the organization may be spread over a long period.

In addition to the dollar cost, employers may feel several other costs once drinking has continued to the point of full-fledged alcohol addiction. When it eventually becomes necessary to remove an individual from the organization because of his blatant deviance or sheer inability to function, management may encounter considerable resistance from the union if workers are organized. Presently, many unions will almost automatically defend deviant drinkers from management action. Weiner (1967) has pointed out that unions are often apprehensive of any management efforts to deal with "mental health"; they view such efforts as potential fronts for the infringement of workers' rights. Disciplinary actions may result in grievance procedures, with costly demands on the time of both management and union personnel. Many union locals will place no limits on involving themselves in the grievance process with the deviant-drinking worker; they feel it their duty to "walk the last mile" with the individual who has totally lost control of his drinking. Some of these costs can be sidestepped through union-management cooperation in the joint development of policy programs, as we outline in Chapter Eight.

If termination occurs and workmen's compensation is awarded, even greater costs may occur. First, the employee may possibly gather adequate medical testimony to provide for workmen's compensation payments for the illnesses that developed as side effects of his alcohol abuse. Second, there appears to be a growing tendency for workmen's compensation decisions to hold the employer responsible for employees' behavior disorders. As we have reviewed elsewhere (Trice and Belasco, 1966a; Trice and Roman, 1971), the trend of broadening employer responsibility may one day lead to compensation awards for the development of alcohol addiction. At present, precedents set in some courts hold the employer responsible for proving that job-related factors did *not* cause an employee's behavior disorders if the company is to win the case. Thus, should decisions continue to reflect a broader scope of employer responsibility, the issue of employer responsibility for alcohol addiction may someday represent a very sharp cost to employers.

Since chronic problem drinking usually begins during the middle years of an occupational career, the employer usually has a heavy investment in the employee whose work performance becomes impaired. The higher costs of deviance among such established employees have been documented by Pritchett (1967). Having been employed for a considerable period of time, the individual may have developed skills crucial to the organization and usually is personally integrated into the organization's functions. Replacing such an employee not only may involve the cost of retraining a new person, but also may represent the loss of unique skills and abilities that can only be developed through long tenure in a particular organization. These indirect costs over the long run may outweigh the immediate costs of the deviant's impaired job performance. These potential costs indicate the need for organizations to confront the deviant drinker early and realistically to attempt to alter his behavior rather than replace him.

The data we have reviewed clearly indicate that the deviant drinker's behavior is costly to the employer and the employee. What about the costs of drinking itself? While a great deal of publicity has focused on the cost of narcotics and the potential security risks engendered by the presence of narcotic addicts in a work force, little attention has been given to the fact that alcoholic beverages are costly as well. Significantly, middle-stage deviant drinkers, particularly those in blue-collar occupations, do most of their drinking in tavern-based groups. Not only is liquor-by-the-drink costly, but most drinking groups require members to pay for "rounds" for the whole group. As the deviant becomes intoxicated, his share of the rounds may increase; his condition frequently engenders outlandish tips and the purchase of drinks for total strangers. Thus deviant drinking can create financial pressures in some instances, tempting the lower-status drinker to pilfer from the employer in much the same way as the heroin addict is forced to use all means possible to raise funds. Garnishments by the deviant's creditors will often add pressures for additional funds (Trice, 1964).

Aside from these costs which may directly affect the smooth functioning of organizations and the employer's profits, community and social responsibility should further impel employers to take action about deviant drinking. Earlier detection and prevention of behavior disorders benefit both the afflicted individual and the community in terms of the resources that must be invested for treatment and rehabilitation of chronic cases. Employers often share heavily in a community's tax base, and tax increases are, at least in part, related to the growing costs of managing persons who have become chronic deviants. Beyond this indirect vested interest, employers will increasingly be required to show social responsibility, as exemplified in the current emphasis on consumer rights and environmental ecology. Finally, and most importantly, the work world has much to gain through the control of deviant drinking. We strongly believe that the work place contains a unique combination of forces for breaking up deleterious deviant behavior before it becomes chronic. Specifically, the employer has a legitimate right to intervene in the employee's personal behavior if it interferes with job performance. This right is the basis for the strategy of constructive confrontation outlined in Chapter Seven.

THE SKID ROW IMAGE

A major barrier to generating organizational interest in the management of deviant drinking behavior is the pervasive stereotype of the deviant drinker as a Skid Row bum (National Institute of Mental Health, 1968:7). This image is present in social stereotypes supported by the mass media and even finds its way into legitimate social programs. The facts about the validity of the Skid Row image are very clear: no more than 3 percent of the deviant drinking population in the United States fits the Skid Row image. The remaining majority are scattered throughout the social spectrum and are actively involved in the community, family, and job roles (Blane *et al.,* 1963), but the influence of the Skid Row image is difficult to overcome for a variety of reasons.

First, Skid Rows are highly visible in most American cities. Nearly every major American metropolis has an area primarily inhabited by homeless men living in seedy rooming houses and hotels and centering their activities in inexpensive taverns and bars. The prevalence of these "joints" on Skid Row, together with widespread panhandling and stereotyped storefront efforts to "save the drunks," leads many persons to characterize these men as alcoholics and readily to equate alcoholism with this mode of living.

Second, the equation between the concepts of Skid Row and of alcoholism serves what sociologists call a boundary maintenance function. While most "normals" drink alcohol (Cahalan *et al.,* 1969), it is very likely that a substantial proportion of drinkers at one time or another have quiet doubts about the normality of their own drinking behavior. The Skid Row image of alcoholism offers an easy way out of personal doubts about the normality of one's drinking: "I'm not like that, so I must not be an alcoholic." Such rationalizations also prevent the labeling of one's "significant others," i.e. family members, close friends, work associates. Deviant drinking thus can go unnoticed in "normal" social circles, avoiding or at least postponing psychological distress about the "normality" of heavy drinking. By assuming that all of a certain type of deviance is concentrated in one place, persons get a stronger sense of social order and a greater confidence in their own righteousness. Furthermore, as Rubington (1962:147) has pointed out, "an achievement oriented society which gives status for effort requires negative reference groups to maintain striving." Skid Row clearly serves this function well.

A third support for the Skid Row image comes from efforts to control alcohol problems. Many social agencies have used the Skid Row image as an attention-getting device to underline the deleterious outcomes of alcohol abuse. Earlier, this image was widely diffused by such prohibitionist groups as the Women's Christian Temperance Union (Gusfield, 1963) in their efforts to illustrate the evils of alcohol. Today, however, the motivation to paint such a grim picture of alcohol's effects is somewhat different. A myriad of social agencies compete with each other for public charity and governmental support. The more severe a particular social problem can be made to appear, the greater the probability that public support will be generated. Thus, as a means for inducing sympathy from the public and serious concern from legislators, the Skid Row image definitely is functional, even though it also puts the problem badly out of perspective.

A fourth, and more subtle, support for the Skid Row image comes inadvertently from Alcoholics Anonymous. A.A. has become a highly respected organization, probably more beneficial to problem drinkers than any other single agency; but, as outlined in Chapter Nine, the functioning of A.A. appears to depend heavily on individual members' assertion of having made "mobility trips" (Trice and Roman, 1970b). In other words, success in the A.A. program may be gauged by the degree of degradation from which the dry alcoholic has risen. Thus, the widely diffused idea that members of A.A. once lived highly disorganized alcohol-soaked lives which come close to fitting the Skid Row stereotype is a factor which tends to promote the pervasiveness of the Skid Row image.

The Skid Row image may block action by both managerial decision makers and first-line supervisors toward the deviant drinker. Many such persons tolerate all drinking which does not approximate the Skid Row stereotype, believing it to be still somehow "normal." This image pervades many quarters: Blane (1966) reports research indicating that even many physicians use a derelict-type definition as a guide in diagnosing alcohol problems. Thus, policy program development and supervisory training activities must underline the fact that Skid Row type drinking is far from representative of all deviant drinking behavior and that such deviation can occur at any or all occupational and organizational levels.

THE ALCOHOLISM INDUSTRY

A heavy contribution to confusion about alcohol problems in American society is inadvertently made by the collection of agencies and professionals we label the "alcoholism industry." Participants in the alcoholism industry include those who design and implement programs for the prevention and treatment of problem drinking, as well as those who attempt to obtain financial support for efforts to deal with these problems.

Nearly every type of deviance in American society, as well as the entire range of "social problems," is surrounded by "industries" that are often microcosms of large-scale marketing organizations. Thus, specific agencies, occupations, and semiprofessions have been developed to deal with the aged, poor, mentally retarded, mentally ill, multiple sclerotics, arthritics, etc.

While it is obvious that a great deal of good stems from the activities of such agencies and professionals, their very nature may prevent them from taking objective views of their respective problem areas. The fact that these "helping" activities have evolved into formal organizations, specific interest groups, and even lobbies makes the overall assessment of the significance of various types of problems difficult. Obviously, each "industry" or collection of concerned specialists has a vested interest in defining its own problem as being the most debilitating, the most widespread, the most tragic, and the most in need of immediate attention. Different sectors of the overall conglomerate of problem industries are in competition with one another for both public and private support. The consequence of this competition is that the total number of individuals estimated (Teele, 1970) to be afflicted with or affected by all of these problems far outruns the total population!

The degree of rationality evident in defining the extent of various problems and the care with which "case counting" is done seems to vary greatly across these different industries. Obviously, some types of illnesses, afflictions, and deviations are better established than others and some miseries, likewise, create more public sympathy than others. It appears that the more recently a problem has come to public attention, the more militant and fervorous is the public in its attitude toward the extent of the problem and its forecasts of potential dire consequences for society. At present the collection of agencies and professionals charged to deal with illegal drug abuse are the most militant in their efforts to persuade the public of the breadth and depth of the drug problem. As outlined in Chapter Two, it appears that several segments of the drug-problem industry are working toward creation and support of national hysteria concerning the extent and consequences of drug abuse.

The alcoholism industry has occasionally captured the limelight with its own brand of militancy and fervor. These efforts, however, are presently overshadowed by the demons associated with other drugs. Without a doubt there are dissimilarities between the impacts of alcohol and other drugs (Pittman, 1967), but it is intriguing and almost humorous to observe the resistances created by the suggestion that alcohol and drug-problem agencies join forces in their activities (usually on the basis of the contention that alcohol *is* a form of drug). Such suggestions sometimes create frantic responses such as intense arguments that alcohol problems are completely unique and that "everyone will lose" if the two sets of efforts are put together. These resistances clearly reflect the vested interests which might be lost through a merger, as well as the greater stigmatization associated with illegal drug abuse: problem drinkers and their caretakers might have their reputations damaged by becoming associated with "drug fiends." The emergence of the illegal drug problem may have inadvertently made problem drinking more respectable in somewhat the same way that the Italian immigration to the United States pushed the Irish-Americans "up a peg" from the bottom in terms of social status.

The irony of the specialized division of labor into various problem industries functioning as formal organizations and, in some instances, as specialized professions, is that their existence effectively precludes elimination of their respective problems. Estimates of a particular problem may not be reliable because of the vested interests involved in estimating the extent of respective problems. The current meaninglessness and uselessness of the term "alcoholism" stems in part from the abuse it has suffered at the hands of the alcoholism industry.

THE DEFINITION OF ALCOHOL PROBLEMS

The term "alcoholism" is widely used by both professionals and the public, often without considering its precise meaning. Some clarity in understanding the alcohol problem may be gained through exploring the background of this term and considering some alternatives to its use in the development of control programs based in work organizations.

Historical accounts of nearly all ancient societies indicate the presence of alcohol use, and there is reason to believe that alcohol was used even before recorded history. Ethyl alcohol appears in nature as a result of a variety of fermentation processes. Thus, where some sort of food storage is attempted, and particularly where methods of storage are primitive, the natural development of alcohol and its accidental discovery are highly likely.

Alcohol abuse appears to have always accompanied alcohol use (National Institute of Mental Health, 1968:2-3). Although different cultures show different patterns of tolerance toward intoxication (MacAndrew and Edgerton, 1969), drunkenness universally creates a high probability of social disruption, the occurrence of which eventually triggers social control mechanisms. For most of recorded history, drunkenness which disrupted ongoing social organization was viewed as immoral, sinful, and, in many instances, illegal. In American society drunkenness and "immoderation" were generally regarded as crimes and signs of immorality up until the second quarter of this century when concerted efforts began to be made to change this definition.

Most influential in attempting to recast drunkenness from the category of sin to the category of sickness was E. M. Jellinek. Jellinek (1960) argued that in certain clear-cut instances abusive drinking constituted a disease which followed a progression from occasional intoxication to frequent and habitual intoxication, finally reaching the state of total psychological and physiological dependency on the drug. Jellinek further argued that there were several different types of the disease alcoholism and that some instances of regular excessive drinking did not constitute a disease at all.

Jellinek's conceptualization of alcoholism as a disease began a small revolution in the societal management of alcohol abuse. Basically, the redefinition set the stage for an approach to alcohol abuse which was in sharp contrast to the punitive strategies previously employed. The new definition fit neatly with an important American value orientation: humanitarianism (Williams, 1970:462). As a society, we are uncomfortable employing punishment to deal with transgression. Christian values which have played a major role in the development of American ideology emphasize forgiveness of sins and the provision of opportunities for repentance. The medical definition of alcoholism not only provides for such repentance, but takes the basic responsibility for the behavior away from the individual. Furthermore, the definition of alcoholism as a disease "fits . . . the microbe-hunters' age of medicine which has shown such signal success in dealing with infections and degenerative diseases . . ." (Cahalan, 1970:5). Thus strong efforts were made and continue to be made to place the management of alcohol abuse in the humanitarian hands of the medical profession rather than in the punitive hands of the police and the law. In nearly every part of the country the diffusion of the disease concept has led to efforts to place deviant drinkers in medical treatment rather than through the "revolving door" of prison (Mulford, 1970).

There is a more indirect reason why individuals and organizations involved in the treatment and management of alcohol problems tend to be attracted to the disease model. Medical professionals in the United States enjoy a very high level of social prestige and power. This prestige and power is in contrast with that enjoyed by law enforcement agencies. The degree to which a particular problem can be defined as medical rather than criminal may greatly augment the prestige and power of those working with the problem (Freeman and Jones, 1970). Thus, persons working with alcohol problems may enjoy much greater professional and personal prestige if alcohol abuse is defined as a form of disease.

Such a tendency is further enhanced by the fact that a large number of new occupations and subprofessions have developed within new programs to treat and rehabilitate deviants. Employees in these new occupations include rehabilitation specialists, counselors, group therapy leaders, and community information specialists. As occupations emerge and develop, they usually attempt to become defined as "professions" (Vollmer and Mills, 1966; Ritzer and Trice, 1969). The definition of alcohol abuse as a medical problem enhances opportunities for professionalization, since it creates identities and alliances with physicians, who unequivocally occupy professional status. This situation contrasts sharply with the professionalization opportunities of occupations associated with law enforcement where the degree of control exercised over work activities by nonprofessionals reduces the opportunities for such occupations to be recognized as professional. Thus, the social status associated with the management of medical problems constitutes a vested interest for the support of the disease model within the alcohol-problem industry.

Calling a certain type of behavior a "disease" carries with it several assumptions: the symptoms of the disease and the behavior patterns accompanying the development of the disease must be common across all cases; the disorder must stem from a detectable cause or set of causes; and the condition must worsen if not treated, but may respond successfully to medical attention. Research on populations of "alcoholics," however, has failed to substantiate any of these assumptions. The course of the disorder varies across cases (Hoff, 1968; Trice and Wahl, 1958); symptoms of alcoholism vary with the definition employed; research has found no one cause or discernable set of causes that uniformly precede alcoholism (Pittman and Snyder, 1962); patterns of pathological drinking can be found where the drinker evidently does not get worse without intervention (Cahalan, 1970) and medical treatment has not been shown to be highly effective in curbing the undesirable behavior (Trice *et al.*, 1969; Belasco and Trice, 1969).

Cahalan's (1970) review indicates that some professionals are increasingly questioning the disease concept of alcoholism, while at the same time the public seems to be adopting the notion. Mulford and Miller (1961) found about half of an Iowa sample accepted the disease concept of alcoholism, although a substantial proportion regarded the alcoholic as *both* "sick" and "morally weak." A later study by Haberman and Sheinberg (1969) showed that about two-thirds of a representative metropolitan sample accepted the disease concept.

One might wonder why the disease concept is problematic even if erroneous. We have argued elsewhere (Roman and Trice, 1968; Roman, 1968) that medical labeling may make deviant drinking irreversible by absolving the drinker of responsibility for his behavior, as well as creating a situation where delabeling is difficult. While such an approach may be humanitarian in the short run, the long-term effects of this labeling may be deleterious.

Nonetheless, the problem of defining abnormal drinking behavior remains. Delimiting and unequivocally defining "alcoholism" has been fraught with difficulties, and myriad definitions exist for what behavior patterns are appropriate "symptoms" to indicate the presence of the "disease." The alcoholism industry's efforts to create the image that alcohol problems constitute one of the most horrendous afflictions in American society has led to the use of the term "alcoholism" for such events as the single experience of a blackout, becoming intoxicated more than 12 times a year, and the experience of becoming intoxicated in the morning (for a review of these, see Keller, 1962 and Cahalan, 1970:1-17). While such behaviors may well match with true cases of alcohol addiction in many instances, their use outside the context in which such behavior occurs can reduce their usefulness to absurdity. The use of "floating" definitions may explain the fact that the estimated number of alcoholics in American society seems to rise steadily each time representatives of the alcoholism industry offer a new estimate.

Progress was presumably made on the definitional problem with the introduction of the element of normative relativity. Representative are Keller and Seeley (quoted in Straus, 1971:247) who define alcoholism as the use of alcoholic beverages to the extent that it repeatedly "exceeds customary dietary use or ordinary compliance with the social drinking of the community and interferes with the drinker's health, interpersonal relations, or economic functioning." While this definition takes into account the context of the drinking behavior, it could allow practically any operational definition to be employed. For example, what does "repeatedly" mean? Twice? Fifteen times? By how much does the drinking behavior "exceed customary use?" How does one measure interference with interpersonal relations? Thus "social" definitions do not clear up the problem, but do enable some determined agencies to cast extremely wide nets in their definition of alcohol problems that deserve the allocation of public resources and attention.

Some have argued that the disease concept is unnecessarily complex and that chronic alcohol abuse is much more efficiently and usefully defined as "a bad habit" (Reinert, 1968). It is not our purpose in this book to debate the validity of the disease concept of alcoholism or to solve the definitional issue once and for all. Our concern rather is with the development of pragmatic guidelines for effective company programs, and to meet this concern we offer three categories of drinking behavior.

The first category is normal drinking. Such drinking does not undesirably alter behavior, does not interfere with the effective and efficient performance of role assignments and obligations, and does not significantly affect day-to-day functioning. While any consumption of alcohol can be objectively viewed as impairing functioning, normal drinking is confined to those contexts of relaxation and conviviality where instrumental role performances are not necessary. Thus, the major criterion in defining normal drinking is simply that it does not interfere with expected role performances.

Deviant drinking, the second category, is drinking behavior which both exceeds the bounds of community definitions and impairs role performance. An individual who becomes intoxicated on a few isolated occasions when his intoxication does not interfere with his expected performances would not be called a deviant drinker. On the other hand, the individual who regularly drinks to excess and who impairs his role performance either by hangover or by attempting to carry out role obligations while actually under the influence of alcohol would be defined as a deviant drinker. The essential point in the definition of deviant drinking is its total reliance on the norms of a particular localized setting.

Alcohol addiction is the third category, and it is defined as physiological loss of control over drinking behavior. Long-term, regular drinking can increase physiological tolerance so that individuals must drink more alcohol to achieve the same psychological effects. Over a long period, often as much as ten to fifteen years, this tolerance can reach the level where the organism is unable to function without the ingestion of alcohol. If such an individual is deprived of alcohol, he manifests sharp physiological withdrawal symptoms, such as delirium tremens, severe "shakes," and psychological syndromes such as Korsakov's psychosis (considerable loss of memory). For the sake of clarity, we define alcohol addiction only on the basis of these physiological withdrawal symptoms and do not include psychological withdrawal. Obviously, over a long period of excessive drinking a person can come to organize much of his interpersonal life, as well as his self-image, around the consumption of alcohol. When alcohol is withdrawn, he may sense extreme stress and discomfort. This psychological withdrawal, however, is highly subjective and likely can be survived without permanent damage to the individual.

Since we use physiological withdrawal symptoms to differentiate between deviant drinking and alcohol addiction, it may be obvious that we believe deviant drinkers can control their drinking behavior, given appropriate motivation. If we used psychological withdrawal symptoms to define alcohol addiction, most deviant drinkers would be redefined as alcohol addicts which would lead to the recommendation that they receive medical treatment. This broad use of disease definitions, however, may have undesirable side effects. Using our definition of deviant drinkers sets the stage for meaningful action by the individual's significant others, while medical referral may only generate ambivalence toward the drinker and ambiguity about his status. In order to make our definitions useful, we focus on behavior rather than subjective internal states. The usefulness of these definitions, in contrast to the global concept of "alcoholism," should prove evident in the following chapters.

These definitions provide the employer with a relatively simple route out of the "disease" dilemma. Although some have argued that certain types of performances are enhanced by alcohol use (e.g. some artistic and creative activities and abilities to influence others) and that alcohol may calm certain individuals and thus improve their performances (Straus, 1971:232), the employer will clearly have little to lose by unequivocally prohibiting the use of alcohol in conjunction with employment. Thus, as we outline in depth in Chapter Seven, the employer's attention can be focused on those who drink in conjunction with performing their jobs, without concern for what constitutes alcoholism or the point at which the deviant drinker is "diseased."

AMERICAN DRINKING NORMS

The "problem" of alcohol in American society can be partially understood by an examination of the integration of alcohol into American life. Alcohol has been on the American scene since the founding of this country (Kelly, 1964), and there is evidence that excessive drinking was more prevalent in some segments of society earlier in history than it is today. The colonial period and the opening of the Western frontiers were eras marked by considerable stress and deprivation. Living conditions were primitive, entertainment and culture were practically unknown, and most of the citizenry lived at the mercy of the forces of nature. In such a context, alcohol use was attractive and may have even been seen as a functional release from the everyday stresses of life. Furthermore, alcoholic beverages were easily produced as an activity auxiliary to agriculture. Bacon (1967) has documented the relaxed attitude toward alcohol during this period. Drunkenness was not tolerated, however, and numerous documents indicate the existence of penalties for such behavior in colonial America (National Institute of Mental Health, 1968).

As the nation became more urbanized and industrialized, drinking and excessive drinking became more problematic. Drinking and factory work were simply incompatible, particularly since such work was much more dangerous than it is today. Furthermore, extensive immigrations of persons from European cultures transplanted a whole range of different attitudes about appropriate drinking behavior (Straus, 1971). The native-American culture looked upon the specter of "masses of drunken foreigners" with great alarm. Gusfield (1962) has argued that concerns over alcohol emerged as a symbol of resistance to the urbanization of American society and the decline in influence of the rural, agricultural, and more abstinent segment of society. Consequently, there emerged efforts oriented originally to advocating moderation, but eventually moving to advocacy of the prohibition of alcohol. Prominent among these groups were the Prohibitionist Party and the Women's Christian Temperence Union which made extensive efforts to eliminate alcohol from the American scene in what now appears to have been a sort of front for an effort to slow down the forces of social change and urbanization. As is well known, these efforts eventually resulted in the "noble experiment," national prohibition.

These historical changes have left lasting marks on American attitudes toward alcohol use. While drunkenness has always met with sanction, the first definitions of mere alcohol use as immoral behavior emerged with prohibitionist activities. Before that time regular alcohol use was an integral part of American life which rarely received attention except in instances of blatant deviance. Even though prohibition was abandoned as an unsuccessful experiment, ambivalences about alcohol use remain embedded in American culture.

This ambivalence may be traced to the central American value orientation emphasizing individual self-control (Williams, 1970). Emphases on self-control and personal achievement are strongly contrary to hedonistic activities of pleasure-seeking and escape from worries and responsibilities. In their purest form, American values definitely reject alcohol use altogether. Regular alcohol use seems to have been tolerated in colonial times simply because it attracted little public attention. Both the manufacture and consumption of alcoholic beverages were primarily private rather than public activities. But while the negative attitudes inherited from the prohibitionists still pervade contemporary American culture, the facts are clear that alcohol has once again become integrated into the everyday social life of American society. The many occasions upon which alcohol use is seen as appropriate and even necessary need not be catalogued here. Suffice it to say that if alcohol were totally eliminated a good deal of social interaction would proceed with much more tension and discomfort than obtains when alcohol is available as a social lubricant (Bacon, 1962). Thus, while we remain uncomfortable about the idea that people use alcohol for pleasure, fun, or escape, alcohol is used in numerous modes that have become thoroughly, although subtly, legitimized.

Alcohol appears to have been accepted into American life by means of "pragmatic justification." In other words, alcohol use is acceptable as long as it serves some larger goal of achievement. If we examine the occasions on which alcohol use is legitimately accepted, we can easily see the dominant presence of pragmatic justification.

Take, for example, the twentieth-century institution of the cocktail party. In nearly every instance, cocktail parties are organized to bring people together for further acquaintance, the consolidation of mutual beliefs, or the development of plans and strategies for future instrumental relationships. Many cocktail parties are symbolic assertions of status and power or constitute a means for balancing social exchange relationships, thus paving the way for further fruitful interactions among individuals. Other cocktail parties are organized to bring people together in anticipation of future instrumental interaction, i.e. laying the ground for business relationships. Although it seems a cynical observation, many such cocktail party events are approximations of the "softening up" operations that occur during drinking business lunches. Cocktail parties, in short, are pragmatically justified as events of sociability rather than as occasions for the loss of inhibitions, relaxation of tensions, and relief of depression.

Regularized afternoon cocktails or weekend drinking in household settings likewise are accompanied by pragmatic justifications. The before-dinner cocktail is seen as a necessity for "unwinding" after a hard day's work. This unwinding serves the pragmatic function of setting the stage for a more effective rewinding for the work ahead. Weekend and vacation drinking have a similar pragmatic justification: they are "earned rewards." Persons who have worked diligently during the week or through the year are believed to deserve occasions of relaxation, again with the intent that this relaxation will recharge them for the work ahead. A close examination will indicate that legitimized drinking within the family closely follows such a cost-accounting system, where drinking is legitimized only to the extent that it does not "overdraw" a "bank" of conformity.

A type of drinking which need not fit our definition of deviant but which is universally viewed in a bad light is solitary drinking. Here pragmatic justification is usually missing. No one is around to keep track of the cost accounting or to exert social controls should the drinking get out of hand. Furthermore, our society has internalized the notion that drinking is a social activity and should be a secondary activity when one is attempting to achieve a more significant goal. Thus, drinking without sociability is deviance; it lacks pragmatic justification.

Drinking in this society is accepted as a means of social lubrication. Relaxation is permitted on the assumption that instrumental activities have preceded and will follow the relaxation period. The lubrication of social groups for more effective interaction clearly sets the stage for ease in dealing with strangers and developing acquaintances for future instrumental relationships. It is within these contexts that drinking is acceptable in American society. Americans who deliberately drink to escape their problems will rarely admit this to their fellows.

Our definition of deviant-drinking behavior fits neatly within this normative context. Role impairment definitions have sharp meaning in a culture that relies upon pragmatic justifications for its pleasures and there can be very few pragmatic justifications for directly mixing drinking and work. Given this fit between definitions, the control of deviant drinking in the work place seems more reasonable than may be the case with use of disease definitions.

A subtle feature of American norms regarding alcohol use is the manner in which persons are socialized in this society to repress alcohol's subjective effects. This norm often makes deviant drinking difficult to control, as well as making rejection of the deviant drinker difficult. Alcohol use is a paradox in the sense that alcohol is used to obtain certain desirable effects while at the same time the user is supposed to deny and repress those effects. In the typical social drinking situation, the primary motivation of participants is to control themselves, an effort which is often contrary to the effects of alcohol. Persons who can "hold their liquor" generally are viewed with esteem, while those who cannot are often seen as problems.

This tendency to repress alcohol's effects reflects American ambivalence toward alcohol and the value on self-control. Adult alcohol-use patterns sharply contrast with the manner in which marihuana is used in youth subcultures. Here the emphasis is clearly on "getting something" from the drug as quickly and as economically as possible. Thus, novice users are trained in various techniques of inhaling and swallowing marihuana smoke to maximize the speed, depth, and duration of the drug's effects. In this respect marihuana-smoking groups stand in sharp contrast to drinking groups; individuals who become high are viewed as successes and may even be positively rewarded in the marihuana-smoking group, whereas the drinker who rapidly becomes high is usually viewed as a failure by his fellow drinkers.

Research evidence shows that experience in the use of either alcohol or marihuana affords the user greater ability to cover up the drug's effects. Significantly, such cover-up skills are actively encouraged among alcohol users as part of everyday drinking. By contrast, the marihuana user does not attempt to cover up the drug's effects unless he finds himself among persons who may exert negative sanctions if they know he is using the drug. This type of socialization and societal support for the cover-up of alcohol's effects makes the deviant drinker more difficult to detect and may set the stage for toleration of deviant drinking as long as the drinker is able to show that he can hold his liquor. Over the long run such toleration will often lead to heavier drinking and eventual loss of control, making successful intervention more difficult.

DRINKING IN AMERICAN SOCIETY

While alcohol use has always been a part of American life, one index of changes in American drinking practices over time is the amount of alcohol consumed per capita. Per capita consumption of alcohol remained virtually unchanged for 110 years, from 1850 to 1960, but a slight increase in this figure was shown in data collected in 1968 (Straus, 1971). Such a rise may reflect the increase of deviant drinking in American society, but may also be a statistical artifact. For example, Keller (quoted in Straus, 1971) contends that the legalization of alcohol sales in many areas of the country during the past decade has simply resulted in a more accurate recording of the actual amounts of alcohol consumed. Since there has been a general decline in the per capita amount of alcohol consumed in the form of hard beverages and an increase in the consumption of light beverages such as beer and wine, Cahalan and his associates (1969) contend that the increase in per capita consumption may simply reflect moderate drinking by a greater proportion of the American people.

A significant advance in the understanding of alcohol use in American society was marked by completion of a national survey of the alcohol-use patterns of 2,746 respondents, comprising a random sample of the non-institutionalized American population, reported by Cahalan and his associates (1969). This study is one of the few in which researchers have been concerned with normal, rather than pathological, drinking. It should be emphasized, however, that while data on normal drinking provide a framework within which deviant drinking may be understood, the validity of data gathered in such household surveys may be questionable. For example, our own experience in interviewing 571 normal employees from five work organizations in New York State (Roman and Trice, 1971a) with an instrument that includes questions about drinking behavior left us with some doubts regarding the candor of responses to such sensitive questions. American ambivalence toward alcohol use, combined with the fact that respondents simply may not feel obligated to reveal behavior which they themselves regard as questionable, leads us to regard data from such a survey as probably underestimating problem drinking. The establishment of methods which assure validity in such surveys, however, is practically impossible; thus, the data reported by Cahalan and his associates (1969) are superior to the guesswork that has marked many earlier discussions of national drinking patterns.

Among this sample of "normal" Americans, 32 percent were found to be abstainers from alcohol (reporting one drink or less a year); 15 percent were infrequent drinkers (reporting at least one drink a year, but less than once a month); 28 percent were light drinkers (reporting at least one drink a month, but rarely more than two drinks on the same single occasion); 13 percent were moderate drinkers (reporting several drinking occasions per month, but no more than three or four drinks per occasion); and 12 percent were heavy drinkers [reporting that they "drink nearly every day with five or more per occasion at least once in a while, or about once weekly with usually five or more per occasion" (Cahalan *et al.*, 1969:19)]. These data indicate that two-thirds of the American population drink at least once a year; but "when the infrequent drinkers and abstainers are added together, the total adult population is seen to be fairly evenly divided between the 47 percent who do not drink as often as once a month and the 53 percent who drink once a month or more" (Cahalan *et al.*, 1969:19).

The highest percentage of abstainers and lowest proportion of heavy drinkers was found in the oldest age group. Highest rates of heavy drinking were found among both men and women between the ages of forty-five and forty-nine. Women in general were more likely to be abstainers and infrequent drinkers, with four times as many men (21 percent) classified as heavy drinkers compared to women (5 percent). The proportion of abstainers is directly associated with socio-economic status, with the fewest abstainers found in the high social classes and the most in the lowest social classes. The proportion of those classified as heavy drinkers remains relatively constant across all socio-economic levels, with those near the top socio-economic levels showing slightly higher proportions and those near the bottom showing slightly lower proportions.

In terms of marital status, the highest proportions of abstinence were found among the widowed (who also showed the fewest heavy drinkers), while single persons showed the lowest proportion of abstainers and the highest proportion of heavy drinkers. Divorced or separated persons showed a somewhat higher degree of drinking than those who were married. In terms of size of community, higher rates of drinking were shown in large cities and lowest rates in rural areas. A greater degree of abstinence was found among black respondents who also showed a slightly higher proportion of heavy drinkers — 14 percent as compared to 12 percent for whites.

Cahalan and his associates present data on other demographic and behavioral correlates of different types of drinking behavior. They also explore variations in attitudes about drinking and variations in the consumption of beer, wine, and spirits. While these data are of considerable interest and value, important for present purposes are the finding that drinking is widely prevalent in American society, the finding of a relatively high incidence of what the researchers label as heavy drinking (which is probably underestimated), and, most importantly, the uniformity of drinking patterns across socio-economic levels of American society. These data clearly prevent the conclusion that drinking and problem drinking are confined only to certain segments of American society; they underline the misleading nature of the Skid Row image and indicate that any effort to cope realistically with drinking and its correlates must be oriented to all segments of society.

AMERICAN PROBLEM DRINKERS

The national survey on drinking behavior, as well as a follow-up of a subsample of initial respondents, has provided useful data on patterns of problem drinking in American society (Cahalan, 1970). Cognizant of the difficulties and ambiguities inherent in the application of the concept of alcoholism, these researchers attempted to define problem drinking. The definition does not concern itself with quantities or frequencies of alcohol consumed, but rather with the degree to which the individual's behavior and life organization is marked by alcohol-related problems. These problems included the following: frequent intoxication, binge drinking, pathological drinking patterns, psychological dependence, problems with family, problems with friends, job-related problems, problems with legal authorities, health impairment, financial difficulties, and belligerence associated with drinking (Cahalan, 1970). Assessment of individual cases allowed for the computation of problem scores for individuals. Nine percent of the total sample, which was representative of the American adult population, indicated a level of drinking-related difficulties adequate for the researchers to regard the respondents as problem drinkers. This group included 15 percent of the men and 4 percent of the women in the sample.

Unlike most of the studies that have focused on labeled alcoholics, this research revealed a higher proportion of drinking-related problems among those in their twenties. The authors add that such a finding does not necessarily undermine the fact that many years of such difficulties may be necessary before socially consensual labeling of the individual as a deviant drinker takes place.

Contrary to previous research showing a relatively even distribution of drinking problems across social classes, this portion of the national survey revealed a somewhat higher preponderance of problem drinking in lower-status groups. The researchers interpreted these differences as possibly reflecting a "relative lack of protection or tolerance from society and one's significant others, fewer options for recreation and tension release, a greater level of alienation and anxiety, and more of a tendency to act out one's aggressiveness on the part of lower status persons." In other words, these problems may reflect the consequences of social-class placement rather than drinking *per se* (Cahalan, 1970:141). Higher rates of problem drinking were found in more highly urbanized settings; this fact was interpreted by the authors to indicate "a lower level of social controls and a more permissive drinking climate in the larger cities." Overall, these results do not diverge sharply from previous studies of deviant drinking which have focused on much more selective populations. The manner in which social status may differentially operate to expose or protect the deviant drinker is explored further in this book in Chapters Four and Five.

One issue of concern that has received little research attention is deviant drinking by females. While most of the generalizations and conclusions drawn here apply equally to employed males and females, a large proportion of females either are employed sporadically or spend practically all of their adult years occupied with household management. Numerous mass media presentations have indicated that female drinking is an insidious and socially invisible problem. The boredom and stress accompanying the housewife role, together with the social invisibility of the home-bound female, are alleged to combine to create a higher risk of deviant drinking. The few studies that have considered the female alcoholic (e.g. Kinsey, 1966) have been inconclusive and usually limited to very small and questionably representative samples. The national survey (Cahalan *et al.*, 1969) indicated much smaller proportions of both drinking and problem drinking among females as compared to males, underlining the alleged masculinity of both drinking and deviant drinking (Blane, 1968). While the data of Cahalan and his associates do not indicate a sharp degree of female problem drinking, they have not yet explored some of the specific dynamics associated with those females who are problem drinkers.

THE CAUSES OF DEVIANT DRINKING
AND ALCOHOL ADDICTION

The diffusion of the disease concept of alcoholism has triggered a considerable amount of research to discover its cause. As mentioned, the disease concept implies that a discernable cause or a set of causes for the phenomenon exists. This assumption has set the pattern for medical research on the causes of other diseases, and the location of etiological factors in physical disease has marked significant breakthroughs in preventive medicine. Location of the cause of alcoholism would presumably also offer similar opportunities for successful treatment and prevention.

The cause of deviant drinking or alcohol addiction, however, has not been discovered. A similar failure to locate causal factors has marked research on other behavior disorders that have been labeled diseases (Roman and Trice, 1967; Silverman, 1968). This failure has led in part to the widespread questioning of the validity of the disease model (Cahalan, 1970).

The search for the cause of alcohol abuse has been carried out at many levels, as perusal of the *Quarterly Journal of Studies on Alcohol* will indicate. Biochemists and physiologists have attempted to locate peculiar mechanisms of metabolism which characterize deviant drinkers and have studied the processes revealed when lower animals are experimentally addicted to alcohol (Williams, 1959). Geneticists have attempted to trace the transmission of alcohol addiction through family pedigrees (Partenen *et al.*, 1966). Social psychologists have endeavored to find the "alcoholic personality" (Menninger, 1938; McCord and McCord, 1962; Blane, 1968; Armstrong, 1958), and sociologists have studied the possible causal effects of different socialization experiences (Robins *et al.*, 1962) and of overall societal conditions (Snyder, 1964). Anthropologically oriented researchers have attempted to explain different rates of deviant drinking associated with variations in cultural configurations (Snyder, 1958; Barnett, 1955; Bales, 1946; Glad, 1947).

These endeavors have generated numerous hypotheses and theories to account for the development of deviant-drinking behavior. Nearly every theory possesses a degree of credibility, but each seems too simplistic by itself to comprise a full explanation of a complex pattern of human behavior. Furthermore, most research has been marked by methodological problems which preclude specification of causal factors. First, practically none of the research has included before-and-after measures, thus raising questions of whether the revealed characteristics of deviant drinkers preceded or followed long-term experiences of excessive drinking. Biochemical and personality differences, for example, may well be the consequences of excessive drinking rather than its causes. Furthermore, most researchers have not concerned themselves with the representativeness of the deviant drinkers they study and often have focused exclusively on aggregates of problem drinkers who are readily accessible: members of Alcoholics Anonymous and deviant drinkers who are inpatients in medical facilities. Obviously, neither of these groups is representative of all deviant drinkers. For example, successful affiliation with Alcoholics Anonymous may require unique personality features (Trice and Roman, 1970a). A.A. members may unintentionally provide inaccurate accounts of their past since A.A.

socialization tends to create the belief that members were victimized by alcohol (Trice and Roman, 1970b). Medical inpatients may, likewise, tend to overrepresent the lower socio-economic strata.

Sociologists have been particularly concerned with the effects of social disorganization on deviant behavior (Cohen, 1959), and some of their hypotheses are applicable to deviant drinking. Merton's (1957) theory of anomie and deviant behavior, for example, posits that the operation of a complex society frequently results in a gap between societal goals and the legitimate means by which these goals may be achieved. The poor, for instance, are cajoled to work toward achievement and success, but are not provided with adequate means for such achievement. Similar gaps may exist for ethnic minorities or for those who possess social or physical characteristics which brand them second-class citizens (Sagarin, 1971). This "bind" may lead to deviant behavior as a means of coping. Persons unable to reach society's goals may attempt to change those goals or may use illegitimate means for goal attainment.

Another category of deviant reactions to anomie is labeled "retreatism." Deviant drinkers would fall into this category (Snyder, 1964), the notion being that one method of coping with a discrepancy between valued goals and the absence of means of achieving them is to "drop out" of the real world and create a less stressful private world. Regular intoxication may be such a coping mechanism. As credible as this notion appears, the anomie theory is not an adequate explanation for deviant drinking behavior in American society. While high rates of deviant drinking are found in certain alienated segments of society, the majority of deviant drinkers appear to be in the mainstream of American life where the gap between goals and means would be minimized (Cahalan, 1970). Thus, motives other than escape from anomic situations apparently play a role in the genesis of deviant drinking.

Looking only at American society, the concept of anomie may be used to explain deviant drinking behavior in a somewhat different way. Anomie indicates the absence of clear-cut rules governing behavior (Cohen, 1965), and one of the main features of American drinking practices is the absence of clear-cut prescriptions of appropriate drinking behavior. Only the abstinent seem to have definite sentiments about appropriate alcohol use. Among others there seems to be a sharp ambivalence about alcohol, with most of the populace lacking specific reasons for explaining why they drink, while at the same time drinking in a regular fashion. The absence of *consistent* and *concrete* definitions of the appropriate uses of alcohol may describe a situation of relative normlessness or anomie.

The definition of deviant drinking becomes problematic when no accepted definition of normal drinking exists. This lack of definition generates a reluctance to recognize the deviant drinker even when clearcut role impairment is evident. This reluctance may result in the relatively inadvertent establishment of patterned deviant drinking: the deviant receives few negative sanctions and the absence of such negative sanctions may actually reinforce his behavior. In sum, anomie appears more useful in explaining deviant drinking in this manner than through positing that deviant drinking stems from social failure.

Despite the elegance of many of the theories of alcohol abuse, none has been scientifically verified. Studies have shown that many of the theorized conditions exist in some cases of excessive drinking, but no single condition characterizes all cases, nor are all persons who experience the theorized sets of conditions problem drinkers. For example, some, but not all, deviant drinkers come from broken homes, but most persons who come from broken homes are not deviant drinkers; thus neither necessary nor sufficient conditions for the development of deviant drinking have been established.

The development of deviant drinking may be better understood by abandoning the search for a single preceding cause. This search may be replaced by a postulation of differential risks of becoming a deviant drinker and the consideration of social reactions to this type of deviance. Our work on alcohol problems has been aided by a model which poses two basic dimensions for the development of problem drinking: (1) personality features or sets of experiences which make individuals vulnerable to becoming excessive drinkers and (2) opportunities and pressures which develop in the social environment and allow deviant drinking behavior to develop and persist (Cahalan, 1971; Trice, 1966). An overview of research indicates that both predispositions and opportunities may be necessary for deviant drinking patterns to develop. There are many vulnerable persons who never encounter the appropriate opportunities or stresses and thus never become deviant drinkers. Likewise, there are those who face opportunities and pressures which might lead to problem drinking, but whose personalities and backgrounds are incompatible with excessive alcohol use. There are also those with both the predispositions and the opportunities who never become deviant drinkers, but their risk for developing such patterns is much greater than that of those without these features.

VULNERABILITY FACTORS

Considerable research attention has been devoted to the psychological characteristics of deviant drinkers. Dependency seems to be characteristic of numerous problem drinkers (Witkin *et al.*, 1959), but it is unclear how this makes one especially vulnerable to excessive alcohol use. A personality feature that reflects one aspect of dependency and which clearly appears to constitute vulnerability is the degree to which an individual has established a firm and satisfactory identity (Connor, 1962). The development of a distinct identity appears contingent upon consistent sets of experience in which the same patterns of behavior are repeatedly reinforced by the social environment (Wiley, 1959). Consistency of both behavior and social reinforcement may likewise lead to consistency in self-image. Persons with erratic or inconsistent patterns of interpersonal relationships may be unable to answer satisfactorily the question, "Who am I?" The regular use of alcohol may resolve such an identity problem: even though the deviant drinker identity may be socially undesirable, it is nonetheless a fairly clear-cut identity. Furthermore, the deviant drinker may be able to organize a consistent set of activities and life patterns around alcohol. Groups of deviant drinkers often come to constitute subcultures with fairly well-organized normative structures (Trice, 1966:55-61), even though these norms are deviant. Thus, undesirable as it may seem, deviant drinking may resolve the problems of both identity and social acceptance, albeit only partially and temporarily.

The individual with a consistent but unsatisfactory self-image may likewise find deviant drinking attractive (Connor, 1962), for the effects of alcohol may turn him into the type of person he really wants to be. McClelland and his associates (1971) have recently concluded that some excessive drinkers appear to be attracted to alcohol because of its creation of subjective feelings of aggressive power. An otherwise weak individual may find himself a new man when he is under the the influence of alcohol. In other instances, excessive drinking may make a colorless individual into the life of the party, making him witty, gregarious, and humorous; and at the same time he obtains a subjective sense of being able to control his environment. Individuals who have spent most of their life "in the shadows" of social relations may find such personality transformations highly desirable.

Aside from problems of self-image, some persons may find alcohol use directly rewarding in relieving their anxieties and depressions. Other means for finding such relief may be unsatisfactory (Reinert, 1968). Furthermore, some who are relatively normal and happy in their everyday functioning find that the sensations created by alcohol are pleasureful and provide them with a desirable sense of well being. Such compatibility with alcohol's effects may definitely comprise vulnerability.

A deviant drinker in one's family background may create a vulnerability for deviant drinking. A child may discover that his parents are especially friendly, generous, and happy only when they are drinking. Experiences with an alcoholic father or mother can also provide cues to alcohol's usefulness in gaining attention and social power. Even unpleasant experiences with a problem-drinking parent can create vulnerability. One way to cope with a cruel and aggressive parent to whom one must submit is to take on the characteristics of the powerful individual. This subtle psychoanalytic mechanism is called "identification with the aggressor" (Freud, 1965) and has been shown to occur in such extreme circumstances as when concentration camp inmates take on the behavioral characteristics of their captors (Kogon, 1950). On the other hand, presence of an alcoholic in one's family of orientation may protect against future deviant drinking; mental associations with drinking may be so negative that the individual remains abstinent his entire life.

Although frequently exaggerated as a cause of alcohol abuse (Ullman, 1960) an individual's socialization into alchol use can create vulnerability for deviant drinking. Introduction to alcohol within a peer group where alcohol is used symbolically to prove masculinity may set the stage for a long-term attraction to the effects of alcohol (Maddox and McCall, 1964). Likewise, socialization in exciting contexts where the new user has highly pleasant and rewarding experiences can create positive associations with excessive alcohol use, i.e. persons may find their initial intoxication experiences marked by strong social approval, successful sexual exploits, etc.

On the other hand, certain individuals have highly negative experiences with alcohol the first few times they use it, becoming physically ill or being extremely frightened by the sensation of intoxication. This may act as a buffer against subsequent deviant drinking. Punishment by outside agents as a consequence of initial experience with alcohol may create either a vulnerability for, or a buffer against, future abuses of alcohol, depending upon the symbolic significance of the agents and the setting of the punishment. Perhaps the most significant aspect of socialization into alcohol use is the reaction of others surrounding the individual, i.e. positive rewards within such group settings during these initial learning experiences may set the stage for future alcohol abuse.

Social definitions accompanying alcohol use during an individual's socialization experiences may create vulnerability to deviant drinking (Plaut, 1967). Drinking may be viewed in a family or subculture as an appropriate means for relieving tension and anxieties and as an appropriate escape to employ when one is troubled. On the other hand, alcohol use may be defined as appropriate only on ceremonial occasions and may come to symbolize familial and religious solidarity, as in Orthodox Jewish subcultures (Snyder, 1958). Generally speaking, the extent to which an individual is trained to view alcohol as an adaptive mechanism and as an appropriate solution for personal troubles is directly related to vulnerability for subsequent deviant drinking.

This description does not include all possible vulnerability factors. Obviously, vulnerability is also a matter of degree. Not only may an individual experience "multiple vulnerabilities," but each of the vulnerability factors may vary in intensity. The importance of these factors is not that they lead persons directly to deviant drinking, but rather that they may differentially "set up" persons for deviation should opportunities and pressures develop.

OPPORTUNITIES AND PRESSURES

Our research has impressed us with the extent to which occupations and organizations offer differential opportunities and pressures for deviant drinking. These factors include the absence of clear-cut standards of work evaluation, freedom to set work hours, work addiction, occupational obsolescence, and occupational mobility. We outline these and other such occupational risk factors in depth in Chapter Four.

In addition to these work-based opportunities and pressures, several general features of social life may be considered as potentially fitting with vulnerable individuals' backgrounds in the creation of regularized alcohol abuse.

The first of these is the extent to which alcohol abuse is an available behavioral alternative. Some social settings, relatively few in contemporary America, preclude alcohol abuse. For example, one may affiliate with a religious denomination which forbids alcohol use, or reside where alcohol is not legally available and is difficult and expensive to obtain, or simply lack the financial resources necessary to procure alcohol. Conversely, one can take up residence in communities and neighborhoods where alcohol consumption is strongly encouraged and even required as a part of everyday social life. Apparently, the social status that one occupies may definitely affect the extent to which excessive drinking is an available behavioral alternative, with seemingly greater opportunities for regular drinking in the middle and upper classes.

Pressure for deviant drinking may be created by the accumulation of tension and stress which cannot otherwise be relieved. Individuals can be driven to drink by circumstances where they find unrelieved tension and stress unbearable without some sort of relief, at least on a temporary basis. For example, drinking may be a much more straight-forward and simple means of dealing with stress than using other drugs or seeking psychiatric help.

Sheer boredom and lack of a sense of personal fulfillment, conditions which apparently characterize many middle-aged, middle-class house-wives, are other examples of pressures toward deviant drinking. The general absence of specific responsibilities and the low degree of visibility that characterizes the housewife during the "empty-nest" phase of the family life cycle may constitute an opportunity for deviant drinking. Examples of opportunities and pressures could be listed in great detail, but in general they are of three main types: availability of alcohol and the opportunities for excessive drinking; low social visibility; and stresses from which escape must be sought.

SOCIAL REACTIONS TO THE DEVIANT DRINKER

The vulnerability-opportunity-pressure model attempts to account for the attraction of certain persons to deviant-drinking behavior; however, the major feature of problem drinking is its repetition. Essential in determining the continuation of a certain pattern of behavior are the social reactions of others to the behavior. In other words, the reactions of others may "make or break" the developing deviation. Thus, a full account of the development of deviant drinking must include consideration of these reactions and their effects.

The sociological study of social reactions to deviant behavior is loosely called labeling theory (Lemert, 1951; Becker, 1963; Lofland, 1969; Schur, 1971). Labeling theory is not concerned with the initial causes of deviant drinking in the same way as the etiological research we outlined previously. Instead, labeling theory focuses on the effects of social reactions in increasing the chances that deviant behavior will be repeated and even perpetuated.

Labeling theorists view the development of regularized or career-deviance as occurring in phases. First, a vulnerable individual under some kind of pressure is exposed to alcohol and finds intoxication or other effects of excessive drinking rewarding. Most deviant behavior eventually comes to the attention of others in an individual's social milieu, and this event then constitutes an initial social reaction. A variety of different social reactions may occur when others become aware of deviance. Others may react negatively and exercise social sanctions against the deviant; in many instances these sanctions may be sufficient to prevent repetition of the deviant act. It is also possible, however, that the others may react positively, depending on the way they themselves drink, as well as on the deviant's previous patterns of behavior. Observers who are heavy drinkers will probably react positively to instances of deviant drinking among their fellows since the development of a new deviant tends to legitimize their own behavior. Intoxication may also improve the social abilities of a previously boring or reclusive individual, and others may find this a welcome change, see him as the hit of the party, and positively reward his deviance.

More likely, however, than either positive or negative sanctions is the attempt to ignore the deviance, i.e. normalization (Roman and Trice, 1971b). Others may tend to see the deviance as acceptable or to assume that "he'll snap out of it." Our observations indicate that normalizing is much more likely to occur than other reactions for many reasons, including the risks involved in labeling someone else a deviant. Persons who are so accused may engage in "boomerang labeling": in response to the accusation that he is deviating, the accused deviant manages to throw the label back on his accuser. He may either call the accuser's own possible deviance to the attention of others or label the accuser a "prude," a "goody-goody," or even a "paranoid." The realization that such accusations can occur makes many people reluctant to recognize deviance among their fellows. It is much easier and often more practical not to get involved.

There are other pressures which may lead to the normalization of observed deviance. Some persons have observed drunkenness so many times with no adverse consequences that they simply do not see it as abnormal, even if it is repeated regularly. Furthermore, most people do not want to disrupt the flow of interaction and make a scene; they generally desire that social life proceed as normally as possible. Finally, people tend to normalize deviance because it is customary to do so. They feel that deciding who is or is not deviant is "none of my business."

Since most deviant drinkers do not come to the attention of a clergyman, a physician, or a psychiatrist until they have developed well-established patterns of deviance, we can infer that various types of normalization are typical responses to the early and even the middle-stage deviant drinker. For the reasons we have outlined, others tend to "put up with," absorb, and tolerate deviant drinking for an excessive period of time before they do anything. What they often decide to do when their patience is exhausted is usually about the worst thing that could happen to the deviant drinker: they become so "fed up" with his deviance that they exclude him from social drinking and even from social interaction altogether, thereby inducing him to seek drinking companionship elsewhere. This companionship can generally be found in pathological drinking groups, usually made up of persons who have undergone the same type of exclusion (Trice, 1966). Here extreme deviance is tolerated and, in a sense, normalization is complete, since deviant drinking and intoxication are the norms.

As a result of these processes the deviant may actually come to think of himself as a deviant, thus adding a further element of encouragement to his continued excessive drinking. Outside agents such as the police may terminate normalization when drinking results in other types of social offenses, but by this time heavy drinking and its rewards may have become a central part of the deviant's life, even though he may still have his job and family. When intervention occurs at this point, terminating the deviance is much more difficult than it is during its initial phases.

Exclusion processes are tantamount to the effective labeling of an individual as a deviant. At this point the individual may lack significant others who would confirm his identity as normal while at the same time he is surrounded by persons who confirm his identity as deviant (Goffman, 1961). While some persons possess adequate ego strength to resist such efforts to label them, most individuals are responsive to social judgments. When marked by consensus, such judgments quickly tend to erode belief in one's own normality.

The labeling of deviant drinkers through exclusion and segregation into drinking groups is only one route by which regularized deviant drinking can be developed. The postulated exclusion process ignores the fact that most families have enough interest in their members to attempt some sort of action on behalf of deviants if they believe that they are in need of help. A huge amount of publicity has passed through the mass media attempting to persuade the public to refer deviant drinkers to appropriate agencies rather than neglecting or excluding them.

While it is possible that a family may refer a deviant drinker directly to the local alcoholism agency, a psychiatrist, or a mental hospital, it is more likely that some "intermediate" or "holding" action will be taken. Most people see direct referral to the agents mentioned as drastic action; family members may be viewed in a bad light by the community if they attempt such explicit referral. Therefore, referral to, or seeking advice from, what Lofland (1969) calls a "middleman imputational specialist" is much more likely. Such "middlemen" include clergymen, family physicians, social workers, teachers, or perhaps even friends who are regarded as highly knowledgeable about mental health (Kadushin,

1969). These middlemen may try to treat the deviant drinker themselves, although in recent years many training efforts have been directed at such persons to persuade them to refer deviant drinkers on to psychiatrists or specialized physicians.

It is doubtful that the deviant would feel fully labeled as a true deviant after processing by the middleman since the middleman does not possess the societal authority for such official labeling. It is also doubtful that such agents would possess effective techniques for changing the deviant's behavior, especially if the deviant drinking has persisted for a long period. Middlemen have little to offer other than counseling or attempted persuasion of behavior change. Thus, referral to middlemen may essentially constitute a delaying action with little effective change of the deviant's behavior in most instances, especially in the case of the chronic heavy drinker. Such attempts may engender the feeling on the part of both the deviant and his family that they have "done something" about the problem, even though the deviant patterns resume. The middleman, however, may decide to refer the deviant to an official labeling agency, such as a psychiatrist or a physician specializing in alcoholism treatment.

Persons socialized in this society think of psychiatrists and similar specialists as having the "right" to decide about the presence or absence of deviant behavior. Referral to mandated labeling agents can often result in successful labeling of the individual as a true deviant drinker; these agents have a mandate and license to engage in legitimate labeling. At this point the official term "alcoholic" is typically employed. With the authority of his mandate behind the professional, such a label will probably stick in terms of both the deviant's self-concept and the definition that his family and others hold of him.

The labeling of an individual as an alcoholic is typically viewed as the successful fruition of appropriate social action. Official labeling and recognition mean little, however, unless some means are provided to take effective action toward changing the undesirable behavior. At this point the process often collapses, simply because adequate psychiatric or medically based treatments for altering deviant drinking behavior are lacking. The individual, having been labeled an alcoholic and having accepted the widely diffused notion that alcoholism is a disease, accepts the fact that he is "sick." This acceptance would be helpful were he compelled to remain on a treatment regimen with a high probability of success; however, without enforced and successful treatment, the sickness label may simply serve as an excuse for the continuation of the deviant behavior. In other words, the deviant may previously have regarded alcohol abuse as his own wrongdoing, whereas the "sick" label may remove his personal *responsibility* for engaging in excessive drinking. It must be understood that the deviant-drinking behavior is rewarding and probably will be until costs are created that outweigh the rewards of drinking. If there is no compulsion for the individual to remain in some sort of treatment following labeling, he will probably return to the community and continue to drink heavily, now accompanied by the legitimate excuse of sickness.

The labeling approach to deviance exposes the greatest shortcomings of the current vogue of classifying many types of deviant behavior as illnesses. Obviously, illness definitions remove individual responsibility for illness-related behavior (Parsons, 1951). Since a sick person is also expected to seek treatment, the use of illness labels is basically sound, as long as some sort of effective treatment exists. If, however, effective treatment is lacking, the labeling process creates populations of relatively permanent deviants remaining in the community until total impairment occurs. The labeling process which they undergo has sufficient official strength to make the label legitimate to both the deviant and to those around him; it constitutes an effective defense for the continuation of deviance.

Unlike most forms of deviation, however, alcoholism has a very successful treatment agency, Alcoholics Anonymous, the dynamics of which we explore in Chapter Nine. Ironically, this form of treatment is nonmedical, although some "disease" assumptions are involved. Successful affiliation with A.A. requires a cessation of drinking behavior altogether, and some intervening crisis may be necessary to reduce the rewards of drinking and create the motivation for affiliation. For persons who are labeled alcoholic and who do not successfully affiliate with Alcoholics Anonymous, the future may be marked by continuation of deviance to the point of total impairment.

Labeling theory implies that the use of the illness label is risky and should be minimized or avoided if long-term costs to both the individual and society are to be minimized. The successful route around labeling is made up of (1) avoiding exclusion processes and (2) avoiding labeling events which provide excuses to the deviant for continuing his behavior. According to this reasoning, it may be much more useful in the long run to consider deviant drinking *inappropriate* behavior rather than sick behavior. Alcohol addiction, however, is clearly a form of illness.

This reasoning precisely relates to the work world. Work essentially involves a contract between the employer and the employee, specifying that a certain performance by the employee will yield certain rewards from the employer and that, should either party breach the contract, the other has the right to demand a change in behavior. Thus employees who are not appropriately rewarded for their job performance may quit their jobs, unionize, strike for higher wages, or bring about legal action requiring the employer to provide them their just reward. On the other hand, inadequate performance by the employee provides the employer the legitimate right to intervene. The impairment of job performance through drinking constitutes such a breach of contract. While the cost factors we have outlined preclude such a simple act as firing, the employer does have this legitimate right to intervene. It is within this frame of reference that we pose in Chapter Seven the strategy of constructive confrontation for work-based policy programs regarding deviant drinking.

POSITIVE FUNCTIONS OF ALCOHOL

As we have done in this chapter, agencies, professionals, and researchers concerned with alcohol have focused their attention almost exclusively on alcohol abuse and the adverse consequences of deviant drinking. This problem orientation of alcohol specialists has in many instances created a neoprohibitionist image of programs designed to deal with alcohol abuse. Such a narrow orientation may be understandable among persons dealing exclusively with the consequences of alcohol abuse. Furthermore, many of the laymen and professionals concerned with alcohol problems are recovered alcoholics themselves, usually members of Alcoholics Anonymous who, while trying to view alcohol objectively, may naturally see alcohol in a negative light.

Alcohol does, however, serve positive functions for both individuals and society (Dock, 1963). Basically, alcohol may alleviate tension and stress that accumulate in complex social life. Statistically, most people who use alcohol never become deviant drinkers even though they may drink regularly throughout their lives. This fact implies that the personal relaxation and tension release provided by alcohol is often a useful adjunct to other coping mechanisms available in everyday life. It is noteworthy that although mental illness is a significant problem, the vast majority of persons live out their lives without the need for psychiatric attention or hospitalization, suggesting that alcohol may play a positive role in the maintenance of personal equilibrium for a large segment of the population.

The social lubricant function of alcohol should not be minimized or ignored. Complex societies create an infinite number of combinations of different statuses and roles to the extent that many individuals have little in common with one another. The conduct of social life often requires that persons with such variant backgrounds come into contact with each other, for both social and instrumental reasons. The cocktail party is probably the best example of this encounter, and the relaxing effects of alcohol can greatly reduce the potential tension in such circumstances. Even when persons are well-acquainted with each other, alcohol may serve to make social interaction flow more smoothly than would be the case in its absence.

Alcohol plays a central role in many of the social ceremonials that characterize role passages. At baptisms, weddings, Bar Mitzvahs, graduations, house warmings, and even funerals, alcohol's contribution to warmth and conviviality add to the occasion's significance. In role passage settings where new interactions between previously separate social units must develop (e.g. the meeting of family and relatives at weddings), alcohol may serve to reduce tensions and promote solidarity which might otherwise be cumbersome and uncomfortable. Similarly, alcohol's effects can enhance social solidarity at such ceremonials as the gathering of family or friends during holidays or other occasions when persons who infrequently interact are brought together. Needless to say, the annals of everyday life are marred with numerous anecdotes of social disasters engendered by excessive alcohol use on such occasions. Overall, however, it appears that the group feeling generated by alcohol is more functional than the tense and stilted interactions that pervade many social ceremonials which are for one reason or another "dry."

Positive functions are also served by taverns and similar types of "watering holes" which are well distributed throughout American society. In many working-class neighborhoods, the tavern provides a center for social interaction and relaxation for males who have few other opportunities to escape from crowded homes (Clinard, 1962). While tavern-based drinking groups can develop pathological norms which encourage and sustain patterns of deviant drinking, most tavern patrons do not engage in such deviant behavior. Instead, they are attracted to these settings by the sociability provided. In many taverns there are social controls which actually prevent deviant drinking and which may not be available to the patrons in other settings.

Finally, alcohol sales provide a huge tax base (Straus, 1971). It can be argued that many worthwhile federal, state, and local governmental programs would have to seek other sources of support were it not for alcoholic beverage taxes. In some localities such funds are specifically designated for social problems. For example, North Carolina allocates a set portion of the taxes derived from alcoholic beverage sales for local communities to develop programs such as alcoholism information centers, educational efforts, and treatment programs. Mulford (1970) has recently pointed out that alcoholic beverage tax revenue is far greater than the amount spent to manage the problems created by alcohol use; in essence, he argues that deviant drinkers are paying for services that are not being provided.

It is evident that each of the functions outlined above has its negative side. Many would argue that the benefits which alcohol provides for society do not outweigh the sharp costs it exacts in terms of alcohol-related problems. While this may be the case, it must be admitted that attention to the positive functions of alcohol has been sparse. National prohibition clearly showed that alcohol cannot be effectively eliminated from this society, but must be lived with and handled wisely.

II

Drugs, Youth, and the Work World

THE concern of business and industry with deviant drinking and alcohol addiction has recently been overshadowed and even upstaged by the national reaction to the use of illegal drugs, a reaction which at times approaches hysteria. While on the one hand many of the journalistic accounts of drug abuse have been accurate in reporting a sharp rise in the consumption of illegal drugs, other pronouncements have escalated national concern to include the belief that drug use foreshadows a total national disaster. A 1971 nationwide poll by Opinion Research Corporation showed 74 percent of the general public "had read or heard" about "unsafe drugs," more than had heard or read about "violent crimes" (67 percent) or air pollution (67 percent). These were the top selections from a list of twenty-five items (Goeke, 1971:81).

While much of the concern has been focused on drug use in the settings of higher education, high school, and even junior high school, the past few years have seen a sharp increase in publicity about drugs and the work world. Employers are often warned by the mass media that a significant proportion of their youthful employees may use drugs on the job, that the work place has become a major distribution point for drugs and a setting where "innocents" are introduced to drugs, that employers can expect a decline in the quality of their products or services due to employees' drug abuse, and that the first line of defense for the work world is the establishment of elaborate screening programs to detect drug-use patterns among young job applicants. This publicity has led to a "felt need" in many work organizations to establish programs to combat drug abuse in their work forces before doom and disaster take their toll. In some organizations programs to deal with the deviant drinker are unfortunately neglected or down-pedaled as a consequence, while elsewhere drug-abuse programs are being formulated without sufficient knowledge of the extent of the problem and in a mood bordering on hysteria and panic.

DRUGS, YOUTH, AND THE WORK WORLD

Our purpose in this chapter and throughout this book is to present both a series of research data and some objective observations on the problem of drug abuse in industry in the hope of precipitating a mood of rationality in understanding and dealing with the problem. While we do not contend that employers should ignore or forget the problem of drug abuse, we strongly feel that the facts have not received a reasonable hearing. In strict research terms, the literature available is limited, but it does help us to place the problem in a perspective that indicates that much of the current hysteria may be unjustified.

Illegal drug use among American youth should not surprise observers of the American scene during the past fifty years. The American culture is and has been drug oriented for a considerable time (Farber, 1970; Lennard *et al.*, 1971). We use chemicals to alter undesirable moods and as solutions to personal problems. The mass media are filled with advertisements for nonprescription items to relieve tension, induce sleep, create sociability, increase energy, and even save marriages. The modern drug industry has created cures for nonexistent diseases, i.e. "the Blahs." We are told that "we only come around once in this life" and that consumption of a certain brand of beer will open the door to solving the existential dilemma. A caffeine-loaded soft drink can presumably expand one's breadth of accomplishments: "You've got a lot to live and Pepsi's got a lot to give." Likewise, Coca-Cola is "the real thing." Apart from nonprescription items, physicians prescribe a whole range of psychoactive drugs to their patients at an astounding rate (Lennard *et al.*, 1971). The use of caffeine, a fairly potent energizer, and of nicotine, a drug whose addictive properties are parallel to those of heroin, are totally integrated into our social customs and their abuse receives practically no meaningful negative sanctions, even though caffeine may contribute to heart disease and tobacco use creates sharp risks of both lung cancer and heart disease. Finally, the picture is not complete without mention of our prevalent use of the addictive drug, alcohol.

This cultural context provides precedents and channels for the diffusion and use of illegal drugs. In many ways, the justifications and use patterns that have developed around illegal drugs in the youth culture are strikingly parallel to the use of legitimate drugs in other quarters of society. This situation allows for two generalizations: (1) the diffusion of illegal drugs occurs in a context prepared by the older generations in American society, and (2) an accurate definition of our drug problem must encompass all drug use, legal and illegal. We cannot rationally assume that some drugs are harmless because they have been legalized (or simply because they were never illegal) or because they are prescribed by members of the medical profession.

We will now attempt to estimate the costs of drug abuse to industry to establish the basis for concern by managements and unions. We then examine the stereotypes of drug users in American society and the social supports which reinforce these images. After delineating the nature of the current social conflict over drug use, we then outline the nature, use patterns, and work-world impact of three prominent sets of illegal drugs: marihuana and the psychedelics, the amphetamines and barbiturates, and the opiates. Finally, we compare illegal drugs with alcohol to assess the relative bases for concern in the work world.

DRUG-USER IMAGES

The popular image of the illegal drug user tends to constitute a barrier to rational planning and policy formation in work organizations. While the Skid Row bum dominates popular imagery of the deviant drinker and alcohol addict, two overlapping images cloud our thinking about drug abuse.

The first and more long-standing of these stereotypes is the "drug fiend." Stemming in part from literary and journalistic accounts of opiate-using Orientals on the West Coast of this country, this image casts the drug user as "out of this world," shiftless, and dominated by a bizarre value system. Added to this picture is the more recent image of the black or Puerto Rican ghetto-based heroin addict moving about in a dazed condition, undernourished, lacking ties to job or kin, and thinking only of theft to provide his next "fix." In contrast to the older image, the modern drug fiend is seen as both a menace to society and a leech on society's resources. Popular imagery, supported by the mass media, also casts the drug fiend as hopelessly incurable. The reaction to this image is one of hatred and rejection, calling forth and supporting the most punitive measures that society can generate.

The second image, again widely diffused by the mass media, depicts the user of marihuana and psychedelic drugs as a dazed hippie: long-haired and dirty, his sole motive is "tripping out," an activity occasionally supplemented by peace marches, promiscuous sex, and panhandling or peddling underground newspapers. He favors violent overthrow of the U.S. government, has dropped out of college, occasionally receives financial support from parents who have lost all hope, and aspires to live in a commune in New Mexico or California. This stereotype has not developed accidentally, but has been generated and supported by the mass media and by the visible presence of such types in the East

Village of New York, downtown Atlanta, New Orleans' French Quarter, and many parts of San Francisco.

These images of illicit drug users are the basis for very inappropriate generalizations. They have generated widespread hostility toward young blacks, Puerto Ricans, and Chicanos on the assumption they are probably heroin addicts and toward "long-hairs" and other youths who affect "hippie" fashions that are regarded as instant cues of illegal-drug users. Such stereotyping is convenient for the mass of the public who seek to resolve instantly the whereabouts of drug-induced evils. In addition to providing for inappropriate discrimination against those who may fit the image but are not drug users, these stereotypes may miss the core of the problem: the drug-use patterns which threaten work impairment and organizational functioning may be marked more by the user's *cover-up* practices than by overt cues that he is "one of them." We generally assume that chronic drinkers and drug users are totally enslaved by their habits and unable to control their behavior. In truth, the typical deviant drinker or drug user often develops vested interests in his deviant practices due to the psychological and social rewards these patterns provide. Such users are not necessarily irrational and "out of this world," but more likely are very much "in this world" since they must be alert to the negative consequences of being discovered. Thus, although the drug-fiend and dazed-hippie images are handy for scape-goating, the stereotypes are highly inaccurate for describing the total population of illegal-drug users. A subtle point which is frequently overlooked in the sociology of deviance and which is very relevant to the matter of stereotypes is clearly articulated by Simmons (1969:7):

> ... there is success and failure in the business of deviating from local standards just as in every other kind of human endeavor.... Most of those who get caught are patently more inept and "uncool" — either because of inexperience or because they didn't care enough about themselves to take reasonable precautions.... This special subgroup is most certainly unrepresentative of all deviants. In many ways these are the "flunk-outs" of the deviant world.

THE DRUG-PROBLEM INDUSTRY

Another factor contributing to irrational and fearful reasoning about work-based programs aimed at problems of drug use is the aggregate of professionals and semiprofessionals who locate, define, treat, and rehabilitate drug abusers. This segment of the social-problem industry has burgeoned greatly during the past five years; this has resulted in a large number of relatively uncoordinated, competing agencies. Collectively, however, the drug-problem industry aggressively campaigns to convince both funding agencies and the public that the drug problem is more significant, more acute, more prevalent, more complicated, and more threatening than any other of our current social ills. There has been a stampede of individuals and organizations to get a "piece of the action" for themselves. They hasten to be "where the money is," creating cut-throat competition with secondary interest in drug dependency per se.

The vested interests of the drug-problem industry in attracting the greatest social attention and allocation of resources are obvious. While recognizing the dedication and humanitarianism of the professionals and nonprofessionals in these agencies, we must also recognize that their work is embedded in organizational structures and superstructures strikingly similar to the organization of business and industry in terms of the significance of the competition. Simply, the aim of various problem industries is the accumulation of new programs, jobs, and resources, which in turn may yield greater social prestige and power. Thus, we warn against ready acceptance of definitions of the scope of problems from those whose future authority and power hinge heavily on public acceptance of these definitions. Unfortunately, adequate data on the extent of illegal drug use *throughout all levels and ages of the population* that has been collected by qualified outsiders who have no vested interest in the problem definition are simply unavailable.

THE ROOTS OF SOCIAL CONFLICT OVER DRUG USE

Never before in the history of American society has the issue of drug use produced the sharp social concern and severe social conflict that mark the contemporary scene. Even the intense, prolonged, and emotionally charged debate over alcohol which covered more than a century (and is still quite active in some quarters), does not match the present ideological battle; alcohol, after all, was only one drug. Now, however, the struggle includes numerous illegal drugs with fiendish reputations and allegedly awesome strength in altering behavior. The depth of the social reaction is reflected in heavy legal sanctions—in some states punishment for marihuana distribution is second only to that for first-degree murder. The heart of the conflict is in the obvious strain between the youth culture and the dominant adult culture regarding the contrast between the acceptability and legality of alcohol, tobacco, and psychoactive prescription drugs, and the condemnation of marihuana and psychedelics. Tobacco and alcohol obviously produce as many abuse problems as the drugs of youth, if not more, yet these are ignored or "lived with" while the use of pot and the psychedelics produce adult hysteria and severe repression. The result:

> Common parlance about the "use" of socially disapproved or illegal drugs usually conveys the impression that any or all use is abusive and constitutes addiction; conversely, references to socially approved drugs such as alcohol and nicotine usually imply that almost all use, including abusive and addictive use, is normal (Fort, 1970:322).

Moreover, the relatively mild social regulations regarding the use of alcohol are not uniformally enforced; compared with enforcement of marihuana laws, those applying to alcohol are weak indeed.

The real struggle centers on youthful (usually student) use of marihuana, LSD, and other pharmacological agents which has "almost replaced student drinking as the major focus of adult concern" (Straus, 1970:42). The depth of the conflict becomes clearer when it is realized that the illegal drugs of the youth culture lie symbolically at the center of the "generation gap." It is important to underscore that this present generation gap is not typical in historical terms. Arnold Toynbee puts the matter in clear perspective:

> Of course there is always a "generation gap." The rising generation never sees life with the same eyes as its elders — not even at times and places in which society is relatively static and in which the younger generation shares with its predecessors a wish to conserve tradition rather than to make a break with it. A generation gap of normal breadth is a symptom of social and cultural health. If it could be closed completely (but it never can be), society would stagnate. But in present day America, and in most of the rest of the world, too, the breadth of the generation gap is abnormally wide (Toynbee, 1969:333).

Margaret Mead underscores this basic point: "The primary evidence that our present situation is unique, without any parallel in the past, is that the generation gap is world wide" (Mead, 1970:68). Drug use, excluding that of the elder generation, has become a significant symbol of these changes. Moreover, it is white, middle-class youths, on whom American society has traditionally lavished deep emotional concern, who are the ideological champions of the new mood-altering drugs; blacks, Puerto Ricans, and Spanish-Americans have been using marihuana and heroin for years without public hysteria. Middle-class youthful support for drugs may result from deep-seated rapid change in social values that has marked the past decade. Mead (1970:78) comments on the extent of social change impinging on the current elder generation:

> No generation has ever known, experienced, and incorporated such rapid changes, watched the sources of power, the means of communication, the

45

definition of humanity, the limits of their explorable universe, the certainties of a known and limited world, the fundamental imperatives of life and death — all change before their eyes. They know more about change than any generation has ever known and so stand, over, against, and vastly alienated, from the young, who by the very nature of their position have had to reject their elders' past. . . . So we are set apart both from earlier generations and from the young who have rejected the past and all that their elders are making of the present. At this breaking point between two radically different and closely related groups, both are inevitably very lonely, as we face each other knowing that they will never experience what we have experienced, and that we can never experience what they have experienced.

In short, the struggle over drug use is largely one of ideology and not of science. In this regard it magnifies a hundredfold the moralistic conflict over alcohol use. Adult hysteria about middle-class youth's drug use and the social sanctities it offends has been aptly termed "pharmacological Calvinism" (Klerman, 1970:316). Thus, "if a drug makes you feel good, it's either somehow morally wrong, or you're going to pay for it with dependence, liver damage, chromosomal change, or some other form of secular theological retribution" (Klerman, 1970:316). In terms of adult ideology, desirable behavior arises from rejecting bodily and emotional satisfaction; drugs used recreationally destroy individual will power and thus constitute a threat of the first magnitude. The prevailing Protestant Ethic allows power and status to be given only on the basis of accomplishment. The dominant culture distributes rewards for effective performance, not for expressive subjective experiences that cannot be seen, counted, or evaluated. Reinforcing these ideologies is the belief that rationality and logic are the genuine paths to truth and the Good Life, and that the emotional experiences of self-exploration and intuition stemming from drug experiences are unsound and misleading. Dominated heavily by existentialism, youth culture doubts that reason and science will bring about a reduction of interpersonal tensions. It advocates immediate experience as far more valuable than delayed gratification and believes that being accepted by peer groups is more important than individual achievement.

If we examine in depth the mode by which alcohol, caffeine, and psychoactive drugs have become acceptable in American society, we again see the effect of pragmatic justification. American society strongly values self-control, achievement, and efficiency (Williams, 1970) and disapproves of "pleasure" or "fun" as *ends in themselves*. Pleasure instead must be earned or serve some valued goal. Thus alcohol is sanctioned for use in group settings where it serves as a "social lubricant" to promote conversation and affability which may lead to friendships and future business dealings. The cocktail party is not seen as a pleasureful orgy, but rather as a future-oriented event which will serve to widen the participants' interpersonal spheres of influence. In a like manner, hard-working Americans earn their before-dinner or evening cocktails by putting in a good day's work after which relaxation is essential to "recharge" for the next day's activities. Caffeine is not used to get high but rather as a "pick-me-up" which allows more alert pursuit of work activities. Psychoactive drugs are not prescribed for the patient's pleasure or for his achievement of new perceptions, but rather to inhibit feelings of anxiety, unhappiness, and depression which may interfere with effective work. The mood-altering substances acceptable in American culture have become so through the practical functions they serve in aiding persons to "get on with the business" of work and achievement.

Clearly, no such pragmatic justifications have been attached to illegal drug use among youth; "smoking a joint" or "tripping out" are defined as purely pleasureful. Rather than serving the goal of "getting ahead," illegal drug use is stereotyped as a way of "getting behind" and losing ground in the competitive struggle. While some youths are apparently patterning their use of drugs (especially marihuana) in ways strikingly similar to their elders' use of alcohol, i.e. smoking at the end of the work day or on weekends when relaxation has been legitimately earned, this pragmatic justification has not been emphasized to make drug use acceptable. Furthermore, the relative lack of responsibility associated with youth status reduces the probability of elders seeing the pleasure of a drug experience as earned. These illegal drugs have entered our culture in such a way that older Americans can see *no good reason* why drug use should be accepted or legalized.

Even though the results of scientific and objective studies of alcohol have emerged in the last 30 years, they have not replaced traditional beliefs and moralistic definitions but merely have become intermingled with them. As Mulford and Miller (1964a) discovered, many who see alcoholism as a disease *also* believe it represents a moral lapse on the part of the alcoholic. In much the same way, but to a greater degree, the primary societal response to the widespread youthful use of drugs is moralistic and ideological (Goode, 1969b). As science attempts to inject objective information into the emotional stuggle, partisans select those bits and pieces of scientific research that fit their preconceived emotional positions. Agents of formal social control and community institutions — police, church, schools — select facts and attempt to enforce their prejudiced position against the use of a particular drug.

On the other side is a sizeable proportion of the rapidly growing youth culture (possibly a majority) who choose their facts in support of newer forms of drug use. That they have time on their side no one would dispute; soon they will have numbers on their side for more than 50 percent of our population is under 25 years of age. The Bureau of Labor Statistics forecasts that by 1975 there will be a 30 percent increase of people 15 to 25 years of age and a 40 percent increase of people 25 to 34 (Koprowski, 1969). Although we have no idea what the carry-over of drug use into adult life will be, recreational and psychedelic drugs are central to the new world of youth and their use is a challenge to the traditional American value system. The drug scene has become the battleground for generational social change.

Whereas most adults have experienced the effects of alcohol, and many have taken psychoactive drugs, the experience of smoking a joint is totally uncharted territory to them. This *absence of empathy* for the variety of drug experiences which their children have had or are having creates a receptivity to the drug-fiend and dazed-hippie images we outlined earlier. In addition, drug use creates many automatic mental associations with Orientals, Latin Americans, and others stereotyped as "strange" and "ne'er-do-well." These elements combine to add considerable fuel to the conflict, with many adults feeling a total and absolute lack of understanding of why their heirs have delved into this underworld of deviance.

The elders' sensitivity has been building for two decades. Widespread heroin use by underprivileged adolescent males in large urban centers such as New York City, Chicago, and Detroit generated demands for more police regulation of illegal opiate traffic. In the early sixties the thalidomide tragedy brought on an international fright about drug safety, greatly aiding the late Senator Estes Kefauver in securing legislation that amended the Food and Drug Act in 1962.

The issue, however, is concerned with more than addiction or specific drug effects. Gouldner has called the "psychedelic culture" the vanguard for current social change:

> . . . for Psychedelic Culture rejects the central values to which all variants of the industrial society are committed. Not only does it reject the commercial form of industrialization, holding money or money making and status striving in disdain, but more fundamentally, it also resists achievement seeking, routine economic roles whether high or low, inhibition of expression, repression of impulse, and all the other personal and social requisites of a society organized around the optimization of utility. Psychedelic Culture rejects the value of conforming usefulness, counterposing to it, as a standard, that each must do his "own thing." In short, many, particularly

among the young, are now orienting themselves increasingly to expressive rather than instrumental politics, to gratification directly achieved with the aid of drugs, sex, or new communitarian social forms rather than through work or achievement striving via individual competition (Gouldner, 1970:78–79).

Elsewhere this new ideology has been labeled the "hang-loose" ethic:

One of the fundamental characteristics of the hang-loose ethic is that it is irreverent. It repudiates, or at least questions, such cornerstones of conventional society as Christianity, "my country right or wrong," the sanctity of marriage and premarital chastity, civil disobedience, the accumulation of wealth, the right and even competence of parents, the schools, and the government to head and make decisions for everyone — in sum, the Establishment (Simmons and Winograd, 1966:12).

Although such intense rejection of current social values by the young certainly does not characterize the entire youthful population (Bazell, 1971), the hang-loose ethic probably influences a sizeable majority (Jennings, 1971; Feinberg, 1971). The work world has indicated a concern with this mood. In an article in *Business Horizons,* appropriately entitled "Today the Campuses, Tomorrow the Corporations," it is asserted that: "Top managers today are talking the way academic deans and university presidents talked ten years ago — it can't happen here. My own feeling is that what has happened to us on the campuses is going to happen to the corporation tomorrow" (Fielden, 1970:13). Such prominent establishment magazines as *Fortune* conclude that the psychedelic culture will have an important impact on most aspects of our lives. Applied behavioral science publications such as *Trans-Action* and *Psychology Today* say much the same thing.

The increased use of marihuana, and to a lesser extent of other "hard" drugs, also has to do with "growing up rather than going awry" (Brenner *et al.,* 1970:108). One of the major tasks of a youth in any society today is to form a stable identity. Erik Erikson (1968) has shown how a youth must find out who he is, distinct from both his family and his peers. He must come to some sense of what his life means, what reference points will guide his behavior. The social context for this transition is crucial, calling for relatively stable adult roles into which he can move, supported by a consistent value system. Rites of passage that signify to the world the change in status are also necessary. Marihuana smoking and other drug use may tend to stabilize an identity with the counter-culture. Since marihuana smoking is predominantly an intimate behavior, carried out in groups and set in ceremonial forms, it not only provides identity with specific and distinctive values, but also acts as a well ritualized rite of passage into an identity. Whereas alcohol use once served the function (and probably continues to do so in numerous segments of the youthful population) of establishing an identity with adulthood (Maddox and McCall, 1964), the use of drugs today underlines an identity with the youth culture and all of the aspects of adult culture it rejects.

The clash between the values of the two generations is dramatized in the public frenzy over the use of marihuana. The rigorous condemnation of this new and strange intoxicant is obvious. Suchman describes the opinion of an "over-30" judge that "alcohol is the socially approved drug of choice for the well adjusted, responsible, hard-working member of society seeking sociability and pleasant relaxation, while the use of marihuana represents the neurotic and anti-social behavior of a juvenile delinquent" (Suchman, 1968:146). On the one hand, adults tend to repress their memories of the days of prohibition and their knowledge of the serious problems posed by alcohol abuse; and, on the other hand, they sharply condemn the use of a drug that may have, in the judgment of many, far less potential damage to role performance. Youthful adherents of marihuana add to the climate of ignorance by not acknowledging that even the most sympathetic observers find that acute reactions and chronic psychic incapacities can emerge from heavy marihuana use. The young thus boldly increase their use of marihuana. The reactions of both young and old tend to be repression, even of objective scientific research. Marihuana use is a rallying point in the deep conflict between young and middle aged, between those who want change and those who support the status quo. For example, John Kaplan, a noted professor of criminal law, concludes that it is almost impossible for our society to form rational policies about marihuana (1970).

Zinberg and Weil indicate that the lack of hard information on marihuana has resulted in a vicious circle: because administrators of scientific and government institutions feel marihuana is dangerous, they are reluctant to allow experimental work on it. Because no work is done, people continue to think of it as dangerous (Zinberg and Weil, 1969). In this same connection Brenner and associates (1970:27) report the following:

> *Medical World News* of September 1969 reported the following story of a physician, a clinical investigator in Texas. Earlier that year the physician was arrested by the state police for possession of marihuana, despite the fact that he had a federal permit to grow marihuana for research use. He showed the arresting officer the permit, but nevertheless spent the night in the county jail before being released the next morning on a one thousand

dollar bond. The physician maintained that he had suffered considerable harassment from both civil authorities and members of his own profession in the area. In the same issue of *Medical World News* Dr. Andrew Weil of the National Institute of Mental Health, who with Zinberg and Nelsen wrote a research paper on marihuana for the December 1968 issue of the journal, *Science,* is quoted: "The fact is that it is very difficult to do marihuana research, no matter what anyone tells you. The legal problems are still extraordinary, but I think the real problem is the emotional attitudes you run into in institutions. People are just scared of it, and they set obstacles in your path and force you to go through things that you just don't encounter in doing research of any other kind."

To summarize, many in the youth culture are attempting to develop new values and behavior patterns which are in defiance of the dominant social ethic; the use of marihuana and other drugs is one of the main symbolic instruments for accomplishing this purpose. In many ways, the elders' severe condemnation can be understood. Ironically, there is no historical precedent in American society by which generational conflict is reduced and "generational equilibrium" established (Feuer, 1969). Adult moral indignation has activated all the powerful forces of community life to prohibit and restrict the use of marihuana and all other "new" drugs that may be used by the younger generation as a symbol of defiance and change. Now intensive efforts are being made to involve the work world as well. Consequently there has emerged an amazing preoccupation with illegal drugs that tends to blind American society to the problem of how to deal with the vast array of legal drugs that are proliferating daily. It has prevented the formation of a rational uniform policy on drugs, leaving us stymied at a time when we desperately need to evaluate knowledge about new drugs. As Klerman (1970:318) puts it: "This is a period of rapid change in the drug field.... It is only a question of time. Modern chemistry is radically transforming our lives."

It is in this atmosphere that the work world may significantly contribute to the welfare of its new and established employees, for job-related research concerning all of the drugs used by the American labor force is desperately needed. Legal drugs such as tobacco, alcohol, caffeine, and the psychoactive drugs are probably producing as many health problems and role impairments as any of the current illegal drugs. "The wrong drugs are receiving most of the attention; alcohol and nicotine are seriously undercontrolled and overavailable" (Fort, 1970:333). Cumming (1969:2) after a brief review of the wide array of addictive drugs, observed that her list "leaves out the greatest of them all, alcohol." One of the most constructive possible measures would be powerful management-union support for objective and detailed research concerning the pharmacological, psychological, and sociological aspects of new drugs, including legal drugs. Perlis of the AFL-CIO Department of Community Services, for example, has recently launched a constructive policy of planning for prevention and treatment even though current studies reveal only a minimal problem of drug abuse among union members (Perlis, 1970). Business and industry, with their vested interests in preventing impaired work behavior, could set the social climate for enlightment by encouraging and supporting such objective research. Essential to such investigations would be researchers who have no vested interests in their results. We would like to believe that the voice of science might be, at least timidly, heard in the land.

COST OF DRUG ABUSE TO WORK ORGANIZATIONS

The issue of costs is basic to the relevance of work-world concern about drug use. Does this problem constitute a major hidden cost to work organizations? Establishing such estimates is extremely risky in the absence of data on the extent of the problem. Whereas we were able in Chapter One to provide some formulas for computing the costs of deviant drinking, these estimates were based on knowledge of the problem's extent and on existing research on the actual job behaviors of deviant drinkers. In contrast, nearly nothing concrete is known about either the extent of drug abuse among workers or its effect on job-related behaviors.

The greatest danger in estimating drug abuse costs is that some single figure will be repeated until it becomes scientific gospel. As outlined in Chapter One, estimates of the costs of deviant drinking, about which much more is known, are tenuous at best; nonetheless, slogans such as the two-, three-, and even four-billion-dollar hangover are widely used without scrutiny of the sources of such estimates. The current drug hysteria is such that any figure will be enthusiastically grasped by the problem industry to exaggerate the extent of the problem. Consequently any estimate will be highly impressionistic.

Estimates of the costs of drug abuse, similar to those involving alcohol abuse, revolve around several factors: impaired performance of the drug user, morale problems of fellow workers and supervisors, grievance problems, retraining, security risks, and workmen's compensation.

We have very little data on the relation between specific work behaviors — such as absenteeism, inefficiency, and accidents — and drug abuse. The available information on drug users' job behaviors is covered in Chapter Five. In general, the cost impact of drug abuse on work performance appears much lower than that of deviant drinking. Absenteeism among deviant drinkers depends heavily on the effects of hangover or the inability to work while intoxicated. Absenteeism among drug-using workers may be a result of the hang-loose subculture which emphasizes low job commitment, rather than of drug effects. Persons whose behavior is sharply impaired by drug use — and who consequently would present problems in terms of their ability to work — are just those who would probably have little interest in becoming involved in a regular job or whose overall demeanor would prevent them from ever passing muster in the personnel office: the true marihuana "head," the "speed freak," and the street addict. Following this same reasoning, there are no special reasons to expect a high accident rate among occasional drug users.

Just as the deviant drinker becomes more costly for his employer as he becomes physiologically addicted to alcohol, the drug user may also be more costly if he becomes addicted. Addictions in general are characterized by increased preoccupation with the addictive substance and less and less attention to the demands of jobs; however, marihuana and the psychodelics in general are not physiologically addictive, although the heavy user may develop a strong psychological dependence on their effects. Even such dependence in no way approximates that which alcohol can create. Amphetamines may be addictive and barbiturates definitely are addictive when taken regularly in large doses, but the extent of such heavy use, although unknown, is probably low. Opiates are clearly addictive, but research evidence, outlined in Chapter Five, appears to indicate that work impairment will not be significant unless the source of supply is threatened and the addict forced into the underworld for procurement.

Overall, it does not appear that drug use is costly in terms of effects on work behaviors, although impairments can be sharp for heavy users of amphetamines and barbiturates who become addicted, for opiate users who lose their normal source of supply, and for heavy users of psychedelics who are inadvertently hired by organizations.

The morale costs of the deviant drinker center on the vacillation of his supervisor and work associates in deciding whether or not he is really a deviant. These responses may comprise the tolerance and normalization shown in response to the deviant drinker on the job, but there is no reason to believe that co-workers would show such tolerance for a behaviorally impaired worker known to be a drug user. Knowledge of the connection between impaired behavior and drug use will rapidly lead to action simply because the foreignness of such behavior reduces tendencies to normalize. Even if impaired behavior is not associated with drug use by significant others, some action undoubtedly would be taken toward such a mysteriously impaired individual — probably referral to the medical department since his behavior would appear to be symptomatic of illness. Thus morale costs do not appear to be a relevant issue in the cases of drug abusers in the work place.

Grievance problems likewise do not appear to be a cost factor in regard to drug users. Should disciplinary action occur, it is highly questionable whether union members would show the same sympathy toward the drug user as toward the deviant drinker. It is doubtful if union officials would risk the stigma of "walking the last mile" with this category of deviant. There may, of course, be exceptions such as older employees who develop drug-abuse problems and who have high rapport with the union, but the likelihood of this occurring appears low.

The costs of retraining stemming from the need to replace impaired employees cannot be estimated without knowledge of the extent of the problem. The currently available estimates, crude as they are, indicate that very few of the long-term workers who represent heavy training investments are replaced because of drug-abuse problems. The retraining costs of drug abuse may be accruing, however, in a more subtle way. Companies taking a hard line against illegal drug use among employees, both on and off the job, may find themselves replacing many young workers whose occasional drug use may be detected through elaborate screening devices. Here retraining costs may be high, even though the employer has little evidence of the impairing effects of the drug-use patterns he is attempting to police. Other than such isolated instances of avid drug protection programs, it is doubtful that retraining replacements of the terminated drug abusers would represent significant costs to employers.

As employers know, the dollar costs of separation and replacement are high. In blue-collar and lower-status white-collar groups, lost production would probably cost somewhere around $60, exit interviews would cost in the neighborhood of $15, and the paperwork involved would probably be roughly the same, around $15. Costs involved in the procurement and training of a new worker would probably be somewhere in the neighborhood of $10 for advertising, $30 for interviews and physical examinations, around $12 for testing and placement, around $150 for training, and perhaps $65 to $70 for extra spoilage and mistakes. Extra supervision and "coaching" in many situations would run up to approximately $90. In all probability, additional paperwork for these steps would run around $15.

Thus, the cost of the turnover of one employee, on the bases of broad estimate, would conservatively approximate $400.

Security risks may represent the single highest cost of drug abuse to industry, but here the risks appear limited to opiate addicts. The costs of marihuana, psychedelics, amphetamines, and barbiturates are relatively moderate and are probably lower for the heavy user than the costs of alcohol for the deviant drinker. According to Goode (1970a:993):

> Even if the marihuana seller smoked ten joints a day, an enormous quantity, he would consume a pound every three or four months which means that his "habit" would cost him one dollar a day at the most. If he smoked a much more common two joints a day, his "habit" would cost him about twenty cents a day at the near wholesale price, fifty to seventy-five cents a day at the retail one-ounce price, and nothing if he did some judicious selling.

Heroin, however, is extremely expensive, costing the full-fledged addict between $75 and $100 per day in many instances. Fear of the extremely stressful withdrawal symptoms pressure the addict to maintain his supply, no matter what. Pilferage from an employer may constitute an excellent means of meeting these costs, and most likely the addict will steal in a highly organized manner to avoid detection for as long as possible. Morale costs may arise if the addict turns to stealing from his fellow employees. Although cases of such costly addicts within organizations have been reported, the individual who becomes addicted with such an insecure source of income to maintain his supply is likely to have other social characteristics which would prevent his employment in the first place. Such street addicts also steal from work organizations, but through burglary rather than pilferage. This crime represents a community-based cost rather than a cost relevant to our present concerns. In sum, while opiate addicts who are security risks may be employed, the likelihood of such an occurrence is probably lower than mass media publicity would indicate.

In Chapter One we reviewed the possibility that workmen's compensation awards may represent a cost of the deviant drinker to industry. This possibility appears less likely with drug abuse. Given the widespread adverse feelings toward drug abuse, it would be difficult for an employee to find physicians to collaborate in covering a drug-abuse problem with a diagnosis of some related physiological impairment. Furthermore, it is highly unlikely that the courts will move in the direction of making awards to drug-impaired employees on the basis that employment factors "caused" the drug abuse — this being a possible parallel to workmen's compensation awards that have been made for mental illness cases that have allegedly been work-precipitated. On the other hand, prolonged opiate medication, prescribed as a result of an employment injury and producing drug dependency, could be the basis for compensation benefits. Willig (1971) has explored in detail the implications of such possibilities in various workmen's compensation acts.

The employer may make drug abuse costly to himself by the assumption that the problem is rampant in his organization and in the labor pool. He may invest substantially in additional security personnel such as guards and inspectors, becoming easy prey for entrepreneurs exploiting the current drug hysteria by selling all manner of identification devices, screening gimmicks, and methods of training about drug abuse which are primarily designed to frighten management into buying more of their devices and hiring more security personnel. At the moment numerous organizations are involved in "witch hunts" for drug abusers largely brought on by the hysteria produced in the mass media and widely circulated through hastily prepared conferences, "seminars," and hysterical literature aimed at management. Practically none of this publicity urges the employer to assess the nature of his company's drug problem. Much of it, however, tries to induce fright and concern so that he will readily invest in preventive and protective techniques which he cannot adequately evaluate. Sizeable amounts of money are currently being made by a new arm of the problem industry from hysteria-oriented conferences, booklets, and specialized speakers and consultants. It is probably reasonable to estimate that the amount of money the work world invests in these fear-producing materials and programs is substantially greater than the cost of drug abuse to companies, with the clear exception of alcohol which is often ignored in the pitch of these promoters.

Should some managements eventually realize that well grounded research by uninvolved outsiders is the only route to an accurate understanding of their drug problem, we may be in a position to offer accurate estimates of the costs of drug abusers. Following the estimates of Winslow and his associates (1966) of the costs of deviant drinking, we would first need to know what degree of actual work impairment is brought about by drug use and abuse and to compare this figure with potential performance. This estimate will be more difficult than the estimates for deviant drinking, since we are dealing with many drugs and many drug-use patterns, whereas deviant drinkers tend to be similar in the patterning of impairment. Once we get a clear picture of the legal and grievance proceedings following confrontation with the drug user, we will be in a position to calculate these costs. Calculations of resulting absenteeism and the costs of treatment procedures will also hinge on further research evidence. The absence of a solid cost figure should not detract attention from the drug problem, but should induce the employer to follow widely used management procedures and to support detached research in assessing the depth and breadth of drug use in his own organization.

III

Opiates, Nonopiates, and Their Users

ONE of the problems in discussing drugs and work is to be as explicit as possible about a particular drug. Even though there are hundreds of substances under the drug category the following ones, apart from alcohol or the opiates, seem to be those of greatest current concern: marihuana, the amphetamines, the barbiturates, and nicotine. A background on both these drugs themselves and the types of users is necessary for a perspective on their job impact. Furthermore, the opiates, especially heroin, have been the subject of great debate, calling for special detailed attention — again to both the drug and its users. Finally, such ignored nonopiate drugs as caffeine need closer scrutiny.

MARIHUANA

Practically everyone exposed to mass media in American society today would assume marihuana use has sharply increased in the recent past. It is difficult, however, to find unequivocal evidence. Typical of the confusion and conflict surrounding drug use is the fact that only scattered bits of evidence clearly document the increased use of marihuana among those soon to enter the labor market. The issue of the continuity of drug use from prework roles to work-force participation remains unresolved; reliable evidence about marihuana use among those already in the labor force is even harder to find. Specialist opinion and scattered data do, however, strongly support a sharp increase in the overall prevalence of marihuana use. For example, Louria (1968) states that marihuana use has been growing rapidly regardless of increased penalties against it. Other specialists express similar opinions (Becker, 1968:5; Brenner *et al.*, 1970:88). Goode states that "marihuana use in high school is less frequent than in colleges, although it is increasing in both" (Goode, 1969a:111). In a follow-up study of drug use on a large midwestern university campus in 1970, Schaps and Sanders (1970:144) report that "whereas our best guess two years ago was that 25 to 30 percent of the student body used marihuana, it is now regularly estimated that 60 to 80 percent of all undergraduates have tried it." There are no current bases for assuming these proportions are decreasing, rather research evidence continues to accumulate that they are increasing (Smart *et al.*, 1971).

For those youths who have been introduced to illegal drugs, there seems to be little doubt that the preferred substance is marihuana. A 1967 study conducted at a West Coast university, using a representative sample of 600 from a student body of 12,200, concluded that, with the exception of alcohol, "there can be little question concerning marihuana's being the recreational drug of choice among this college population, one of five admitting its use, despite its illegality" (Suchman, 1968:147). A study which did not consider alcohol use concluded that, "while students had used a variety of drugs, by far the most widely and frequently used were marihuana and other cannabis substances" (Schaps and Sanders, 1970:137). The Blum (1969b) study clearly showed marihuana experiences to be far more frequent than experiences with hallucinogens or opiates. Blumer (1967:83) found marihuana "is by far the most popular among Oakland [California] youths."

Other data from 1967–68 collegiates parallel these findings. A 1967 study of the all-male California Institute of Technology used an anonymous questionnaire which yielded a 90 percent return of 1,290 responses: 19.8 percent of the undergraduates and 7.7 percent of the graduate students reported marihuana use one or more times. In 1967 surveys at Yale and Wesleyan Universities showed that 18 and 25 percent had tried marihuana at least once (Imperi *et al.*, 1968:1022). Noteworthy is that 20 percent of these users reported having smoked marihuana *only* once, while 40 percent had smoked more than ten times. Samples of undergraduates at five coeducational West Coast colleges revealed from 10 to 33 percent users (Blum *et al.*, 1969b:1969).

Yolles (1968), a former director of the National Institute of Mental Health, summarized: "Surveys of high school and college drug use indicate that approximately 20 percent of the college students questioned reported some experience with marihuana. It is estimated that about two million high school and college students have had some experience with marihuana." It is important to note that the 20 to 30 percent figure includes young persons who are users even in a *single* instance.

Closer to our concern with the work world are two surveys of persons in their later twenties and early thirties. A 1967 study of a random sample of 1,104 San Francisco adults eighteen years of age and older revealed that 36 percent of the adult males under 35 years of age had used marihuana at least once. For males between the ages of 18 and 24 the proportion was substantially higher — 49 percent (Mannheimer *et al.*, 1969:1545). Also relevant is a 1968 study of marihuana use by enlisted men in two Army corps in Vietnam (Roffman and Sapol, 1970). Questionnaire data from a random sample of 584 respondents representing a population of 15,284 men in two southern corps units revealed that only 31.7 percent indicated that they had smoked marihuana. Of these, "61.1 percent first smoked marihuana after coming to Vietnam. Approximately three-quarters of the users only experimented with the drug; one-quarter were considered to be heavy marihuana users." Heavy use was, however, defined as smoking on 21 or more occasions. These findings show marihuana use to be no more prevalent in the military population studied than in many civilian university communities, or in the general population of comparable age in San Francisco (Roffman and Sapol, 1970:35).

Two other military surveys found that between 30 and 65 percent of military personnel in Vietnam used cannabis derivatives at least once in their tour of duty (Talbott and Teague, 1969). Since a large formal organization such as the Army resembles many civilian work situations, these studies may indicate the likelihood of young adult marihuana users entering certain areas of the work force. The stress and uncertainty of military life, however, together with the widespead availability and use of cannabis in the native Vietnamese population may make all such generalizations very tenuous.

Two findings of these studies are particularly relevant for work-world projections: marihuana use tends to be concentrated among young, middle-class males who may comprise an important segment of the work force of most organizations. There is considerable agreement that most marihuana users are males (Murphy, 1966; Mauss, 1969; Blum et al., 1969a; Suchman, 1968; Goode, 1970b). It appears that males use all types of drugs more frequently than females; a 1968 study of drug use in metropolitan Toronto high schools consistently found a larger percentage of male students using both legal and illegal drugs (Addiction Research Foundation, 1969).

Numerous studies have also emphasized the middle-class background of users (Brenner, 1970; Blumer, 1967; Suchman, 1968; Mauss, 1969; Carey and Mandell, 1968). Evidence suggests this trend is not as emphatic as current beliefs would indicate. For example, Goode reports users scattered randomly at all social-class levels (Goode, 1969) but he later concluded that there is almost a linear relation between social status and smoking (1970b). Mauss also expresses skepticism regarding the middle-class status of youthful users. He indicates that there is practically no survey data or "other systematic empirical evidence published about the social statuses of contemporary marihuana users" (Mauss, 1969:358). Research on college marihuana use has drawn attention away from the fact that marihuana entered American society via culturally deprived and low-status ethnic groups. There is little reason to believe that use within this population segment has declined; rather, it appears likely that, like alcohol, marihuana is now spread widely across the social spectrum.

The reader should likewise note that most of the studies on which these estimates are based are "cross-sectional," i.e. they do not follow users over a period of time, making it difficult to assess changes. The one study including this follow-up dimension concludes: "In light of the rapid changes we observed taking place in the campus drug community, we would caution investigators of deviant subcultures to pay particular heed to the developmental stages through which the deviant group moves" (Schaps and Sanders, 1970:145). Overall cultural trends may also makes a difference; for example, Cummings sees a

> ... strong element of faddishness about [drug use] .... In the early 1960's there were epidemics of glue sniffing both here and in Scandinavia, and the literature was full of accounts of this dangerous practice, but who hears of it now? In Japan, just after World War II, there was a frightening epidemic of amphetamine use, but it has subsided. Use of LSD was much more widespread in the middle sixties than it is now (Cumming, 1969:3) .

With this background on marihuana, we now turn to the drug itself. It is first necessary to realize that the effects of the drug vary with dosage, the personality of the user, and the social setting in which it is used. Past experiences, expectations, and even the mood of the day may also affect the nature of the "high." The description of modal effects that follows assumes wide individual variations.

In many ways marihuana's short-term effects are similar to those of alcohol. It produces intoxication, typically accompanied by a feeling of well-being, relaxation, sociability, talkativeness, laughing, and, in the sizeable majority of users, a feeling of floating. There is mild exhilaration, a loss of inhibitions, and a changed sense of time. Sometimes physical relaxation leads to drowsiness, but a talkative gregariousness tends to permeate the interpersonal relations among the smokers. The world seems less harsh and abrasive, and one feels separate from general institutional order: social controls are suspended. In some, an ecstasy and euphoria are produced that have a dreamlike quality, accompanied by enhanced sensitivity. Unlike alcohol,* marihuana typically produces little aggression or violence, tending rather to lead to passivity and mild lethargy. Inexperienced users sometimes show anxiety and panic with relatively small doses, but this rarely gets out of control. Much like alcohol, moderate use (such as one cigarette every-four or five hours) does not tend to produce a hangover or any apparent physical impairment.

In short, the results of moderate use of marihuana and alcohol are similar: some unstable personalities may be adversely affected, while the majority of users will suffer no apparent dire consequences. In addition, and in contrast to the visibility of alcohol use, many "pot" users become so familiar with the drug's obvious effects that they can control their own behavior, preventing others from detecting that they are "stoned" (Murphy, 1966; Zinberg and Weil, 1969; Mayor's Report, 1944). Again like alcohol, larger doses of the drug can produce acute effects; while mild doses are usually productive of euphoria and confidence, larger doses may be hallucinogenic.

Like alcohol, marihuana reduces and alters learned inhibitions and, thus, may reveal repressed drives and emotional conflicts, yielding problem behavior. Most observers agree that antisocial behavior is less common with the use of marihuana than with the drinking of alcohol, but there is, however, a definite possibility of an acute paranoid reaction. One recent report describes twelve cases of military personnel in Vietnam who, upon *first* admitted use of marihuana, revealed behavior that justified the diagnosis of "marihuana psychosis" (Talbott and Teague, 1969). Reported symptoms included marked suspiciousness, delusions, and hallucinations combined with such physical symptoms as impaired coordination and throat irritations. It is important to note that the marihuana used in this instance was apparently twice as potent as that typically available in the United States. Furthermore, the acute psychosis faded within a few days, leaving no detectable impairment. The "psychosis" may have been "a reaction to the reaction," the severe and uncontrollable anxiety of a naive, first-time user who believed that the "temporary symptoms of the drug represented a permanent derangement of his mind" (Becker, 1967:163).

Most likely, other novitiates have reacted similarly but were in an otherwise stress-free environment (unlike Vietnam), immersed in a group of experienced users who reassured them and reduced their anxiety. Initial reaction to the effect of any mood-altering drug is

---

* For a humorous and accurate account of alcohol use and bodily violence, see Tannenbaum's (1971) description in the *Wall Street Journal* of the increase in broken jaws during Christmas drinking and celebrating.

related to the tempermental set of the user and to the social setting in which the use occurs. One who is deeply suspicious of the motives of those encouraging him to smoke may well show spells of paranoia under relatively large doses. The social setting may reinforce an intense feeling of being overwhelmed and dissolved into the surroundings; such reactions can strongly reinforce feelings of anxiety and panic. Beyond a doubt, many first-time users feel isolated and lost without the usual reference points for ordinary behavior. Irrationality and paranoia likewise accompany alcohol intoxication among some inexperienced users; but the familiarity of drunken behavior rarely leads psychiatric observers to apply to it the potent psychiatric label of "acute psychosis" (Murphy, 1966; Popham and Kalant, 1970; Brenner et al., 1970).

Little is known about any long-term effects of marihuana use. Cannabis psychosis is rare and apparently requires both heavy use of the much stronger hashish and a preexisting disturbance. Studies of long-term marihuana use in India and North Africa (which may have limited applicability to the United States) show that heavy users neglect personal hygiene and diet; such users are thus undernourished and more susceptible to infection. Chronic bronchitis and emphysema are frequently reported concomitants of regular, heavy chronic use, as with heavy smoking of tobacco cigarettes. Evidence of chronic mental deterioration is nonexistent. In one group with an average of seven years of regular use, no evidence of either mental or physical deterioration was found (Murphy, 1966). Sloth and lethargy, which are the main reported accompaniments of heavy chronic use in foreign settings, may result from social and cultural conditions that accompany the use of the drug rather than from the drug itself. Informal observers of the American collegiate scene report the existence of the unmotivated drug head who eventually may drop out of academic pursuits, but the extent of such syndromes, the role marihuana plays in their development, and the degree to which such individuals restrict their drug use to "pot" are all unknown. Heavy use of the drug may, in most social settings, lead to situations similar to those found by foreign researchers; however, it is not until adequate long-term research is performed that we can actually answer this question (Kalant and Kalant, 1968; Archibald et al., 1969; Murphy, 1966; McGlothlin, 1966). One such report has speculated that long-term use might cause liver damage or might aggravate the toxic effects of alcohol on the liver (Kew et al., 1969).

To what extent does marihuana produce dependency? The concept of "drug dependence" was formulated by the World Health Organization in 1964 after repeated failure to develop workable definitions distinguishing "drug addiction" from "drug habituation." Drug dependence is "a state arising from repeated administration of a drug on a periodic or continuous basis" (World Health Organization, 1964:9). Drug dependence "will vary with the agent involved," and, consequently, any use of the term must include designation of the particular type of drug involved.

A component of drug dependence, physiological dependence, is usually well defined and specific. When the drug produces physiological changes, i.e. body cells adapt to the drug, withdrawal of the chemical produces clearly observable physical distress. Physiological dependence may be partially based on tolerance, which is the body's adaptation to the presence of the drug so that an increase in dosage is required to bring about the same effects previously produced. The classic example of this kind of physical dependence occurs with the use of the opiates where tolerance may rapidly increase and withdrawal distress may be pronounced only after weeks of relatively heavy doses. Tolerance or physical dependence, however, sometimes occurs without the other.

Psychological dependence is much less precise, however. Lindesmith (1947), in his study of opiate addiction, demonstrated that unless a drug user was conscious of what was producing his withdrawal distress and of how it might be relieved by readministration, he did not become fully drug dependent. The World Health Organization (1964:13) describes this aspect of dependence as "psychic dependence upon the effect of the drug related to a subjective and individual appreciation of those effects." A group of Canadian researchers have attempted a quite inclusive definition of psychic dependence that is linked to relatively common human habits:

> Psychological dependence can occur with any type of drug and with many types of behavior not involving drugs. It is important to reiterate that psychological dependence is merely a descriptive label for a pattern of behavior which can vary from a trivial and inconsequential reliance upon some generally harmless substance or practice, such as one's morning paper or coffee, to an intense need for a drug which dominates virtually the whole pattern of an individual's life. The potential range of intensities from trivial to severe is well illustrated by the different shades of psychological dependence upon cigarette smoking (Archibald et al., 1969:17).

An example of psychological dependency is a person with no physical disorder who for years repeatedly takes a barbiturate compound to bring on sleep, even without having to increase the amount and without any physiological harm (Brenner et al., 1970:12–13). Cumming puts the dichotomy into practical focus: regardless of whether a person is "addicted" or "habituated," what is significant "is the dependence itself;

one form can be as enslaving as the other" (Cumming, 1969:1). Perhaps the definition offered by Bell in 1958 is sufficient to encompass the essence of addiction: it is a "craving or a compulsion to eat, drink or inhale a specific substance, which if frustrated, results in a most unwelcome effect" (Bell, 1958:585).

Goode finds "psychological dependence" vague and "not easily measured. . . . the designation permits such looseness in interpretation as to be almost without utility as an analytic category" (Goode, 1969a:46). He quotes one author as pointing out that men have a strong "psychic dependence on wearing pants." Drug dependency may be as much related to the user's personality as to the pharmacology of the drug; this would certainly seem to be the case with marihuana. In other words, there is probably a dependent personality type susceptible to extreme reliance on a variety of persons, situations, and drugs. The American Medical Association refers to the personality dimension in its definition of psychic dependence: "Persons who use marihuana continually and as the symptomatic expression of a psychological conflict, [as] a means of gaining social acceptance, or as a way of escaping painful experiences of anxiety or depression, may be said to be psychologically dependent on the substance" (American Medical Association, 1967:369). Hollister (1971:26) concludes that "psychological dependence [on marihuana] has been well documented, but physical dependence manifested by withdrawal reactions is unknown."

In short, there is no addiction to marihuana as the term *addiction* is typically interpreted, i.e. *physical* dependence upon a drug. The World Health Organization's definition of the "problem" marihuana user is as follows:

> Drug dependence of cannabis type is described as a state arising from repeated administration of cannabis or cannabis substances, which in some areas is almost exclusively periodic, in others more continuous. Its characteristics include: (1) a desire (or need) for repeated administration of the drug on account of its subjective effects, including the feeling of enhanced capabilities; (2) little or no tendency to increase the dose, since there is little or no development of tolerance; (3) a psychic dependence on the effects of the drug related to subjective and individual appreciation of those effects; (4) absence of physical dependence so that there is no definite and characteristic abstinence syndrome when the drug is discontinued (World Health Organization, 1964:15).

Marihuana creates a lower risk of dependency than alcohol. The World Health Organization's Committee on Alcohol and Alcoholism described dependency as follows: "Since, on the interruption of continous drinking, the distressing withdrawal symptoms provoke the drinker to seek relief from them by the use of more alcohol, the committee refers to this condition as a 'physical dependence on alcohol' " (Jellinek, 1960:144). Jellinek describes "a Gamma species" of alcoholism in which there is "(1) acquired increased tissue tolerance to alcohol, (2) adaptive cell metabolism, (3) withdrawal symptoms and 'craving,' i.e. physical dependence, and (4) loss of control" (Jellinek, 1960:37). He argues that Gamma alcoholism is apparently "the predominating species of alcoholism in the United States and Canada, as well as in other Anglo-Saxon countries." Cumming (1969:9) places alcohol among the hard drugs since it develops tolerance, causes abstinence distress, and intoxicates.

In addition, the Committee on Alcohol and Alcoholism delineated a psychological dependency component in alcoholism:

> During a period of abstinence, even in the absence of withdrawal symptoms, one observes clinically the building up of psychological tensions which provokes a 'pathological desire' for alcohol as a means of relieving this tension; in this condition the individual may be said to be psychologically dependent on alcohol" (Jellinek, 1960:144).

Psychological dependence on marihuana apparently matches psychological dependence on alcohol; subsequent physical dependence may develop upon alcohol but not upon marihuana. Excessive drinking, however, does not necessarily produce physical dependence: "There may be heavy, frequent drinking which does not go beyond psychological dependency, but still may cause social damage and damage to the user's health . . ." (Jellinek, 1960:152). In sum, marihuana use does not create physical dependency risks in contrast to alcohol, barbiturates, and the opiates.

THE MARIHUANA USERS

The psychologically dependent user of marihuana is the first type of marihuana user we shall consider. Brenner and his associates estimate that the number of "those who are psychologically dependent on marihuana is very small, at least at the present time." Goode (1969a) estimates that "the true heads represent less than one percent of all who have smoked marihuana." These psychologically dependent users probably show a "general disposition toward psychoactive drug use" (Bluem et al., 1969b:109) and reflect "a widespread willingness to use a variety of drugs as tools to alter states of consciousness, biological cycles, and social relations." Thus the marihuana-dependent person is in all probability deeply involved in the use of other drugs as well (Goode,

1969c:58). Although Schaps and Sanders (1970:138) do not regard the heavy user as necessarily psychologically dependent on marihuana, they do indicate that frequent and regular users of marihuana also tend to be frequent and regular users of a variety of recreational drugs. Thus the dependent marihuana user who only uses marihuana may be non-existent. We would include in our definition of this psychologically dependent type the presence of significant role impairment resulting from marihuana use.

The heavy user, our second type, may be more relevant to the work world. He is a frequent user, but although "marihuana is an important element in his life, it does not disrupt his functioning" (Goode,. 1969a:110). The Vietnam study of military marihuana users defined heavy use as smoking on 21 or more occasions during the two-year time span the study covered. Goode's estimates place approximately 11 percent of users in this category, while the Vietnam study included 25.4 percent in their comparable category. Schaps and Sanders (1970:138) define heavy users as "those who are frequent and regular users of a variety of recreational drugs," not only marihuana. They placed 26 percent of the drug users in their sample in this category.

This type of smoker continues to perform many of his role functions satisfactorily. Even though he often works while "high," he readily compensates for the drug effect so that those around him are not aware of his psychic condition. This surprising capacity of frequent users to "compensate" has been clearly documented (Zinberg and Weil, 1969). At the same time, such users clearly risk psychological dependence on the drug with subsequent role impairment. The greatest number of potential marihuana-problem employees are of this type. In all probability, the psychologically dependent user is so immersed in a drug subculture that he is not on the payrolls of American industry, while by contrast the frequent-heavy user will probably continue to work despite his regular smoking. Consequently, it is among the frequent-heavy users that employers can expect to encounter marginal work performance. Conservatively (realizing there is a likelihood that as young, male heavy users enter the labor force their usage will taper off), it seems likely that 4 to 5 percent of those who use marihuana may have job behaviors that are not consistent with typical work norms.

Closely paralleling the "social drinker" is a third type who can be termed the "social smoker." These are the occasional users who smoke on social occasions where marihuana is available. Apparently, marihuana is coming to serve for many of its youthful users the same social functions that alcohol serves for the adult generation. While data from other cultures indicate that marihuana is used primarily in private contemplative patterns, practically all American studies of the drug suggest it generates sociability, talkativeness, and a relaxation conducive to pleasant group interaction. Social use of the drug does in fact appear to be normative in some youth subcultures; informal interviews conducted by Roman indicate that "smoking alone" is defined as deviance among occasional users. A side effect of social-use patterns is protection and orientation provided for first-time users or others who may get an unexpected reaction and feel they are "losing their minds." The social smoker category broadly corresponds to the "light-moderate" and the "moderate" users described by Schaps and Sanders (1970:137). Twenty-four percent of their users fell into these categories, while Goode estimates 33 percent of all users to be social smokers.

By far the most frequent type of marihuana smoker is, ironically, the infrequent user. Sometimes called the "experimenter," he tries the drug a few times, but probably never learns the process of becoming a marihuana smoker (Becker, 1953) and shows little determination to become a user. Pearlman (1968) reports that in an urban, college-student population about one-third of the users had had only a single experience, while another 60 percent had used it only a few times. The study of Army enlisted men in Vietnam reported that "most marihuana users appeared interested only in experimentation, not continued use" (Roffman and Sapol, 1970:16). Goode's campus study of marihuana use reports:

> . . . infrequent use is far more common than frequent use. Most individuals do not "progress" to using marihuana often. The infrequent use of marihuana does not inevitably "lead to" frequent use. Most users either discontinue the use altogether, or continue use infrequently (Goode, 1969c:62).

This category also corresponds to the 42 percent of "light" users described by Schaps and Sanders (1970). On the basis of these data, the social smoker and the infrequent user comprise roughly 90 percent of all users.

Considering that some of these will cease to use marihuana when they move into jobs, the percentages are hardly consistent with the public hysteria in numerous quarters. The chief risk run by these young users is the definite possibility that they may be branded as "criminal" and left with a record for life.

The young person who abstains from marihuana has received almost no attention. In Suchman's (1968) study 22 percent reported no drug use, and a large majority of the Vietnam soldiers, approximately 69 percent, had never smoked marihuana (but the extent to which they may have used other drugs is unknown). The Blums (1969) defined abstainers somewhat misleadingly, indicating only 4 percent of the students on five campuses had used no drugs, including alcohol and tobacco. Since only the Vietnam study strictly reports on abstainers from marihuana, it is the best guideline currently available. It seems likely that at least 50 percent of young persons entering the labor market may never have used marihuana. The other 50 percent are distributed among the types described above, with most in the "experimental" and "occasional" or "social" user categories.

To what extent will these use patterns carry over into regular employment? This question raises a prior one: to what extent are young people socialized into marihuana use before entering college? One study found "high school students rating high on the Scale of Anticipatory Socialization Toward College were about twice as likely to have used marihuana as those not rating high" (Mauss, 1969:363). This finding was significant among upper middle-class youth, less so in the middle-class group, and actually negative in the lowest-status group. The findings held for males only. In sum, upper middle-class boys who anticipated going to college while still in high school were more likely users of marihuana than middle-class or lower-class boys in this study. Thus some students may come to college with a readiness for continued experimentation with drugs.

What about post-college use? Eighty percent of the users in Suchman's study indicated that they had never gotten sick using marihuana, although 25 percent of these reported at least one "bad" drug experience. Less than 10 percent of the users wanted to stop or had even tried to stop using the drug, even though 20 percent said that they were rather "worried" about continued use (Suchman, 1968). These data infer the absence of any significant motivation to cease use in the personal experiences of many users.

Another set of data is relevant to the carry-over question: while 28 percent of the users in the Vietnam study said they had smoked marihuana before entering active service, "the greatest percentage of users in this category merely sampled the drug, smoking it five times or less" (Roffman and Sapol, 1970:16). Specifically, 72 percent of users with previous experience were casual users in Vietnam; 28 percent were heavy users. Upon entering the service, but before arriving in Vietnam, approximately 61 percent continued to use marihuana, but of this number only a quarter were heavy users. Thus there was a carry-over of use into military life among the majority of users when they moved into active duty, but the number of heavy users remained roughly the same. Some stopped use upon entering the service but were joined during this period by a sizeable number of new users. In any event, this study does give us some information about the extent to which marihuana use carried over into a structured work situation, although soldiering in Vietnam is not typical of most American work settings. It suggests that there are a sizeable number of users who drop the use of marihuana, but their numbers may be countered by some who initiate use upon entry into a regular job role.

If we assume that marihuana use parallels alcohol use in the generation of the 1930's and 1940's, then two types of heavy users may be expected to develop. First are those whose heavy use reaches the point of psychological dependency during college and who carry this use over into the early stages of the work career. The second type is comprised of those who develop heavy use or psychologically dependent use as they grow older and must accommodate more fully to the demands and role expectations of organizational life (Trice and Belasco, 1970). These, of course, are strictly inferences from data which may not accurately represent the young worker; adequate data on marihuana-use patterns among representative groups of young workers are simply not available.

AMPHETAMINES

Although a group of drugs with vast potential for damage to both the work world and the community at large, the amphetamines have received relatively little attention in the American literature. Available data are meager and confusing. These drugs apparently have more potential for creating dependency than marihuana. Use is by no means concentrated among youth although some well publicized, spectactular use patterns have been noted among younger persons. In contrast to marihuana, amphetamines are widely available legally, a market augmented by an unknown number of illegal distribution points. Most significantly, the drug "fits" into the American work ethic, since it affords the user persistent hard work and concentration over a sizeable period of time. Kalant (1966:65), reporting on the work of Connell, states that "all walks of life and occupations were represented [among amphetamine users]. . . .It is worth noting, however, that people in the medical and paramedical professions, and, in recent years, married women and housewives, are highly represented" (Kalant, 1966:65).

Whether or not the use of the drug has recently increased either in student-youth populations or among persons already actively working in the labor market is difficult to ascertain. Blum and associates state that "limited evidence suggests that excessive and chronic useis increasing.

. . . among drug oriented groups intravenous injection has replaced oral administration" (Blum *et al.,* 1969a:114). They also indicate that "physicians and staff at college health services are uneasy about the insidious but recognized increase in the use of the amphetamines" (Blum *et al.,* 1969b:301). Some relatively unrepresentative data from their study on five college campuses indicate a slight increase in usage; however, "the amphetamines have been widely used on many campuses for years for such innocuous purposes as staying awake all night to study for examinations and to concentrate more intensively during examinations" (Becker, 1968:5). Rawlins (1968) describes how amphetamine use became a pharmacological part of the end-of-the-semester ceremony during the late forties and early fifties, setting the stage for abuse of the drug by students today. A study of amphetamine use among medical students at the University of Oregon in 1965 found that almost half had used amphetamines, and most of these had used them more than once (Smith and Blachly, 1966). In 1955 Los Angeles police seized 6,987 amphetamines; in 1964 this number jumped to 99,884 (Rawlins, 1968:57). While some of this increase may be due to better police detection and population increase, the magnitude seems far too great to attribute solely to these factors. In St. Louis, Robins and Murphy (1967) found that 16 percent of the black males who were born between 1930 and 1934 and had attended school were regular amphetamine users.

The Blums (1969a:114) state that "epidemics of use center among the 15 to 30 age group in Japan, Sweden, England, and the United States — four of the most technically advanced nations." In other words, if amphetamine use has increased, it has been not only in the youthful category, but also in the late twenties and thirties age group. Moreover, "high school students also appear to be showing an increasing rate of amphetamine use" (Cox and Smart, 1970:727). This review cites a research paper by D. E. Smith which indicated that "22 percent of the eleventh and twelfth grade students in the research population had taken amphetamines once or twice, while 75 percent of the users had taken them three or more times."

A belief in an increase in the use of the amphetamines pervaded a recent Senate hearing on a bill to control stimulant drugs. Former Senator Thomas Dodd held that the illegal use of these drugs was rapidly increasing among juveniles and young adults and that the use of these drugs was directly related to increased crimes of violence. He also claimed that amphetamines were in many instances replacing hard narcotics such as opium, heroin, and cocaine and that amphetamine abuse was becoming more prevalent among middle-class youth with no prior delinquency or criminal records (Walsh, 1964:1419). Witnesses testified that truck stops on major highways were the major centers of distribution for illegal amphetamines and that at least half of the nine million doses of barbiturates and amphetamines produced in 1962 had found their way into the black market. A 1965 World Health Organization report unequivocally states a concern over the world-wide spread of amphetamine type drugs, especially among the young (World Health Organization, 1965). Robbins (1970) refers to a 1966 report which indicated amphetamine use was on the rise in both the United States and Sweden. Moreover, the Select Committee on Crime of the House of Representatives, U.S. Congress, clearly implied an increase when it reported, "there is an incredible overproduction of speed by legitimate manufacturers. Eight billion speed pills are being spewed out upon this country every year. This is enough for 40 doses for every man, woman, and child in the United States" (U.S. Congress, 1971:2). Later the Committee's report states: "Testimony . . . uniformly attested to the relationship between abuse of amphetamine-type drugs and violence and crime" (14). All in all, it seems reasonable to conclude that there has been a recent increase in both the legal and illegal use of the amphetamines (Kramer *et al.*, 1967; Griffith, 1968) and the drug has truly dangerous potentials.

Manufacturing statistics indicate amphetamine use has been increasing since the end of World War II. An estimate of annual production in the United States for 1962 indicated four and one-half billion tablets, or twenty-five tablets per citizen; the Food and Drug Administration estimates half of these were consumed without a medical prescription (Blum *et al.*, 1969a). Seever's rough estimate concluded that

> Seventy tablets of amphetamine-type drugs are produced legally in the United States for every man, woman and child. This is almost three times the estimated yearly production of barbiturates. Although illicit manufacture of amphetamines exists and is apparently on the increase, no estimates of production are available. It is safe to state that total production is greatly in excess of proper medical need, some estimates using a factor of ten or more (Seever, 1968:7).

Kalant, whose amphetamine study is probably the most comprehensive, strongly suggests there may be many more amphetamine users and abusers in the general population than is typically suggested and points out:

> official statistics may underestimate the true incidence of drug abuse and addiction by two orders of magnitude, both because of the failure to report diagnosed cases and because of a lack of interest and attention to the problems of diagnosis. It should be emphasized that about ten percent of all cases of drug abuse involve amphetamines (Kalant, 1966:115).

The Blums (1969b) found that 21 percent of the students studied on five campuses had taken amphetamines at least once, while Goode used different sampling procedures and found 43 percent to have taken one of the amphetamines at least once (Goode, 1969c). The data recorded in student drug diaries collected by the Blums indicate that the extent of amphetamine usage varied widely, ranging from 5 percent in one school to 33 percent in another. These diaries showed that most used amphetamines rarely, although there were a few who used the drug between seven and fourteen times per week. These users seemed to *concentrate* their use, suggesting to the researchers periodic and acute cycles rather than steady, regular use (Blum *et al.*, 1969b).

The amphetamines occur in numerous forms and combinations, benzedrene and dexedrine for example. Seevers (1968) lists 70 different classifications of amphetamines and amphetaminelike drugs. Amphetamines are synthetic stimulants that arouse the central nervous system. The action is chemically similar to that of adrenalin, a hormone that prepares the nervous system for the organism to go into action. Amphetamines are most frequently used to produce a sense of wakefulness which in turn produces a marked increase in emotional and motor activities. Thus, with moderate doses the user becomes more alert and more energetic and can continue psychological and physical activities for long periods before becoming tired. Many users report a marked increase in ability to concentrate, an elevated mood, and a state of well-being. Kalant summarizes the stimulant effect of the amphetamines as being "perceived subjectively as a sense of increased energy and self-confidence, and of faster and more efficient thought and decision making; it is usually accompanied by a feeling of well-being and even of euphoria" (Kalant, 1966:5).

The amphetamines, through preparing the system for action, inhibit appetite and are widely used for weight control. In addition, moderate dosages may alleviate depression. These two functions of the drug fit neatly into a society that admires the slim figure and rewards the optimist. In low and moderate doses of approximately 10 to 20 mg. per day, the drug has been beneficially employed since its development in the 1930's; however, substantially larger doses can produce intoxication and over-stimulation of the sympathetic and central nervous system, sharply altering mood and producing a high risk of psychotic symptoms such as frightening auditory and visual hallucinations and delusions of persecution (Kalant, 1966; Archibald *et al.*, 1969; Blum *et al.*, 1969b). Chronic use of large doses, through appetite inhibition, can result in malnutrition and reduced resistance to infectious disease. Concentration becomes more difficult as thoughts go racing through the mind. Psychotic results are not presently predictable, but observers infer that since tolerance for the drug increases rapidly, the risk of psychotic reaction also goes up with increased intake. Not only high dosages, but also the anxiety and fear of new users may bring on these reactions. It has also been observed that "in certain individuals the intake of one or a few doses of amphetamines can produce a transitory psychotic episode" (Kalant, 1966:23). That such psychotic reactions are transitory does not alter the fact that they can be extremely disturbing and even dangerous in a work situation.

Amphetamines, however, may apparently be used for long periods of time without damaging effects or without the need for modification of dosage. Kalant presents numerous examples to show "that the amphetamines can be taken in considerable doses and for prolonged periods by some individuals without any marked physical or mental toxic effects" (Kalant, 1966:34). Individual responses to the drug vary widely (Cox and Smart, 1970); apparently these are unpredictable and thus an overall condemnation of the drug may be inappropriate. The amphetamines may, through their behaviorally enhancing effects, fit very neatly into certain role demands and job situations. These drugs are often valuable to the student who is cramming for exams, the athlete who wants additional nervous energy and a feeling of fatigue reduction, the truck driver involved in long cross-country hauls ("West Coast Turnabouts," i.e. a driver can go to the coast, take on a supply of "dexies" and a new truck load and return nonstop), the moonlighter who must keep alert for two jobs, the entertainer who needs energy and self-confidence, and in many other roles where "efficiency" counts heavily.

Recent testimony before a Senate Subcommittee on drug abuse in the trucking industry indicated that amphetamine use is required for a successful job performance among many long-haul truck drivers (Angle, 1971). The argument was advanced by Senator Harold Hughes, a former truck driver, that the pressures for maintaining alertness over long hauls did not make amphetamine use an option but rather required it: "Too many drivers face a cruel choice of taking pills or falling asleep at the wheel." Further testimony was advanced that truckers are forced to use amphetamines because of extremely short notice given before haul assignments and the trucking companies' circumvention of federal rules governing duration of a particular hauling assignment.

Professional sports, especially football, provide another example of the compatibility between the chemical effects of the amphetamines and the demands made on many workers for strenuous performances. Malcolm (1970) reports on two studies of drug effects in sports, one on swimmers and the other on track men. They compared the effects of barbiturates, amphetamines, and a placebo. For the swimmers "the amphetamines significantly improved performance and had no conclusive effect on judgment" (Malcolm, 1970:5), while "eight out of the nine [track men] ran faster with the amphetamines than with the placebo." In addition he describes studies of motor coordination and control in which the amphetamines improved performance. He concludes that it is "likely that the stimulants caused both attitude change and performance changes, and that these factors are at least initially independent of one another" (Malcolm, 1970:6). Using drugs to assist players such as punt and kick-off return specialists obviously raises serious ethical questions; but, since winning has become all important ("winning is not everything; it is the *only* thing") in practically all sports, the value of the amphetamines in providing the narrow margin between winning and losing is obvious. Seevers (1968:11) concurs by stating that ". . . carefully controlled studies have demonstrated that amphetamines are capable of driving trained athletes to increased performance in individual athletic events involving strength and endurance," and their use in athletics is more widespread than is generally admitted.

Bernie Parrish a well known, and, until recently, employed, professional "cornerback" openly admits in his book (Parrish, 1971) that he relied heavily on Dexedrine and other drugs to face the rigors of professional games. Zimmerman believes that "bennies" and Dexedrine "pop up in many dressing rooms" (1971:243). Scott (1971) reports that a veteran captain of a major professional football team filed a 1.79 million dollar law suit against his team because he was administered harmful and dangerous drugs without his consent. Scott divides the drugs used among athletes into those that are restorative and those that are additive. The former, such as painkillers, anti-inflammatants, and muscle-relaxers are far less controversial than those additive drugs used "with the intent of stimulating an athlete to perform beyond his 'normal' capability — The use of these drugs is usually cloaked in secrecy, for they are extremely controversial from a legal and ethical, as well as medical, standpoint" (Scott, 1971:108). He also uses reports from a popular sports magazine to emphasize the role of the amphetamines as an additive drug in sports:

> Bill Gilbert, in a series on drug usage in athletics for *Sports Illustrated,* pointed out how amphetamines have what he termed a triple-threat effect. They work indirectly to suppress hunger, and, consequently, are often used by athletes such as jockeys, boxers and wrestlers when they have to lose weight quickly in order to make a specific weight limit. They also speed up the user's respiratory and circulatory system, enabling him to remain hyper-

active when he might otherwise have been overcome with fatigue. And, finally, they act directly on the brain, producing a sense of euphoria and an "I-can-lick-the-world" feeling (Scott, 1971:109).

It is not difficult to expand this list of occupational roles whose incumbents might find the use of the amphetamines valuable to them. The executive who must deal with large numbers of organizational problems, put in many long hours, and show an "energetic" posture in order to move up the promotion ladder might readily benefit from the controlled moderate use of these drugs. In postwar Japan, when that society was rebuilding,

> amphetamines became their favorite drug. In time, however, use grew to such an extent that it became a serious problem and it became necessary to bring the sale not only of amphetamines, but also all raw materials from which it was possible to manufacture amphetamines chemically, under the strictest possible control (Jacobsen, 1961:5; see also Malcolm, 1971).

Consequently, we have a situation in which the drug is admirably compatible with many of the norms and demands of the typical American work organization even though it is potentially dangerous.

Aside from the definite possibility that untoward and even psychotic behavior may result from heavy or prolonged use of amphetamines, a drug dependency of a kind substantially different from that stemming from excessive use of marihuana but somewhat like that present in alcoholism can emerge. The alertness, energy, and sense of power which amphetamine use can produce could easily lead the user to continue and even increase his dosage, and evidence also clearly suggests that physical dependency is a definite possibility. Not only heavy use but even less spectacular, ordinary use may expose the user to addiction: "Eventually both psychological dependence and tolerance may develop, leading the user to steadily increase his dosage and finally to switch to intravenous injection, a method which produces stronger and quicker effects" (Robbins, 1970:188). Kalant, after a careful review of information available in 1966, concluded that addiction to the amphetamines definitely occurs:

> Development of tolerance was common, and often marked, and the problems of obtaining the large doses required led in many cases to financial hardship, neglect of family, and anti-social behavior such as theft and forgery of prescriptions. In addition, physical dependency has been indicated recently by the discovery of certain abnormal electro-encephalographic and electro-oculographic patterns during amphetamine withdrawal which are abolished immediately by restoring the drug. It is possible that the absence of severe withdrawal symptoms is related to the relatively low rate of elimination of the drug. It is therefore concluded that addiction to amphetamines does occur (Kalant, 1966:120).

Earlier, in 1964, the Expert Committee on Addiction Producing Drugs had concluded there was a "general absence of physical dependence so that there is no characteristic abstinence syndrome when the drug is discontinued" (World Health Organization, 1964:15). Other experts currently believe "it has still not been decided whether continual regular use of 'speed' actually leads to physical addiction" (Cox and Smart, 1970:725). Robbins (1970:190) believes, however, that "regular intravenous consumption of amphetamines produces more serious psychic and organic damage than long-term opiate addiction." In short, the amphetamines are far from free of dangerous effects. This concern appears to be reflected in the fact that the medical profession lists in the *Physicians' Desk Reference to Pharmaceutical Specialties and Biologicals* only two obscure disorders for which amphetamines are indicated: narcolepsy or inappropriate deep sleep and hyperactivity in children who are often called minimally brain-damaged children. At the same time agreement among specialists about the drug's capacity to produce physical dependency is less than their consensus about dependency risks associated with alcohol, opiates, or barbiturates.

THE AMPHETAMINE USERS

With this background it is possible to delineate different types of amphetamine users. First, are those who find amphetamines compatible with their jobs. Seevers believes amphetamines have

> ...legitimate medical usage in situations where the individual must continue to perform adequately for comparatively long periods of time.... the greater use for alerting and insomniac purposes in the United States is by truck drivers and students. From a medical point of view, reasonable use of drugs for this purpose would appear to be proper (Seevers, 1968:10).

Apparently such users do not experience unfortunate consequences such as paranoid reactions and are actually stimulated, sustained, and provided with a competitive advantage by the drug. A 1964 review of data on amphetamines and delinquency indicated that in moderate amounts amphetamines may yield desirable reactions and cited several clinicians who had "treated delinquents with amphetamines and reported dramatic improvements in up to half the patients in work performance and social attitudes" (Scott, 1964:452). Certainly there is no way of predicting in advance who such fortunate persons will be.

A second type of user is the relatively infrequent abuser who takes average doses and experiences a substantial degree of intoxication. His tolerance for the drug rises rapidly and he may subsequently experience acute reactions. The overrestless, excited, voluble, and manic behavior brought on by this type of use can be quite disruptive in work relationships and can adversely affect work productivity (see Chapter Five). Although the infrequent abuser may not be technically addicted to the drug, his intoxicated behavior poses a definite risk of antisocial behavior within the work setting. Moreover, if use continues to the point that withdrawal occurs, overt depression can damage job performance and pressure the user into resuming the drug. Furthermore, the drug may aggravate and reinforce a psychological condition recently called "work addiction" (described in Chapter Four). The term "overreacher" used to describe peak intravenous abusers may be apropos to the extremely compulsive work addict: "He is always straining to do more than he has done in the past. This is not done as a matter of setting new records, but as a matter of uncontrollable use of bottomless energies derived from a distant factory which knows him not" (Fiddle, 1968:82).

Finally, there is the user who becomes addicted to the drug and whose addiction can drastically affect role performance not only at work but also in the family and community. Even if the addiction is short-lived, the experience can have lasting effects on the user's personality.

> There is a tendency toward identity loss. When a user is "up" on speed he feels elated, masterful, intellectual and socially sparkling. After the stimulant wears off and the user is "down" he may feel tired and depressed, dull and ineffectual . . . and see one's "real" self as dull and empty. The amphetamine addict may become convinced that he has no identity except by virtue of his stimulants and his dependency will be thereby reinforced (Robbins, 1970:190).

It is now generally accepted that amphetamine and combined amphetamine-barbiturate dependency is much more widespread in the United States and most Western countries than narcotic dependency (Griffith, 1968:17). There is also reason to believe that amphetamine abusers tend to use alcohol and barbiturates heavily. Clinical evidence suggests that they are "adept at concealing addiction" (Bell and Trethowan, 1961:490).

Apart from these types is the "speed-freak" or "meth-head" who Yablonsky (1968:33) describes as "a new breed of drug addict." He believes that, while some may also use heroin, most only "shoot speed." Carey and Mandel (1968:165) describe these persons as users of amphetamines who regularly take 100 to 1,000 mg., compared to the typical daily doses of 5 to 10 mg., mostly by intravenous injection. The crystalline form of the drug is mixed with water and injected directly into the veins with effects that are immediate and far more intense than the results of oral administration. The sensation of extreme euphoria and intense pleasure has been described as "an orgasm all over your body" and "nirvana" (Carey and Mandel, 1968:167). A "rush" or feeling of sudden and unusually heightened exhilaration immediately follows the injection, but within a few minutes the intense euphoria subsides and an adrenalin-like effect experienced as a flood of uncoordinated physical and mental energy emerges. Having achieved the high, the user can go even higher by continuing injections; if he does not, a "down" begins after two or three hours and the user becomes exhausted and often very depressed. If, however, he continues "shooting" he can prolong the "trip" during which he is a very different person. Carey and Mandel (1968) list hyperactivity, compulsive behavior, paranoia, and extreme volubility as behavioral characteristics of the high speed-freak. They report that it is not uncommon for them to stay awake for two, three, or even four days, a duration that is called a "run." Appetite is almost nonexistent, but physical activity and energy are incredible. If the trip is quite long — as much as four or five days — the user becomes emaciated and may "freak-out," i.e. may experience a severe toxic psychosis in which very rapid perceptions are completely out of his control.

During the trip, concentration may become so enhanced that actions are often highly repetitive while the user's productivity is immense. Carey and Mandel describe one chronic user who during a series of runs turned out a largely unintelligible 453-page book when he had been requested only to make minor comments on a simple research project. Aggressiveness may also characterize this hyperactivity, especially when the user is "coming down" and approaching a "crash." The aggressive antisocial behavior appears unprovoked, is unpredictable, varies in nature and intensity from person to person and varies with the nature of the high and the runs accompanying it.

In addition, toxic paranoia, often present in the acute reactions of other users, may pervade the behavior and mental processes of the meth-head. Perhaps this can be explained by the constant threat of arrest and by "self-reaction" to his own frequent outbursts of aggression. These users are also extremely voluble. Carey and Mandel (1968:169) report that "verbosity is so intense [among users] that four person conversations are often impossible because everyone is speaking at once." This unusual characteristic alone can limit the effectiveness of the meth-head's interactions. When the speed-freak crashes, he may sleep for 24 to 36 hours and will be intensely sensitive when he awakens. Any inconvenience angers him; arguments and even physically aggressive behavior are frequent. Any simple demand made upon him is seen as inconsiderate and wholly inappropriate. The down is so diametrically opposed to the high that it explains why heavy users eventually experience confusion of personal identity. This may subjectively parallel the intense agony of opiate withdrawal.

Obviously, the speed-freak and meth-head cannot engage in regular and steady work life. While the speed-freak is "unlikely to have a job" (Carey and Mandel, 1968:173), "maintaining a pattern of just weekend use would be difficult..." (Cox and Smart, 1970:728). Thus the major impact of amphetamine abuse on the work world will come from moderate users who experience acute intoxication reactions. Likewise, there may be employed chronic users who do not "shoot crystal," but whose drug use may at times produce some of the speed-freak's behaviors in less exaggerated forms. These chronic users may show aggressiveness, work overactivity, sensitivity, and extreme talkativeness, but perform adequately enough to remain in work settings.

Heavy amphetamine use may develop in an effort to find a way out of other drug dependencies or to assuage the effects of a bad trip on another drug. Robbins reports

> ... an interesting pattern in which the drug becomes popular in youthful drug scenes as a "remedy" to mitigate the consequences of another drug. Persons become involved in amphetamines as a device for reintegrating themselves after disruptive psychedelic experiences and subsequently use heroin to alleviate the ravages of speed (Robbins, 1970:192).

The sketchy research information available makes it difficult to estimate the distribution of these various types, but the chronic meth-head or speed-freak appears to make up a very small proportion of the total of amphetamine users. As we have outlined, however, probably no other drug, except alcohol, presents greater potential for adverse impact on work organizations.

BARBITURATES

Barbiturates are depressant drugs, employed to relieve anxiety, produce relaxation, and induce sleep. Although epidemiological evidence is lacking, indirect evidence suggests that barbiturate abuse is increasing. phenobarbitol (Luminal), Nembutal, and Seconal are reportedly being used in new patterns which clearly contrast with sole use of the drug or its use in conjunction with alcohol (Smith *et al.*, 1970). Smith and his associates have found barbiturate use to be a correlate of amphetamine abuse, with Secobarbital ("reds") employed as a way to come down from intense amphetamine stimulation (tranquilizers are also becoming popular as "downers"). Barbiturates create even greater addictive and dependency risks than amphetamines; thus use of both may result in a double dependency.

LSD and other psychedelics are sometimes augmented by short-acting barbiturates, such as Secobarbital, to counteract uncomfortable muscle tremors that can be produced by psychedelics. In addition, "Many ex-heroin addicts began using intravenous barbiturates as a substitute although heroin was always preferred when available" (Smith *et al.*, 1970:61). Such new patterns clearly suggest a moderate increase in barbiturate use among a minority of the users of other drugs.

Availability may be another factor in increased barbiturate use. Louria (1968:58) estimates that in 1962 "enough barbiturates were produced in the U.S. to supply twenty-four average doses to every man, woman and child in the country." Smith and his associates (1970) estimate that approximately 300 tons of barbiturates are consumed in this country each year and its abuse "has become a major drug problem in the U.S." Legal prescriptions appear to account for a significant proportion of this increased consumption (Lennard *et al.*, 1971). The barbiturates have a long medical history as sedatives and sleep inducers and thus have been a logical accompaniment of the "almost astronomical increase in the production and consumption of tranquilizers" (S. Holmes, 1963:3) which have pharmacological actions similar to those of the barbiturates (Essig, 1970).

Barbiturate use and abuse may be concentrated among adults rather than youth. Devenyi concluded that "barbiturates play a very minor role [among youthful respondents]; studies typically report that less than six percent of respondents have used barbiturates at all, and that most respondents who have used barbiturates have used them only occasionally" (Devenyi, 1970:23). While studying a sample of young people who had been hospitalized for drug problems, Devenyi found that "the use of barbiturates is marginal — these young people use barbiturates mostly as accessories to other drugs whose effects they value more highly."

The potential toxicity of barbiturates is relatively unique. Unlike heroin or amphetamine users, persons physically dependent on barbiturates may die from a dosage increase used to overcome the tolerance developed through chronic use (Devenyi, 1970). Consumption of "a large dose by the disturbed addict may be just as likely to cause death as an ingestion of the same dose by a person who is not addicted to these drugs" (S. Holmes, 1963:6). Barbiturates may also create "cross-tolerance"; an increased tolerance to a depressant such as alcohol produces increased tolerance to barbiturates "even though the second substance may never be administered" (Devenyi and Wilson, 1971a:217).

Barbiturate withdrawal is much more severe than opiate withdrawal, often characterized by convulsions, temporary psychosis, and even, on occasion, death (Essig, 1970). By contrast, "withdrawal from opiates is never fatal" (Devenyi, 1970:24). The severity of the abstinence syndrome varies with the degree of dependency. Smith and Wesson (1970:295) report that while "the dosage and time required to produce major signs of withdrawal are *not* well established for most drugs," they are quite clear for the barbiturates. These researchers estimate that Secobarbital or phenobarbital require 600 to 800 mg. daily for 35 to 57 days to produce major signs of withdrawal distress. The effects of various dosages may vary with social settings and the personality of the user; thus, intoxicated extroverts appear talkative and humorous, especially in a relaxed and recreational setting, while withdrawn, schizoid types exhibit mood swings and ambivalence.

Although relatively little attention has been given to the barbiturates, their dangers should not be underestimated. S. Holmes (1963:3) concludes from a review of clinical experiences that barbiturate addiction shows "more devastating [effects] than opiate addiction." Laurie (1969:63) interprets their effects, when dependency on them develops, as far more "destructive to personality" than opiate dependency, which generates a "quietism."

Unlike amphetamine use, barbiturate use is compatible with neither basic American values nor work performance demands. Thus it is questionable whether barbiturate use will concern work organizations in the future. However, the attraction of relaxation, escape, and sedation in nonwork situations may well produce increased use.

THE BARBITURATE USERS

As we did with other drugs, we can specify several types of barbiturate users that may be encountered in the work place. First are those who use them beneficially with legal prescriptions. Assuming the absence of predispositions to dependency, use in these circumstances may well be beneficial and enhancing to work performance.

The second type is made up of those who are introduced to barbiturate use in a medical setting but who develop an attraction and attachment to the drug's effects and must either pressure a physician or seek illegal sources for continued use. Tolerance will increase, but may stabilize at a level where only minor withdrawal distress results, such as mild apprehension, feelings of physical weakness, gastrointestinal disturbances, and muscle twitches. This route, however, may lead to classic barbiturate abuse, in which the user is heavily dependent on the drugs both physically and psychologically. As the pattern develops, there is a necessarily increased tendency to resort to illegal sources. This type of addiction has been characterized as "an old, established vice of the American middle class and is related in many of its characteristics to our nation's number one drug problem — alcoholism" (Smith *et al.*, 1970:57).

The third type is the combined alcohol-barbiturate dependent. While the two drugs have similar effects, barbiturates are probably more efficient than alcohol in producing the desired effects. Furthermore, their action may enhance the effects of alcohol. According to Alcoholics Anonymous folklore, E. M. Jellinek once stated, "the alcoholic who uses barbiturates is eating his alcohol instead of drinking it." Devenyi and Wilson (1971a) reported studies in which 22 to 70 percent of alcoholics abused barbiturates in some manner. A subsequent careful study revealed that 70 percent of a sample of 129 alcoholics were drug abusers who were "using barbiturates alone or in combination with other drugs, i.e. barbiturates were the largest single group of drugs that were abused by addiction has been characterized as "an old, established vice of the alcoholics" (Devenyi and Wilson, 1971b:219).

Finally, there are the abusers who use barbiturates in connection with LSD and amphetamines or as a partial substitute for heroin. They differ sharply from the third type in that the barbiturates are used to oppose the action of the primary drug rather than to enhance other drug effects.

Available data do not allow for estimates of the probability of any of these barbiturate users appearing in work roles. The second and third types may well emerge, but partial evidence indicates that barbiturate abuse alone tends to be part of the "housewife syndrome." In the third type, alcohol abuse may well be the more prominent symptom; and it is doubtful that the fourth type would attempt or could obtain regular employment. In any event, barbiturate abuse should be quickly evident in the work situation since the symptoms closely approximate those of alcohol and since it does not fit with the demands of the work place as does amphetamine use.

OPIATES

Although many claim that rates of opiate use and opiate dependency have been rising in recent years (Brenner *et al.*, 1970; Cohen, 1968), the evidence is mixed. Overall, it indicates that an increase in use has occurred among middle- and upper-middle-class college-age youth who soon will enter the labor force, but it contains considerable uncertainty about the size of the increase and the form this increase has taken. For example, Blum and associates (1969b:192) conclude that "it is likely that some opiate increase has occurred" among students they followed up in 1968; but in their original study the number of opiate users was very small, only 18 students out of 1,314 in their sample. Ten of these were classified as "intensive" users and eight as "less intensive." These numbers are so small that statistically meaningful comparisons with other types of users are practically impossible.

Schaps and Sanders (1970) found opiates to be the drugs least used among students. Darnton believes "many on campus [are] shifting to softer drugs and alcohol" (1971:7). Blumer (1967:84), studying drug use in Oakland, reports that "in the course of our study we encountered only four adolescent addicts; however, many had experimented with heroin." Goode is dubious about the alleged increase in the use of opiates:

> Some commentators notice something of an increase in heroin use among middle-class drug users in the past few years. No solid evidence has documented this rise as yet and if it does exist, it involves a miniscule number of students. If a half dozen students out of a college population of 10,000 use heroin more than a dozen times, a great stir is created, and an epidemic is claimed for that campus. If the figure was one or two students a few years ago, the rise is over 300 percent, but the number is still tiny. Psychedelic drugs are still the category most likely to be used among college marihuana smokers, by far (Goode, 1969c:60).

In addition, he points out that "while marihuana arrests have increased on the order of ten times since 1969, the narcotics and opiate arrests have been increasing very slightly and even declining on a per capita basis." The Blum study (1969b) found the correlation between using marihuana and using any of the opiates was much lower than that between using the psychedelics and using marihuana. Arguing against any unusual rise in the use of opiates among middle-class college students is the tendency for them to think of becoming hooked on the opiates as dangerous and as inconsistent with youth-culture norms. "The intensive opiate user . . . is suspected of being a different chap" (Blum et al., 1969b:142). The apprehension is not limited to the middle class. A study of working-class young adults reports a definite trend toward use of marihuana rather than hard drugs and a negative reaction against use of the opiates, especially heroin (Klein and Phillips, 1968). In mid-1971 a staff reporter for the *Wall Street Journal* even noted a return to beer among many college students (Gallese, 1971).

Still, a definite rise in opiate use — the significance of which is difficult to evaluate — has probably taken place especially in large urban centers and in federally financed and contracted work situations involving those from impoverished backgrounds (U.S. Department of Labor,1970). In New York City there is reason to believe a sizeable increase has occurred, unless the recorded increases are largely the result of stronger law enforcement. Arrests for crimes related to heroin addiction increased from 15,937 in 1968 to 27,290 in 1969. Heroin overdose complications are "now the leading causes of death in New York City between the ages of 15 and 35" (Joseph and Dole, 1970:42). In addition, a recent survey by Smart in Toronto showed that from 1968 to 1970 in school grades seven to thirteen the use of opiates had increased from 1.9 percent to 4 percent. We, and other observers, have repeatedly heard that heroin is now easier to get than it once was. Lindesmith (1971) describes a study made by a student polling agency in 1970 showing approximately 35 percent of Midwest college students sampled knew someone who was using heroin or had used it.

There has been a decided drive in urban industrial centers to hire persons from deprived ethnic groups and from ghetto populations, settings in which opiate addiction has been traditionally concentrated. This tendency has given rise to a great deal of hearsay panic in the work world that such hiring practices might induce an epidemic of heroin use in the work place. While it follows that expanded hiring practices might have brought some addicted persons onto the payrolls, this may be insignificant since street addicts are typically involved in drug sub-cultures that discourage and even prevent regular, steady employment in the "square" work world. Increased marihuana use has brought about, among an unknown proportion of its heavy users, the tendency to experiment with hard drugs which may include the opiates. There is substantial agreement that the very heavy user of marihuana may be tempted to use hallucinogens or opiates. Such broader drug use may be a side effect of law enforcement; the illegal channels necessary to obtain marihuana and other soft drugs bring the purchaser into contact with pushers who market hard drugs and have a vested interest in creating expensive addictions. The opiates, however, seem to rank low as the drug of choice of experimenters, and, consequently, the expanded use of marihuana more likely leads heavy users, especially among middle-class youths, to experiment with hallucinogens rather than opiates. On balance, however we can assume a discernable increase in the number of opiate users either in or about to enter the labor market.

Indeed, Sheppard and his associates (1971:29) conclude that 1970 was the "year of the middle-class junkie." They based their conclusions on studies of the Haight-Asbury area in San Francisco "where new drug patterns are established [for the youth drug subculture] and then tend to 'ripple' out and involve other parts of the country." Thus, "new junkies" have recently appeared in Haight-Asbury: "within the last two years there has evolved a new style of heroin addict consisting largely of alienated white youth suffering from disillusionment, disaffiliation, frustration and despair" (Sheppard *et al.*, 1971:22). It should also be observed that such "ripples" have been unusually dynamic, practically all of them dissipating within a year or so. Moreover, feelings of alienation act to keep such heroin dependent youth out of the labor market. The increase thus appears to be a moderate one and the numbers involved are probably, in a relative sense, rather small. Drug subcultures where opiates are much more readily accessible are located in those disorganized segments of American society isolated from student life and student communities; this probably accounts, in part, for the apparent fact that the increase among students is only modest. Differential rates in opiate addiction in general seem best explained by availability. This probability is borne out by the high rates not only among persons in ghettos but also among doctors and nurses (Lindesmith and Gagnon, 1964). In terms of overall prevalence, it seems unlikely that there has been any significant change in the fact that narcotic addicts are concentrated in the culturally deprived minority groups in large urban centers (Robins and Murphy, 1967).

To form a background for considering types of opiate users, the effects of opiates need to be sketched. These effects contrast markedly with the intoxicating effects of alcohol, marihuana, and the amphetamines and vary sharply between beginners and habituated users. For the novice, a *three-stage process* typically occurs during three or four hours following administration of a dose (Chein *et al.*, 1964). First, transitory nausea brings on effortless vomiting. Second, a wave of euphoria consisting of a

> feeling of impact in stomach, bodily warmth, "pins and needles," and an itching sensation of a rather pleasant and eroticized nature; a feeling of lethargy, somnolence, relaxation, and relief from tension and anxiety; and the experience of the "high." This experience . . . is one of comfortable detachment from and lack of involvement in current experiences (Chein *et al.*, 1964:362) .

The third stage occurs following this "being in the junkie's paradise" and is a return to a much less intense feeling of relaxation and detachment. Routine activities may then be resumed. Alcohol intoxication steadily disrupts the user's inhibitions, coordination, and mental functioning. By contrast, such disturbances are strikingly associated with withdrawal from opiates rather than the intoxication *per se*. The alcoholic may be said to suffer in his intoxication; the opiate addict suffers in his abstinence. The alcoholic pays the piper through the disabilities of his intoxication; the opiate addict pays through the disabilities of abstinence (Chein *et al.,* 1964:362) .

For the developed addict the sequence of stages varies from those of the novice. Stage one largely disappears and the high of stage two is present for only a brief moment, if at all. The experienced addict with an adequate supply spends most of his time in stage three, i.e. in a state of pleasant well-being. *If they take regular stable doses,* opiate addicts can hold regular jobs and appear virtually normal. Intense fear of loss of supply is the major disruptive force.

THE OPIATE USERS

Who, then, are the different types of opiate users and to what extent might they be found in the work world? The first type, whose existence is a shock to many observers of the drug scene, is the occasional or controlled user (Rubington, 1967:10). There are some persons who use opiates, but never become addicted to them. Chein and his associates describe four stages in the process of opiate addiction: experimentation, occasional use, regular or habitual use, and efforts to break the habit (Chein *et al.,* 1964:149). From their data it is clear that some persons only experiment and occasionally use the drug nonaddictively, even though it is highly addictive in a comparative sense. This type suggests one of the forms the increase in heroin use may take. Increased exposure, such as accompanies military service in Indo-China, sets the stage for greater amounts of casual, occasional use in ways other than intravenous injection. Thus use of opiates has increased, but this growth is, in part, made up of the type of user who does not progress into a stable drug dependency. For example, a finding at the University of Michigan was that approximately 17 percent of students had "used" opiates. Such a statistic could be misleading until it is realized that 16 percent of the students had reportedly used opiates only once or seldom and less than 1 percent used them often or regularly (Berg, 1970).

A second type is the medical addict who had become addicted to the drug through a medical or physiological condition which called for prescription of an opiate. These persons were introduced to the drug and learned how to use it in legitimate medical settings. This type of addict was highly visible during the late nineteenth and early twentieth centuries when opiates were easily and legally available and inexpensive. Those who became addicted often did so through self-medication that was a logical outgrowth of their exposure to its legitimate medical use. Although this type has probably declined in relation to the "criminal" type (due to knowledge of addictive dangers in medical circles), a sizeable majority of addicts may still be in this category. This second type corresponds with one described by Ball (1970:81) in his study of hospitalized addicts at hospitals in Lexington, and Ft. Worth: "[This] pattern is typified by the middle-aged Southern white who uses morphine or paregoric and obtains his drugs through legal or quasi-legal means." This type is made up of persons who are

> more frequently residents of small towns than any of the other addict groups. . . . The pattern of drug use among the Southern whites was quite distinct. Onset occurred at a later age, marihuana use was uncommon, opiates other than heroin were commonly used, the intravenous route was less often employed, and drugs were usually obtained from medical or semilegal sources (Ball and Chambers, 1970:15).

A third type of opiate addict, nearly invisible to the general public, is the "professional" addict. Typically members of the medical profession or of paramedical occupations that surround that profession (such as nurses and technicians), these persons have easy access to opiates. As described in Chapter Five, most of these occupations consistently show substantially higher rates of addiction. One study suggests that this type is growing in prevalence: "The incidence of alcoholism and drug dependence among our hospitalized physician-patients was 69 percent and 58 percent respectively, higher than in other reported studies" (Simon and Lumry, 1969:11). Informative studies of this type are also provided by Sherlock (1967) and Modlin and Montes (1964).

Finally, the most frequent, most visible, and most stigmatized type is the "street addict." Legal repression and the probability of being labeled and processed as a "criminal" affect the identity, role, and self-image of these persons, who are characterized primarily by the fact that they must move into the drug addict subculture to maintain their supply (Rubington, 1967).

> [They] take on a new and deviant identity simply as a condition of surviving as a drug addict. . . . A major source of this transformation of personal identity comes from addict argot. . . . In a quite literal sense, the drug addict is saying "my language is me." . . . By means of that language, he found his way through the urban maze to support his habit, to develop innumerable ways for appearing as someone other than himself, for managing the pauses between administration of the drug, for identifying himself to other addicts, and for sustaining a sense of community with others for brief periods in a career fraught with many dangers (Rubington, 1967:14–15).

The opiate addict subculture has an ideology, as well as specific skills, norms, and argot.* Addicts, according to Rubington, exert every effort to "keep their cool" and to maintain a self-image consistent with the state of "being at ease with the world" that coincides with opiate intoxication. The addict subculture teaches, by hard experience, skills for securing drugs, administering them without infection, avoiding the police, and, in general, "scoring." The subculture tutors its members in norms governing their relationship with "straights," namely "working them" for some tangible means of support. These norms also call for addicts to share "good stuff" with fellow users, but at the same time to avoid all interaction with "finks" (Rubington, 1967:16). The opiate addict's beliefs and behavior center on his habit, which holds top priority over all his actions (Rubington, 1967:16). Obtaining a supply of opiates and maintaining the security of that supply are the main factors delineating the "street addict" from the other types. The addicted professional and the occasional user do not have to maintain a "connection" or know a pusher who can obtain the "stuff" for them. Because of their higher incomes and prevalent opportunities, supplies are generally secure, although it is conceivable that these users could be drawn into the maze of the criminal underworld that makes up the drug addict subculture should their supplies be cut off.

The street addict who primarily uses heroin appears to be the most common type of opiate addict and the one with the greatest potential for disorganized behavior. For these very reasons, street addicts are not likely to be regularly employed. Addicts with these self-images and behaviors may be part of a marginal, intermittent work force, and there is always a possibility that they may find their way onto regular payrolls. At the same time it seems quite unreasonable to believe that many of these persons will seek or occupy regular, steady jobs. This situation is not true for the addicted professional or for those who have become addicted as a side effect of medical treatment. Likewise, the experimenter and occasional user may definitely be encountered in the work world. Since the opinion is widespread, even among informed persons, that use of opiates is equivalent to being addicted, the experimenter and occasional user who is discovered may well be branded as an addict when actually he is not. Even if addicted, these opiate users are secure in the source of their supply and it is doubtful that their job behavior will be affected in any clearly observable manner. Since the street addict is the most frequent type, there is little reason to believe that the

---

* For excellent glossaries of addict argot, see Lindesmith, 1968:249-266; Keup, 1971: 347-373; Rubington, 1971: 721-740; and Smith and Sturges, 1969:168-175).

work world will soon face an unusual and menacing increase in opiate addicts.

Brief mention should also be made of heroin use and military life. Both the Civil War and the Spanish-American conflict produced an increase in the number of addicts in the United States because of the careless "use of opiates for wounded soldiers and for those suffering from such diseases as dysentery . . ." (Lindesmith, 1968:225). Though greater caution somewhat reduced this feature of the military use of the opiates in the two world wars, their use was not an exception. Similarly what objective evidence we have regarding the Vietnam conflict suggests that the medical type of opiate dependency has again increased as a result of military life. In reference to addiction among Vietnam veterans, Dr. Samuel C. Kaim, director of the Veteran Administration's Alcohol and Drug Dependency Service, stated recently,

> We anticipate an immediate heavy overload from addicted veterans, primarily heroin users, because of new laws expanding eligibility and providing court commitments and other referrals to V.A. hospitals. While ultimately we will see 20 alcoholics for every veteran addicted to other drugs, alcoholism generally takes longer to develop to the point where it is diagnosed (Kaim, 1971:1).

In the last analysis, however, the impact of drug-dependent veterans is, according to Dr. Kaim, "miniscule" compared to the ultimate influx of alcoholics.

Moreover, the ready availability of drugs in Indo-China is apparently quite high *(Newsweek,* May 24, 1971:26). Since easy access seems to be the major factor in explaining heroin (i.e. opiate) dependency, (Lindesmith and Gagnon, 1964; O'Donnell, 1969), the exposure of thousands of young males is another factor in the present upsurge of heroin use. Much of this increased opportunity may, however, result in merely experimental "skinpopping,"* sniffing, or smoking that will decline or disappear upon return to the United States where access declines sharply. "Only some of the persons who use opiates, perhaps even a minority of them, ever become addicted" (Lindesmith and Gagnon, 1964:182). At the same time many of those with strong predispositions for drug dependency will doggedly seek out illegal sources and become completely dependent when they return home. Thus the aftermath of the war will see an increase in both medical and street addicts, some of whom will find their way onto company payrolls.

This particular drug problem must, however, be placed in perspective. The handling of the issue of drug use among American soldiers in

---

* Use of the drug intramuscularly rather than intravenously.

Indo-China provides an illustration of an undesirable side effect of American drug hysteria. Much interest developed in 1971 about establishing the extent of drug use among American fighting men in Indo-China (Colbach, 1971) and about developing programs for its management. From the beginning it appeared that the investigations would reveal very high rates of drug use and abuse. This result was accomplished, in part, through the very casual use of epidemiological methods. Many of the mass media reports failed to distinguish between the users of different types of drugs. Equally important, much of the reported evidence was not concerned with quantity or frequency of drug use. For example, many of the reports appeared to assume implicitly that any use of opiates was evidence of opiate addiction requiring treatment. The conclusion of the numerous investigations was that a severe drug problem had developed among American soldiers in Indo-China, and one of the consequences was the establishment of several government-operated stations for the screening and treatment of veterans with drug problems upon their return to the United States. Should identification as a drug user become a part of a soldier's permanent military record a lifelong stigma could mark him.

These investigations occurred at a time when American unemployment rates were high and a considerable proportion of veterans of the Indo-China War were having difficulty finding employment. Although attitudinal data are unavailable, the publicity about military drug use could have hindered veterans' searches for employment. As mentioned, most laymen, including those in personnel departments of work organizations, feel uncertain about judging the presence of symptoms of drug abuse or heroin addiction. In the absence of reliable screening devices, stereotypes of who might be a drug user may become involved in employment screening. One business writer believes that a "growing number of personnel chiefs are quietly circulating backlists [sic] of known users through their industries" (Murray, 1971:43). Although apparently not aimed specifically at Vietnam veterans, these lists could work against them since their exposure has been greater than other applicants. Current war

> frustrations create the social climate that typically generates a search for scapegoats. . . . Here I want to do no more than warn of a grave impending danger: of making scapegoats of innocent Americans — mainly servicemen and other young persons — and of letting guilty Americans — mainly politicians and physicians — become inquisitors in a holy war on drug addiction (Szasz, 1972:4).

Thus it appears that efforts initially aimed at aiding veterans with drug abuse problems may have resulted in stigmatization of many more veterans than actually are affected by drug problems (Colbach, 1971), in large part because of the misuse of epidemiological methods. Furthermore, it is possible that the attention given to the prevalence of drug abuse in this segment of the population may have characteristics of a self-fulfilling prophecy, i.e. the use of drugs became defined as an expected association with military status in Indo-China.

WHICH DRUG IS THE GREATEST THREAT?

We now attempt to assess the relative threat of the major drugs to the work world, but first we must develop an "ideal-type" of the drug characteristics most likely to produce a complete drug dependency in a vulnerable user. The construction of such ideal-types is a sociological strategy used to classify different aspects of reality (McKinney, 1966). After examining naturally occurring phenomena in a certain category, the most striking characteristics are derived to construct a model of an "extreme." Comparisons are then made against this extreme for classification. Ideal-types are never found in nature, but are instructive when we put them beside a natural phenomenon such as a specified drug and see the extent that drug fits the ideal type. A model of such an ideal is presented in the chart below.

Drugs and Their "Fit" with the Ideal Model of Dependency

	Physiological dependence	Psychological dependence	Simplicity of manufacture	Simplicity of use	Societal supports
Marihuana	No	Yes	Yes	No††	No†
Amphetamines	?*	Yes	No*	Yes	Yes††
Barbiturates	Yes	Yes	No	Yes	No
Tranquilizers	?*	Yes	No	Yes	Yes
Opiates	Yes	Yes	No	No	No
Caffeine	No	Yes	Yes	Yes	Yes
Nicotine	Yes	Yes	Yes	No	Yes
Alcohol	Yes	Yes	Yes	Yes	Yes

* Evidence is inconclusive.
† Limited but growing societal supports for marihuana use are developing.
†† Much ambivalence exists, combined with covert support.
††† Smoking marihuana is a less simple use-technique than ordinary swallowing.

First, an ideal dependency-creating drug would create physiological dependence. It would rapidly produce cellular tolerance in the user so that regular use would lead to increased dosage to obtain subjective effects. Withdrawal distress would emerge following cessation, thus motivating the user to avoid cessation and continue use.

A psychological effect is the second component of our ideal-type drug. It would possess pharmacological features that rapidly and easily provide a vulnerable personality with a subjective sense of well-being and a means of temporarily avoiding typical anxieties, tensions, and frustrations. See pages 64 to 66 for a detailed discussion of this component.

Third, the ideal-type drug would be readily available to potential users, implying that its manufacture would require a minimum of deliberate cultivation and technical processing. It would, in short, be naturally available without the necessity of invention or complicated fabrication.

Fourth, its use would be simple. Users would not have to learn complex techniques for ingestion and universal folk techniques would provide nearly everyone with the necessary skills for drug use without the necessity of initiation into use.

Finally, the ideal-type drug would have maximal societal supports for its regular and repeated use. Such a drug would be surrounded by a social environment that would make its use easy, convenient, and socially rewarding, despite the hazards to society that its use may present. This social-support network would include positive beliefs about the desirable effects of the drug and, as an expression of these beliefs, the drug would be available at nearly all times and places. Drug distribution networks would be an integral and legitimate part of numerous social occasions, social ceremonials, and even of everyday life. The drug would be available across all levels and segments of society.

How does marihuana compare with the model? Apparently it does not fit the first dimension of physiological dependence; however, it can, like alcohol, bring about an intoxication that is relaxing, depresses inhibitions, and relieves anxieties about self-worth and inadequacy. Thus it can be very attractive to anxiety-ridden personalities and may produce psychological dependency. Although its source, the hemp plant of the genus cannabis, is native to Asia, it has been cultivated in most other areas of the world. Pot users in the United States have successfully grown it, and it still grows wild in the Midwestern areas of the country as a result of the encouragement of its cultivation during wartime for use in rope production. Marihuana grown in this country is generally milder than that produced in Asia and Latin America, but the drug is easily available naturally.

Marihuana use requires a moderate degree of technical knowledge, i.e. learning to "roll a joint," acquiring skill at holding the inhaled smoke, and learning how to become high (Becker, 1963). Experienced users have experimented with oral consumption of chopped leaves, usually in baked goods, which allegedly leads to a longer but less intense high. Smoking marihuana is not as natural an action as drinking alcohol, but the technology is relatively simple. Officially, there is no social support for marihuana use. Widespread availability and the advocacy of its use by many segments of youth culture, however, give it much isolated, illegal support.

The physiological effects of amphetamines are still a matter of debate. There is substantial evidence that they produce very rapid tolerance, a depressive withdrawal, and risks of toxic psychoses. Amphetamines definitely provide psychological rewards tantamount to psychological dependence, being widely used in numerous occupations to enhance alertness, wittiness, and productivity. They permit the user to concentrate longer, compete more intensively, and serve as an effective means for weight control, especially attractive for women who wish to be slim, slender, and sexy.

Amphetamines do require technical manufacture; they do not appear naturally. Thus, use of the drug depends on the presence of a rather sophisticated technology, but drug companies are capable of producing billions per year, making for a relatively easy availability. Furthermore, there is considerable "ease of manufacture [by clandestine producers] and high profits [are] available to entrepreneurs willing to set up a speed laboratory" (U.S. Congress, 1971:25). Most amphetanine consumption is in pill form, making the learning of use-technology unnecessary. This changes when the user moves on to "shooting speed" intravenously, but generally the technology for amphetamine consumption is extremely simple.

Societal supports for amphetamine use are incomplete; while one cannot buy them from a dispensing machine or "across the bar," they are available from many physicians who believe in their medical value and they can be obtained on the black market as well. Indeed, Ball and Chambers conclude that amphetamines, along with barbiturates and tranquilizers, "have had general acceptance by the medical profession. . ." (1970:310). In terms of more general social supports, we repeat the observation of a fit between amphetamine use and competitive pressures indigenous to American culture. While widespread normative support for their use is not presently the case, this may change in the future. Some signs point to stronger legal controls: currently the Food and Drug Administration is reviewing the legal controls on the manufacture of these drugs and may decide to restrict the number of doses produced (Spivak, 1971).

The barbiturates follow a pattern of fit to the ideal-type similar to the amphetamines. Protracted use of barbiturates can create physiological dependence, with potentially more toxic withdrawal than in amphetamine addiction. Their relaxing effects and use with alcohol can clearly create psychological dependency. While they require technical manufacture, they are as available through prescription and the black market as the amphetamines. Their pill form makes consumption easy, but they do not seem to enjoy the latent societal support of the amphetamines.

Tranquilizers fit our ideal drug model in much the same way as barbiturates. Although there has been little research, most tranquilizers are apparently obtained through legal channels, but some observers detect increased black market use because of their popularity as "downers." Tranquilizers appear to have social support, especially in middle-class circles, no doubt because use typically implies a legal prescription. This acceptance may be largely a consequence of labeling: tranquilizers are seen as legitimate, and there has been little publicity about their abuse. The stereotype simply protects the user rather than preventing abuse or addiction.

Opiates clearly create physiological dependency. Tolerance builds rapidly and withdrawal distress becomes extremely painful, although it is not physiologically dangerous and is rarely fatal (Glaser and Ball, 1970). Their enhancing escape effects create a high potential for psychological dependency. Although opium is a natural product, it must be extracted and refined before consumption, calling for a moderate degree of technology. Moreover, the opium poppy requires cultivation and demands special climatic conditions—those in Turkey, Iran, Egypt, and India appear to be the most favorable (Malcolm, 1971). There is a clear-cut technology to properly learning to inject opium or to sniff it, a much less efficient means of obtaining a high. Clearly there are no societal supports for opiate use, except within alienated street cultures that have developed in the poverty areas of American cities.

So far we have paid little attention to caffeine, a stimulant drug which appears naturally in coffee and tea, is found in cola drinks, and is also a primary ingredient in several widely used nonprescription stimulants. Documentation of the extent of caffeine use in American society is unnecessary. The use of caffeine in the work place is especially noteworthy, with nearly all work organizations having caffeine in some form readily available to workers. In many instances the coffee break is a work-based ceremonial in which participation is practically mandatory.

Caffeine is not widely recognized as a drug because it is typically ingested as a food. This nonrecognition of drug content is strikingly similar to the societal definitions of table wine in most European cultures. Probably most adult Americans are caffeine users, but few regard it as a drug. Nonetheless, the patterns and timing of consumption (morning coffee) clearly show it is used as a stimulant. To our knowledge, caffeine abuse has not been defined or explored, except to the extent that persons suffering from certain physical disorders are ordered by their physicians to avoid caffeine. Persons who are heavy caffeine users (over five caffeine-containing drinks a day might be an arbitrary cut-off point) can be observed in nearly every social circle. Often irritable and hyperactive, they sometimes show apparently uncontrollable shaking of the hands when consumption has reached its daily peak.

The impairing results of such heavy caffeine use are practically unknown, but adverse effects on health and performance could be logically expected. Obviously, caffeine has great societal support since it receives practically no attention as a drug. This lack of attention clearly illustrates its nearly perfect fit with what we have described as the societal support dimension of the ideal type of drug. There is, in any event, no evidence of physiological dependence on caffeine. While persons may complain bitterly if time pressures or other contingencies keep them from their morning coffee, there seem to be no withdrawal symptoms. These complaints are, however, symptomatic of psychological dependence on caffeine. Malcolm (1971:255) flatly asserts that "coffee is undoubtedly an habituating drug. It has been shown that about one person in four depends on coffee to get him functioning in the morning." The drug clearly enhances mood by subjectively raising energy level, although caffeine does not alter mood enough to be used for escape. Finally, caffeine fills the remaining two dimensions of the model by being easily obtainable and simply consumed through drinking.

Nicotine competes with alcohol as the most widely used drug in American society. Nicotine can clearly create physiological dependence, as shown by the clear-cut withdrawal symptoms of those attempting to "give up" smoking and the rapidity with which tolerance develops. Direct psychological dependence is questionable since the main motive for use among the addicted apparently is avoiding withdrawal symptoms; however, a rationalized dependence can develop in terms of easing tension or "giving me something to do with my hands." Nicotine addiction seems best characterized as physiologically rather than psychologically based. Persons do not become intoxicated or high on nicotine; the chief noticeable behavioral and subjective symptoms occur when the drug is unavailable.

Tobacco is a plant easily cultivated in many regions of the United States, and drying tobacco leaves and creating cigarettes from chopped leaves are relatively simple processes, especially when compared to the manufacture of amphetamines and barbiturates. The extensive tobacco industry in the United States also makes the drug universally available. Tobacco smoking must be learned to some extent since the inhalation of concentrated smoke is not a natural behavior. Few determined to become tobacco smokers, however, are prevented from addiction because they cannot learn to smoke. Tobacco smoking enjoys extremely widespread social support in American society, although this has been dampened somewhat by federally sponsored research illustrating its health dangers. The negative sanctions smokers are beginning to receive have not yet affected overall tobacco consumption, perhaps because of the intensity of nicotine addiction.* Additionally, tobacco use is widely provided for in this society: cigarette machines, matches, and ashtrays are ubiquitous, and the "no-smoking" havens where the nonsmoker can breathe free have all but disappeared.

Ethyl alcohol fits the entire ideal drug model quite neatly. It can create physiological dependence, but the tolerance buildup is very slow compared with that of heroin or the amphetamines. Psychologically, alcohol has special emotional value for those who compulsively seek independence, have deep anxieties about their adequacy, show a low threshhold for anxiety, and adjust by means of withdrawal and isolation; it is very attractive psychologically to vulnerable personalities. More significantly, the drug "pays off" psychologically for those who are normal users, although such admissions are most difficult to extract. Alcohol is a natural product of fermentation processes and is readily available regardless of complex industrial means of mass production, purification, and packaging. Thus, while the advanced and widespread industrial manufacture of beer, wine, and liquor creates fantastic opportunities for drinking, these industries are not necessary for alcohol consumption to occur — as witnessed historically as well as in contemporary alcohol-consuming underdeveloped societies. Consuming alcohol by drinking it as a part of what are often pleasant tasting beverages is a simple process and requires no special equipment or techniques.

---

* In 1971, 529 billion tobacco cigarettes were consumed in the United States; 1.5 percent more than in 1970 (*Business Week*, 1971).

Nearly anyone can become high from beverage alcohol without undergoing any special sensitization.

Finally, as we outlined in Chapter One, alcohol is embedded in a widespread and sophisticated societal support network. Opportunities to secure the drug are ubiquitous in bars, restaurants, specialized stores, pharmacies, and supermarkets. In America alcohol is readily available in literally hundreds of forms in practically all locales — even those officially dry — despite the many societal hazards it creates: driving accidents, crimes of violence, and costly fires inadvertently set by intoxicated smokers (Irwin, 1971). Observe the "free ice" available in practically all motels and hotels. Most significant in the societal-support network is the mode in which alcohol is integral to occasions of sociability and relaxation, with its consumption almost required in some settings.

Our discussion and the patterns in the chart clearly show that alcohol comes closest to fitting the ideal dependency pattern, closely followed by the amphetamines, caffeine, and nicotine. Were we to assign weights to the dimensions of the ideal-type, societal support may be the most significant factor in the long run, implying that drug use is widespread, accepted, and even legitimatized. Such a setting affords the abuser greater social protection and triggers the forces of normalization which prevent meaningful action toward the abuser until a pattern of dependence is well underway.

ALCOHOL: THE MAJOR DRUG FOR CONCERN

The foregoing review of the social characteristics of use of drugs other than alcohol leaves us with many reasons why alcohol remains the most significant problem drug for the employer's concern. Overall, it seems probable that the impact of the new drugs on job behavior and work organizations is far less than popular concern would suggest. From the public health point of view, the use of marihuana is a minor problem compared with the pathological use of alcohol. "Pot" and associated drugs, however, have received such disproportionate attention and concern that a concerted effort must now be made to put this drug into perspective. Fort (1970:331), describing the results of the enforcing of laws pertaining to mind-altering drugs, insists that such action "precludes giving adequate emphasis to the major drug being abused, alcohol." He states emphatically that "it is most often alcohol, among drugs, which causes or contributes to accidents, violence, and crime."

Although legal, and not typically classified as a "hard drug," alcohol is intoxicating, alters mood and behavior, develops tolerance, and produces sharp withdrawal distress for the dependent user. Even though only a small minority of alcohol users become dependent upon it both physiologically and psychologically, this "small minority" is probably "twenty times greater than the number of addicts to all other drugs. The social damage originating in alcohol addiction is thus incomparably greater than from the so-called addiction producing drugs" (Jellinek, 1960:120). Although this estimate was made ten years ago before the upsurge in the use of marihuana and other drugs, alcohol's damage is still much greater than that of other drugs. Even if Jellinek's estimate were reduced by half, the impact of alcohol abuse on social life, including job behavior, would continue to overshadow that of the other drugs. Even the most exaggerated estimates suggest no more than 300,000 narcotic addicts in the United States; this contrasts with the conservative estimate of 5,000,000 persons with alcohol problems.

Lindesmith emphasizes that "intrinsically marihuana is less dangerous and less harmful to the human body than is alcohol. It is for example not habit forming, whereas alcohol is" (Lindesmith, 1967:223). Relatively long periods of heavy alcohol use are typically required to produce physical dependency, but such addiction has developed in many deviant drinkers. Alcohol is available in a wide variety of potent forms, has a long history of use, and is integrated into American social customs. Many people who reject other hard and soft drugs will feel justified in merely using alcohol since the other drugs are almost universally portrayed as much worse.

Significantly, alcohol and nicotine are still the most widely used drugs among young persons. A 1970 review of current literature on psychoactive drugs concluded: "Obviously, the older, socially approved drugs — alcohol and tobacco — have not been replaced by the newer illicit drugs. The former are still the most important and potentially most dangerous, so far as numbers of persons exposed to their use is concerned" (Smart, 1970:237). Recent research suggests that nicotine cigarette smoking "significantly increased the college student's likelihood of illegal drug use of all kinds" (Goode, 1971:610). Suchman's data revealed that

Alcohol continues by far to be most frequently used, with an overwhelming majority of students (84.1 percent) reporting that most of the students they know drink alcohol frequently or occasionally, as compared to 38.9 percent for marihuana and 10.1 percent for LSD. . . . The ratio of approval to disapproval is 10:1 in favor of alcohol, 1:1 for marihuana, and 1:20 against LSD. It would appear that the campus is split on the use of marihuana, but overwhelmingly in favor of alcohol and against LSD (1968: 148–149) .

Blum and his associates (1969b:177) found in two schools that alcohol was the most widely used single drug, but in another school studied there were twice as many student panelists who took marihuana as drank alcohol. Additionally, "they used marihuana more often, two or three times a week compared with only once a week for liquor." Becker (1968:4), however, feels that "available evidence in the experiences of campus physicians indicate that drugs are a minor health hazard. LSD apparently presents some difficulties but marihuana has no demonstrable bad effects. Campus psychiatrists know that alcohol presents them with far worse problems."

This information raises the possibility that the current generation of illicit drug users may become deviant drinkers as they age. The pressures and contingencies of adult life, combined with the need to conform to "get ahead" and the universal availability of alcohol, may well make heavy drinkers out of current drug users. Drug use may remain an aspect of youth culture, signifying irresponsibility and rebellion, no matter what particular group of individuals occupies that generational status. In other words, drug-use patterns may come to be a function of age, with the users of illegal drugs moving on to alcohol use and abuse upon assumption of adult status. If this proves true, there may be more deviant drinkers in the future than there are today since contemporary youth have become conditioned to the pleasures of mind and mood alteration. Although the problem users of other drugs will rarely be encountered at regular jobs, the developing alcohol addict continues to work for a long period supported by the normalization efforts of his co-workers and supervisors.

The amphetamines may well be alcohol's greatest competitor. While use of these drugs can enhance work performance at practically every skill and status level, they expose the user to a more rapid addictive process, as well as creating the risk of toxic psychotic reactions. Once we know more about the amphetamines and their impact on the work world we will be able to judge more clearly the total impact of expanded drug use on work organizations, but it does appear that they are capable of creating almost as many problems as alcohol. Irwin, (1971:13) ranks them just above alcohol as posing "intrinsic hazard potential to the individual." He, however, did not consider alcohol's greater societal support.

This ends our general discussion of the nature and effects of alcohol and other drugs. We now turn to the specific relations between the use of these drugs and the demands of work and work organizations.

IV

Job-Based Risks for Deviant Drinking and Drug Use

THE management of deviant drinking and drug dependency would be much easier if knowledge were available about their causes. We could then focus our efforts on realistic prevention. Research, however, has produced no such knowledge. While many factors are apparently involved in producing these behaviors, these factors seem to affect individual potential deviants differently. Rather than listing the possible ways in which work-based experiences might encourage a person to drink or use drugs, we choose to focus on "risk factors" (Plunkett and Gordon, 1961) which are features of social life that increase the chances of deviance being continued, often to the point of total impairment. We do not allege that the risk factors discussed here produce deviant drinking or drug use; rather, the employee must already have had rewarding experiences with alcohol or drugs before these risk factors are relevant. While the original "cause" of the deviance may thus be within or outside the work world, risk factors will tend to aggravate and reinforce the deviance once it is underway.

This approach is especially useful in considering the relations between alcohol, drugs, and the job since there is practically no way that the work organization can or should control the off-the-job experiences of employees, and it is generally these which introduce persons to alcohol or drugs. The risk factors presented here constitute real events that can occur in work organizations, and it is within this sphere that work-world attention is most appropriate and potentially valuable.

TWELVE RISK FACTORS

The two general types of risks which may occur in any work organization are absence of supervision and low visibility of job performance. Either type may set the stage for deviant learning which may lead to a relatively permanent deviant "career." By contrast, regular supervision and visible job performances typically allow for early identification of developing deviance, whether involving alcohol or drugs. While at first it appears simple to provide adequate supervision across all levels of an organization, relative absence of supervision may be unavoidable. It may be a fact of organizational structure or may stem from supervisory incompetency. Despite precautions, such situations develop in nearly every work organization.

Low visibility of job performance may be a result of minimal interdependence among jobs. The fact that some jobs are performed independently may allow for simultaneous development and cover-up of deviant drinking or drug-use patterns. Employees who are subject to minimal supervision or who perform relatively independent tasks are not necessarily prone to deviant drinking or drug use, but are subject to few social controls when such patterns develop. This applies to both white- and blue-collar personnel. Ambiguity regarding the nature of assigned tasks often accompanies such low visibility and may generate anxiety, thus creating a setting in which the individual may find excessive use of alcohol or mood-altering drugs considerably rewarding (Snyder, 1964).

In this chapter we consider twelve risk factors within four different groupings:

1. Risks in which lack of visibility is most prominent include occupying job positions with nebulous production goals, occupying positions in which hours of work and schedules of output are flexible and largely an individual option, and occupying positions which keep the employee out of the purview of supervisors and work associates.

2. Risks where the absence of structure is most prominent include work addiction, work-role removal and occupational obsolescence, and entrance into a job position which is new to the organization.

3. The absence of social controls are particularly prominent in job roles where drinking is a part of the work role, job roles in which an employee's deviant drinking or drug use actually benefits others in the organization, and instances of mobility from a stressful job position with considerable control over deviance into an equally stressful position with few or no controls.

4. Miscellaneous risk factors which may be particularly relevant to drug use include role stresses which place individuals under severe strain but generally preclude their acting to reduce the stresses, organizational emphases on intensely competitive struggles for scarce rewards, and the presence of illegal drug users in the work place.

LOW VISIBILITY

Absence of Clear Goals. Jobs in which production goals are nebulous may be increasing in large organizations as a result of the growth of specialized technical functions (Blau and Scott, 1962). Highly specialized personnel may have no one to evaluate their work because they alone have the necessary technical skills. This may allow them to get by with inadequate work performances, while the lack of readily available guidelines for evaluating their activity prevents a recognition of such inadequacies. For example, a technical specialist is assigned to study organizational processes so that strategies for increasing output and effectiveness may be developed. He may send his superior volumes of cryptic reports which are highly repetitious and represent little effort. Regardless of the quality of his performance, immediate evaluation is difficult if not impossible. Such a specialist is only one example of the many job roles in which individuals function independently due to their relatively unique professional skills.

Such job roles may not appear problematic, especially to those who see work performance evaluation only as a coercive device to keep employees within certain boundaries (Strauss and Sayles, 1967). Evaluation, however, is much more than this for many employees. The essential feedback it provides allows them to alter their job behaviors, improve their performance, and increase their job satisfaction. Positive feedback may also be ego enhancing. Industrial psychologists and sociologists have long realized that individuals receive noneconomic satisfactions from their work (Roethlisberger and Dickson, 1946; Landsberger, 1958).

An employee whose work is not evaluated suffers from the ambiguity of being unable to determine his status within his job, within the organization, or within his profession. He may have assurance of retaining his position, but the absence of evaluation may create a situation of essential meaninglessness. Thus he may see himself as isolated within the organization and may likewise be regarded as such by others. This may be a consequence of his having been hired to serve a ritual function for management, such as the resident specialist and the resident black who are used to illustrate the progressiveness of the organization.

These factors may produce anxiety and the employee may find alcohol or drug use an extremely effective way of releasing the accompanying tension. The absence of evaluation and clear production goals leaves the organization with few means for obtaining cues about the individual's developing deviance. When there is no clear definition of appropriate work performance, it is most difficult to recognize impaired work performance. The organizational isolation of these individuals further reduces their performance and it reduces the possibility of recognizing the developing problem. Thus, they may become locked into a pattern of rewarding deviance which goes unrecognized until it has become fixed into their personal adaptive systems.

These risks imply that management should avoid creating isolated jobs. Colleagues are extremely valuable both for individual employees and for the organization. Not only do employees benefit professionally and personally from their colleagues' evaluation of their work, but the presence of colleagues also aids in the integration of individuals into the organization (Pelz and Andrews, 1966). Thus, if an organization is unable to hire more than one of a particular type of professional, it may be better to employ a consulting firm or some other outsider. Even if (as in most cases) the solo professional or technician does not develop patterns of pathological behavior, he will probably not produce at his best level (Pelz and Andrews, 1966).

Freedom to Set Work Hours. Closely related to the isolated employee is the employee who is able to set his own working hours because of his professional or executive status* or because of the relative uniqueness of his job. He may differ from the first case by having specific output goals which must be met. Deviant drinkers and drug users, especially in the early stages of their addictions, can control their deviance and perform excellently at their jobs (Trice, 1962). Such "excellence" may constitute an indirect form of cover-up of their developing impairment. Individuals with regular job hours, however, may be "high" when they are supposed to be at work. In these instances, patterns of absenteeism and on-the-job impairment emerge as cues for organizational reaction.

The employee who sets his own hours of work cannot easily be defined as an absentee. Furthermore, by working during others' off hours, he can easily cover up hangover, withdrawal symptoms, and on-the-job deviant drinking and drug use. Such individuals may "shape up" and work hard for a period of time and then return to alcohol or drugs. In addition, their job requirements may be such that they can work while high during the socially invisible off-hours.

A quality-control inspector who covered a large territory illustrates this type of opportunity. He would rapidly inspect a normal number of sites during the first half of the day and then turn to drinking. He was

---

* An illustrative account of an alcoholic executive's work life can be found in Maloney (1962).

relatively careless in his work, but this was acceptable at the locations which he was supposedly inspecting. Thus there were few signs of his developing alcohol dependency, and considerable time lapsed before these patterns were revealed. He was eventually accidentally discovered by his supervisor after he had faked inspection reports without actually visiting the locations.

In addition, such job freedom may generate anxiety because of the nebulous network of role expectations. This ambiguity indicates in turn a lowering of potential psychological meaning and rewards that might be obtained from the job (Blauner, 1964) and increases the attractiveness of mood-altering drugs.

Low Structural Visibility. A particularly prominent American occupation characterized by low visibility coupled with a potentially stressful work environment is that of salesmen and other field representatives who are away from the home or office for considerable periods. Daily performances are not visible to supervisors or colleagues who would otherwise have opportunities to recognize the development of patterns of deviant behavior. These jobs require individuals to be away from their families, friends, and other sources of emotional gratification and also place them in situations where they frequently encounter strangers and need to kill time. These factors together may create considerable risk of deviant drinking or drug use. Some organizations clearly recognize this risk and include in their training the admonition to "never pack a bottle." Furthermore, the social rounds of salesmen in places frequented by other mobile persons may increase their chances of encounters with deviant drinkers or sellers of illegal drugs.

Sales and other field-representative roles are accompanied by low organizational visibility. The employee may be in contact with his supervisor and work associates briefly, but most of the time he is on his own. Even when deviance develops and is visible to his clients, they may be reluctant to "turn him in," especially if his deviance makes business encounters more favorable to them.

In some circumstances a vicious circle may develop which further encourages drinking or drug use. The individual's absence from his family and other primary groups may lead to estrangement, for they will not be receiving the satisfaction they expect from interaction with him (Levinson, 1965; Gouldner, 1960). If he is regularly absent for long periods, his primary groups may develop substitute figures as the source of need satisfaction. When the individual returns to group contacts, he may find himself left out emotionally. In a sense, his position in the primary group may be lost which may lead in turn to exacerbation of his developing patterns of deviance (Trice, 1966).

To avoid the difficulties of low visibility, management should maintain close contact with all field employees. Furthermore, research should provide personnel departments with a profile of personalities vulnerable to the stresses of traveling jobs (Belasco, 1966). In the absence of this information, a policy of returning salesmen to the home office for periods approximately equal to the time spent in the field should be instituted, thus allowing for social continuity with their families and communities.

Work Addiction. "Work addiction" has received little attention in the behavioral science literature, even though it clearly illustrates the functions of neurotic behavior. (See Chapter Six for a description of the work behavior of neurotics.) An individual may become addicted to work to allay anxieties which have developed within his life space. Work addicts are not individuals who simply work hard, but individuals who "live, eat, and breathe" their jobs. They stay late at the office, take work home at night, work all weekend and on holidays, and refuse to take vacations. Their involvement in work appears to have no bounds; not only do they carry out all of the commitments called for by their role assignment, but they also undertake nearly any other job-related task when requested by others.

The American social structure, with its values of achievement and upward mobility, generates, promotes, and rewards work addiction as a reflection of occupational excellence (Williams, 1970). The work addict has exceeded the norms of adequate performance and thereby is seen as a valuable member of both his work organization and the larger society. Feature stories in the mass media which focus on leaders in politics, business, or the professions latently tend to idealize such behavior in describing the work involvement of their subjects.

The work addict will be rewarded by prestige and deference in the work place and in the general community. By overperforming at work, the work addict may be freed from many of his other obligations, particularly those in the family. His lack of participation in child-rearing, family decisions, and even marital sex may be justified by his total work involvement and the consequent "success" enjoyed by the entire family.

As a type of obsessive neurosis, work addiction is typified by the tremendous energy invested in managing anxiety while the end result may be additional anxiety (Kisker, 1964). The means by which the individual attempts to manipulate his environment become ends, and the work addict is constantly compelled to achieve and be overinvolved in work-related matters. The value he receives is implicit in the "seeking behavior" rather than in the consummation of goals, since the actual achievements themselves are short-term.

A sustained level of compulsive activity may build up tension and emotional exhaustion which must be released. Since work addicts are isolated from social interaction in informal systems both within and outside the work organization, they may find it necessary to release tension in a solitary setting. Excessive use of alcohol or drugs, gambling, or sexual exploitation may be highly rewarding, as well as seemingly appropriate means of overcoming accumulated tension.

Since the work addict's behavior reflects American values, supervisors, work associates, friends, and family members may tolerate his alcohol or drug abuse or other deviance. Supervisors and work associates see him as sacrificing all his energy for the organization. They have probably benefited from his behavior; furthermore, challenging his behavior would highlight their lower degree of commitment to the organization. Family members may also see his behavior as the way he seeks to provide the best for his dependents; thus they also do not feel justified in sanctioning his tension-releasing deviance. The deviant himself may see his behavior as wholly justified; he has worked so hard that he owes it to himself to "cut loose" on occasion. The work addict may, metaphorically, accumulate a "bank" of overconformity from which he may draw to buy freedom from negative sanctions.

The recurrence of this vicious circle over a period of time can contribute to alcohol or drug addiction. At some point significant others may enter the work addict's life and attempt to change his behavior through sanction, but considerable time may elapse before his bank of overconformity is exhausted.

Occupational Obsolescence. Work-role removal and occupational obsolescence may also be conducive to deviant alcohol and drug use. Because of rapid technological change, knowledge and skills acquired during formal education or training may simply not last through a career. Consequently, many individuals now become obsolete because they cannot perform new tasks which come to be associated with their work roles (Perrucci and Rothman, 1969). Retraining individuals is not only costly and uncertain but also involves suspension of work activities. Given a readily available pool of persons emerging from educational systems equipped with the new technology, attempts at retraining may simply be poor management. Thus many managements find it more advantageous to hire individuals who initially possess the abilities rather than attempting retraining. The obsolete employee is then laid off, given early retirement, or placed in a job with few meaningful responsibilities. Due to organizational or union commitment to long-term employees, the latter course appears the one most often followed.

In a recent study of the work histories of alcoholics, engineers clearly exemplified the dynamics of occupational obsolescence and its relation to the development of deviance (Trice and Belasco, 1970). For example, "Engineer D" was superior in his college work and had many job offers upon graduation. During college he drank with fellow students, but reported no role impairments. For approximately seven years after employment his specialty was central in organizational planning and production, and he advanced rapidly in salary and organizational status. During this period his drinking was normal. Overall company planning, however, soon moved to areas outside his specialty. "Engineer D" tried, unsuccessfully, to become knowledgeable in the new areas. As his obsolescence became clearer, his drinking became heavier. He was transferred to an administrative post that did not demand highly specialized technological knowledge, a move which subtly constituted a demotion. Subsequently, addiction to alcohol clearly began to develop. At this point he had been out of college only eleven years. This case demonstrates several possible organizational reactions to obsolescence. Frequently, obsolete individuals must be retained because of the potentially disruptive impact of a dismissal on organizational morale (Goldner, 1965; More, 1962). Thus they may be transferred to generally meaningless positions.

Not only does the obsolete employee lack the skills necessary to be effective in the organization, but his participation in ongoing affairs may actually be disruptive. Since his obsolescence is threatening to the activities of others, it may be necessary to isolate him by relatively subtle means. As a secondary consequence, he becomes a "covert pariah" and slowly becomes isolated within the organization both in terms of task performance and social interaction (Lemert, 1967).

The process of becoming obsolete may be slow or rapid. Where it develops slowly, individuals may be aware of what is happening to them in terms of their value to the organization so that anxiety and depression develop (McNeil and Giffen, 1967). The insidious isolation process may release social controls which previously held the individual's drinking behavior in check. Furthermore, the obsolescence crisis of formal role change can further precipitate deviant patterns which are rewarding as tension release.

Obsolete individuals may be able to spend much time in deviant activities. Other organizational members may want the obsolete individual absent from work, reducing the threat of his interference with their activities. Furthermore, those who participated in the initial decision to decrease his responsibility may feel less personal guilt if the employee is frequently absent. In any event, alcohol use during work hours may not be a problem for the organization since the obsolete individual's role assignment will call for an insignificant performance unintegrated with the activities of others. Finally, obsolescence will probably create needs for tension reduction which are well met by alcohol or drugs.

Deviant drinking or drug use may actually provide a role-deprived individual with a relative degree of structure and meaning. The process of acquiring a supply, maintaining cover-up, and interacting with other deviants may provide vulnerable persons with stimulation, excitement, and activity lacking in many boring, unchallenging, or obsolete jobs. This factor may constitute another source of rewards to sustain the patterns of deviant behavior.

Thus the emergent system of norms surrounding the obsolete individual may actually call for deviant drinking or drug use rather than forbid it and, thus, precipitate drug dependency. The organizational basis for confronting such a deviant is on the grounds that he is injuring his health. When intervention does occur, it will probably lead to termination since this will provide the organization with the excuse needed to remove him once and for all.

New Work Statuses. A newly created position in a work organization may not only cause stress, but also provide opportunities for deviant drinking or drug use. New roles may be stressful for many individuals because of the ambiguity of nearly all their work activities; however, this ambiguity may be countered by the fact that new roles allow their incumbents to engage in some "role-shaping" (Becker and Strauss, 1968:29; Brim and Wheeler, 1966). The individual may set his production norms, develop interaction patterns with line and staff persons without the interference of historical precedent, and design work activities according to his own schedule. Thus the occupant of a new role may in large part be his own agent of social control. If the combination of stress and an absence of social control is coupled with heavy drinking or drug-use experiences, the individual may set up a work role with many opportunities for deviance.

ABSENCE OF SOCIAL CONTROLS

Required On-the-Job Drinking. The salesman and the field representative may have to drink with clients as part of their jobs. Along with low social visibility, stress, and deviant opportunities, this drinking requirement may constitute a very high risk for regular excessive alcohol use. Bartenders and those who work in concerns manufacturing or selling alcoholic beverages may also be unduly exposed to this risk, particularly where employers allow or expect on-the-job drinking. Drinking in these circumstances is generally oriented to the achievement of better rapport rather than to escape from tensions and pressures, assuming there are not an exceptional number of stresses present.

Mutual Benefits. The organizational circumstance in which benefits accrue to others as a result of the deviance of a particular individual is a clear-cut setting for the development of alcohol and drug addiction. Power struggles are very meaningful in organizational life and the elimination of the competitor's claims to power is often an effective means of victory (Dalton, 1959; Bensman, 1967). A two-phased study reported in 1970 explored the effects of such situations on the development of deviant drinking (Trice and Belasco, 1970). First, data were gathered from a national sample of 552 members of Alcoholics Anonymous and 83 were interviewed in depth. The second phase involved anthropological observations in four large organizations where top-level executives were alcoholics. Information was also gathered through key informants.

The study initially focused on the extent to which experiences such as college drinking patterns were related to subsequent alcohol addiction. These factors were then reconsidered in relation to the individual's contemporary life, particularly factors in his organizational life. In other words, to what extent are drinking patterns in late adolescence useful clues to later deviant drinking?

Nearly 90 percent of the executive and professional respondents who subsequently developed alcohol addiction reported few social complications from college drinking. The college drinking patterns they described appeared to be typical of social drinkers in relatively permissive college settings. Similarly, when these individuals entered the labor market there were no complications due to alcohol use, beyond incidental hangovers from social drinking which interfered with work. During this period the respondents were concerned mainly with establishing a career; alcohol was not a significant preoccupation. Less than four percent described fears about becoming dependent on alcohol during early work years. Their accounts emphasized the social role of alcohol in their lives; drinking at home with one's spouse, at cocktail parties, and at various ceremonial and business occasions. Regular bar or cocktail lounge drinking was unusual.

Social complications from drinking began to appear when these respondent's reached their mid-30's and became committed to one organization. An early symptom was "on-the-job absenteeism" (going to work out of a strong sense of responsibility when actually unable to work) as they began to ascend the organizational ladder. On-the-job and noon-time drinking also appeared at this point in their histories, leading to obvious job-role impairments which called for deliberate cover-up of alcohol consumption.

The data suggested that informal power struggles in upper organizational levels may precipitate deviant drinking and promote the development of alcohol addiction. The data indicated very little transfer of deviant drinking patterns from college life into occupational careers, which supports the notion that contemporary career factors may be more relevant determinants of deviant alcohol use than early childhood and family experiences (cf. Sherlock, 1967).

The observation that alcohol-based role impairments apparently did not deter these individuals from upward job mobility led to the hypothesis that deviant drinking is part of a manipulative system which generates considerable individual anxiety, but also makes for organizational mobility. Information on both white- and blue-collar employees indicates there are many individuals who develop drinking-related role impairments early in their work careers which stymie subsequent mobility and relative effectiveness. Many cases of upper white-collar, executive, and professional personnel, however, show that deviant drinking may go hand in hand with considerable upward mobility. A summary of the work patterns of four alcoholic company presidents and their immediate associates may be illustrative.

The reported life histories of these executives did not include college drinking problems, but all were apparently drinking heavily before they achieved the top positions in their organizations. Surprisingly, each company had dramatically increased profits and general organizational success under these alcoholic executives.

In each organization, the chief executive's deviant drinking was a closely guarded secret. At the time of the field observations, when the chief executives were clearly alcohol addicts, many of their subordinates were unaware of their conditions. Further observation revealed that the executives hid their problems from the public and from most members of their own organizations through the exploitive cooperation of a small coterie of "insiders." The presidents had little to do with the actual administration of the companies they headed. While they served as figureheads, actual authority had devolved to a small group of second-level executives. Orders were issued, authorizations signed, and managerial decisions made by this small coterie in the president's name.*

A description of a typical workday is instructive. An executive assistant generally picked up the president at his apartment around 8:30 a.m. By this time the president typically had had four or five drinks to overcome the results of the previous day's excessive drinking. Generally, the executive assistant took about an hour to get the president in condition to begin his activities. Then, the president would spend 45 minutes reviewing stock market transactions and preparing his trades for the coming day. (This particular president was extremely successful in stock market trading.)

To avoid the morning rush, the two left for the office an hour later, by which time the president had had seven or eight drinks but was reasonably alert, although testy and irritable. Once in the office building he went directly to his office by a specially constructed private elevator, which kept him and his condition from public view.

Once in his office the president had a few more drinks and then was ready to see his appointments. He saw individuals from both inside and outside the organization. In all of these interactions he listened, but said little and made no decisions; rather, he made general statements of approval or disapproval. He usually needed a few more drinks before attending the executive luncheon where he rarely drank more than one cocktail. After the luncheon his workday was over. He left for his apartment with an executive assistant who stayed with him into the evening to be certain he was safe.

This arrangement had not always been the case. At the start of his tenure this president, and each of the others studied, had drunk heavily, but was an able and active administrator who had carried out extensive organizational expansion. To help carry out his complex administrative tasks, he had surrounded himself with a group of specialists. His drinking and its concurrence with organizational expansion programs eventually reduced his ability to attend to details, thus creating an organizational vacuum rapidly filled by the ambitious insiders who formed the small coterie. The chief executive's deviant drinking was, therefore, highly functional for others in the organization. Economic rewards and decision-making authority accrued to these others as a consequence of the executive's impairment. Should the executive's status change in any way, the rewards to these others would also be jeopardized; therefore, the insiders simultaneously tolerated and exploited the executive's drinking

---

* Similar patterns apparently developed during the final period of President Woodrow Wilson's administration (Weinstein, 1967).

problem. The situation was also beneficial from the president's point of view for he retained his occupational label, his material comforts, and his social prestige while being able to continue drinking with few negative sanctions.

The case histories of these executives imply several things. First, deviant drinking was supported and protected by a group of significant role definers. A protective clique enveloped the executive in an intricate network of protection which effectively isolated him from the rest of the organization. Simultaneously, the clique members satisfied personal ambitions for power and material gain such that the relationship between them and the alcoholic executive evolved into symbiosis. Clique members maintained their power positions partly through the private use of the label of "alcoholic" as a weapon in the struggle over the allocation of scarce power resources. They effectively controlled the president through a clearly understood, yet covert, threat of exposure, for the president's exposure would obviously mean personal humiliation, loss of status in the organization, and loss of protection for continuing deviant behavior. Thus the executive usually acceded to their wishes rather than risking exposure.

Since they controlled communication channels both to and from the chief executive, the inside group's power was further consolidated. With significant interactions between the chief executive and others in the organization filtered through group members, the executive was prohibited from testing reality. He knew only what was told him by group members, and this information was at times very sparse. The insiders did not trust the executive for fear he might blurt out vital information at some inopportune moment. Likewise, the chief executive's knowledge of vital organizational information would jeopardize the clique's power. The president was also unwilling to risk the personal embarrassment of directly confronting other subordinates for information which had initially been directed to him. The president was therefore effectively removed from both crucial and routine decision making.

The protective clique structure, combined with the symbiotic relationship between the presidents and these associates, aggravated the deviant-drinking patterns. Not only were the executives placed in a position where significant others expected them to perform the role of deviant drinker, but they were offered no alternative. The clique's exclusion of them from meaningful administrative processes brought them to the reality of their failures.

The dynamics described are not limited to executive, upper-status, or white-collar workers. Our research has revealed several instances of subordinates encouraging and covering up the deviant-drinking behavior of their blue-collar supervisors. For example, a building supervisor of an elementary school was in charge of six janitors and custodians. The supervisor became dependent on alcohol over a period of years, during which he regularly became intoxicated during work hours. He became very sociable when intoxicated, often to the aggressive level that he would demand that one or more of his charges leave their work to join him at his nearby home or at a tavern where he would insist they drink with him. Little attention was paid to the janitors' work performances, as the deviant's own immediate supervisor appeared only for announced inspection tours twice annually. It is perhaps obvious that none of the janitors or custodians reported the observed deviance to higher authorities because of benefits to them. Although not validated, there was even some evidence that one custodian held a second job which required his absence during two hours of his assigned tour of duty at the school. The supervisor's deviance was eventually revealed to his superiors by reports from the parents of some school children. This case illustrates further the "reverse exploitive opportunities" present in the supervisor-subordinate relationship.

Obviously, there are many employees who take action when they observe deviant behavior regardless of their own actual or potential interests. Our purpose in presenting these cases is not to suggest universal occurrence but rather to illuminate the modes by which structured opportunities for deviance may develop. Deviant drug use by an executive could easily create the same pattern of circular support. The stigma of drug use might lengthen the time between the executive's initiation of such behavior and the associates' awareness of it, but once the process began there would probably be even greater resistances to breaking the cycle than would occur in the exploitation of the deviant drinker.

These cases support previous evidence that the key to maintaining work-organization status concurrent with deviant drinking is continued appearance on the job, even though appearance is not accompanied by effective work-role performance. In cases where it is difficult to assess the output of an individual or in situations where assessments of production are unrealistic, it is necessary only for the individual to appear on the job to maintain the myth that he is still functioning.

Reduction of Social Controls. Interorganization mobility may be associated with risks for deviant drinking. In the initial organizational environment, alcohol may be acceptable as a means of reducing tension and may become institutionalized within a firm structure of social control.

In the new setting, the need for tension release is still present; alcohol is available, but social control is much weaker.

Research data gathered by the authors on alcohol use among graduate students has been compared with the social structures which these individuals would face once they achieved faculty status (Roman, 1970). Data were collected through anthropological observations and interviews of approximately 75 students in a large Eastern university. The consideration of deviant-drinking patterns was prospective: No one in the sample had developed deviant-drinking patterns, but rather current drinking was considered in relation to the structure of future settings. The data indicated that experiences with alcohol within this culture may be dysfunctional for those moving into settings with loose structures of social control subsequent to the completion of their degrees.

The undergraduate drinking patterns of those in the sample included all types of drinkers except those whose undergraduate patterns seriously impaired academic performance, a reasonable result since undergraduates who were deviant drinkers would not perform well academically. The responsibilities of graduate school, such as the long hours of work and family duties, tend to limit drinking behavior among graduate students. Since in many ways, however, the graduate student is an enforced work addict, he may face many of the risks of work addiction outlined previously. The significant others of a graduate student do not excuse relief drinking as do those of a typical work addict, for the work-addicted graduate student is not deviating from performance norms but rather conforming to them. (By contrast, the work addict is typically a "positive deviant" since he is doing more than expected.)

In addition, the graduate student's status is marginal to both under-graduates and faculty. No longer a carefree student pursuing a broad range of interests, he is constantly exposed to the faculty reference group of which he is clearly not a member; membership in this group, however, would solve his marginality problem and greatly enhance his prestige. In addition, the economic rewards he receives as a graduate student allow for a standard of living which is considerably below that of faculty members. Also, his autonomy of academic pursuit is limited by faculty research interests. Thus the completion of the degree is seen as distinctively rewarding in terms of identity, economic rewards, and autonomy. In these ways most students are motivated to complete the degree as rapidly as possible. This motivation reduces the tendency of students to engage in behavior such as routine daily drinking which may be seen as hampering progress toward the degree. Several informants in this study specifically mentioned their anticipation of enjoying a daily drink when they eventually attained faculty status.

A further factor found to restrain graduate students from engaging in routine drinking in public places was their quasi-faculty status in relation to undergraduate students who were taking courses in which they were teaching assistants. This restraint is parallel to the reluctance of faculty members to become involved in drinking with graduate students on a regular basis.

Similarly to the work addict, the graduate student may release his tensions through overindulgence in alcohol on certain occasions; however, graduate student release generally takes place in a group setting. The "ceremonial" occasions when alcohol is used by graduate students include the completion of regular examinations or projects and the climactic rite of passage when a group member successfully completes final doctoral exams. Many of these ceremonials resemble classic role transition drinking, with considerable drunkenness and an almost total absence of negative sanctions. In addition, spontaneous drinking sessions may develop following an evening of study in the "bull pen," but such events are highly controlled and confined to time limits.

Although the graduate student's subculture does recognize alcohol as a means for release of accumulated tension, it also exercises social controls that prevent the dire consequences of immoderate alcohol use. Participation often leads to a learned association between immoderate use of alcohol and relief from tensions, but within the restraints and shelter of a supportive group. *Many have come to depend on these controls to regulate their drinking for them.* Most students in the sample became high during their drinking group participation and there were certain students who regularly became intoxicated on these occasions.

These points stimulate speculation about the removal of restraints which accompanies passage into faculty status. The entrance of these individuals into systems in which they possess faculty status may be accompanied by initial relaxation of norms governing drinking behavior. This restraint removal, however, may be rapidly followed by the imposition of new restraints such as the necessity of "overadequate" role performance as a means of receiving tenure, promotion, and prestige within the professional specialty. The imposition of new restraints may lead to continuation of the controlled heavy drinking patterns of the graduate years or to a reduction in the amount of drinking, depending upon the character of the new restraints.

This model may be applied to any instance of interorganizational mobility. *The greatest risk of controlled heavy drinkers developing alcohol dependency occurs when they enter a situation which has few structural restraints on heavy drinking* (cf. Sherlock, 1967). Such situations may especially develop either in isolated organizational settings where recruiting is difficult and a greater amount of deviance among employees is tolerated or when the individual enters a relatively large organization and associates with an established deviant-drinking group. This may lead to relatively heavy drinking which may emerge as "patterned deviance" after a period of time. In summary, when controls over drinking are external and subcultural norms allow the heavy use of alcohol to release tension, individuals risk developing deviant patterns should they move into a situation which relies on internal controls.

These data were collected before the "drug revolution." More recent, albeit less systematic, observations indicate that the results of this study may be consistent to a degree with what is known about the use of drugs among graduate students. Marihuana use especially appears to be equally acceptable to undergraduate and graduate students. Since graduate students generally have less free time than undergraduates, occasions of drug use might more readily be viewed as tension-relieving and more excesses tolerated among graduate students. The pressures of graduate student life seem to affect drug and alcohol use similarly, leaving aside for the moment the possibly functional role of amphetamines.

It appears to be a fair generalization that the tolerance of drug use in any American setting today is a function of the degree to which youth dominate and control that setting. Student populations are thus typified by high tolerance of drug use whereas populations comprised mainly of older adults show less tolerance. If one assumes that work organizations for the most part, including college and university faculties, are dominated by older adults, then we see both undergraduate and graduate students who move into the work world encountering an increase rather than a decrease of social control of drug use. Thus the graduate student who joins a college faculty may well cease his drug use, as may other college graduates entering a white-collar occupation. In fact, since many "adult" social settings actually involve pressures *for* the social use of alcohol, the young employee who wishes to please his fellows and advance in the system will probably attempt to conform to the dominant drinking norms. Thus what might well occur with mobility from the university to the work place is a substitution of alcohol for drugs in conformity to the dominant norms.

It is, of course, recognized that a drug-using, young, white-collar employee may locate a group of like-minded peers in the work organization and continue drug use similar to that carried out in college. It is doubtful, however, if there are many noncollegiate settings with the level of tolerance for drug use that is found in college, indicating that in most instances entrance into the work world involves encounter with increased levels of social control and lowered levels of tolerance in regard to illegal drug use. The overall characteristics of the setting point to greater alcohol use and lesser drug use in college-trained entrants into employment.

OTHER RISK FACTORS

Severe Role Stress. Severe on-the-job role stress is an obvious risk factor (Kahn *et al.*, 1964; McLean, 1970). Both drug and alcohol use may be readily available methods of coping with severe job pressures, ambiguities, uncertainties, and anxieties. While such adaptations are nearly universally recognizable as undesirable, many organizations nonetheless knowingly tolerate and accept such employee behavior.

Although managements generally recognize that some work roles are more stressful than others, two assumptions often prevent organizational action to alleviate these pressures: First is the typical assumption that such problems are temporary and that eventually work loads and pressures will even out; second is the natural-selection assumption that no one will remain at a job which is too much to bear physically or emotionally. Obviously, these assumptions are not always borne out.

An employee under such severe stress may unwittingly become dependent on alcohol or drugs over the long run while trying to tolerate stress in the short run. This mode of "coping" may be so effective in the short run that the individual comes to believe he has mastered the stress. In other words, drug use may mask natural stress reactions. The major danger thus associated with severe occupational and organizational stress is that the use of alcohol or drugs is not only rewarding to the employee but may come to constitute an artificial and false adaptation to stress which is actually beyond his natural level of tolerance. Thus, should alcohol or drug use develop as such an adaptation, there are built-in counter pressures against recognizing the deviance and against applying negative sanctions on the parts of both the employee and the employer.

Competitive Pressure. Mild to intense competition among employees for scarce organizational rewards is basic to American capitalistic enterprise. Work organizations obviously have differential distribution of competitive pressures whether for money, deference, or power; and some types of business and industry endemically foster greater degrees of reward competition and survival competition. In the former case, two or more employees are competing for an advancement or an additional "reward" which will be added to what the winner already possesses; in the latter, competition is for a single "set" of valued goals and the winner takes all including the loser's previous "holdings." One might see "reward competition" obtaining in a bureaucratic hierarchy where advancement does not come to all but where one does not advance at the cost of others. "Survival competition" may obtain in advertising, marketing, or sales organizations where the gains of one employee essentially constitute a loss to others, assuming a limited number of buyers. Viewed within this framework, the effects of competition bear a close relation to occupational security. The effects of competition are greatest and most stressful in situations of survival competition. In a free market economy with imperfect communication, there is good reason to expect that many employees are frequently placed in survival competition.

Since work performance is related to alertness and competition will require more alertness, amphetamine use will be attractive to employees in competitive settings. While large doses of these drugs create sharp ups followed by downs, mild dosages may enhance performance without deleterious aftereffects once the individual acquires some drug-use skills. Such an amphetamine user may become an outstanding employee and win in competitive struggles over the short-run, although over a long period there is danger of amphetamine addiction as tolerance is built up and dosage is increased. Addiction to amphetamines may not be inevitable, however, and the length of time one may maintain a moderately enhanced performance level without deleterious side effects is unknown.

Presence of Illegal Drug Users. A final risk factor in work organizations is the presence of illegal drug users. Unlike the deviant drinker, the user of illegal drugs behaves contrary to both formal and informal societal norms. This presence triggers two subtle sets of forces which may increase the risk of illegal drug use among other employees.

First, the use of illegal drugs obviously implies illegal procurement. Purveyors of illegal drugs usually charge high prices to the user but promise price reductions or a share in the profits if the user can expand the drug market. Thus, if a user can interest others in experimenting with drugs, he may reduce the cost of his own drugs or even turn a profit. Thus it would be expected that drug users in the work place, especially if not well paid, would in some instances encourage drug use among other employees.

A second factor pertains to the negative evaluation placed upon illegal drug use by society at large. It is difficult for a single individual to challenge a contrary and overriding public judgment without some form of support; thus the solitary drug user may come to feel a lonely guilt for his behavior. This guilt can be counteracted by joining with a group of drug users who share positive evaluation of drug use. Thus, as a way of legitimizing their own behavior, illegal drug users may seek to convert others to this deviance. Although to a limited extent deviant drinkers may be motivated to encourage others to drink with them, alcohol consumption has already been legitimized by society so that its deviant use may not be as automatically guilt-producing as illegal drug use.

We emphasize that drug use within a work organization constitutes a risk for further drug use which is by no means inevitable. Many drug users keep their deviance completely to themselves while others segregate their drug use from work activities, e.g. neither co-workers nor members of their social circles are induced to acquire drugs from the regular users' source.

There is a final element in the contemporary youth culture which bears mention in regard to the spreading phenomenon we have postulated. Drug use symbolizes membership in the "Now" generation, thus generating social pressures for drug use among young people. These pressures may operate in the work place and may also attract some "over-thirty" persons who wish to be regarded as youthful swingers, particularly in a culture — such as ours — where youthfulness is held in high regard.

V

Job Behaviors of Deviant Drinkers and Drug Abusers: Specific Impacts in the Work Place

THE real costs of employees' alcohol or drug dependency arise from the impact of their deviant behavior on job performance. In this chapter we focus upon the effects of deviant drinking and drug use on the following work-related behaviors: work efficiency, turnover, cover-up, absenteeism, and accidents. This chapter is intended to serve three main purposes: First, we summarize the results of a large set of research studies relating to on-the-job behaviors of abusers of alcohol and drugs. This survey of facts may provide a rational backdrop for policy construction. Second, knowledge of work behaviors which may be useful in company programs oriented to the identification of deviant drinkers and drug abusers is presented. Third, an outline of these behavior patterns will serve to place the problem in perspective, indicating, for example, that the well intentioned actions of top and middle management, first-line supervisors, and fellow workers often serve to prolong rather than shorten the period of alcohol or drug dependency. Our discussion of job-related behaviors will first focus on the effects of deviant alcohol use and the use of nonopiate drugs on the various "costly" job behaviors. We will then turn in a final section to a general consideration of the job behaviors associated with the development of opiate addiction. We set this latter section apart since the patterns and dynamics of the opiate-addiction process are qualitatively different from those of alcohol abuse and nonopiate drug use.

OCCUPATIONAL LEVEL

Research data suggest that deviant drinking is not concentrated in any one social class or occupational group. There are, however, class variations in the extent to which such deviants are identified. When supervisors in a large private utility were asked to identify problem drinkers, those identified were significantly concentrated in lower-class occupations (Warkov *et al.*). This concentration may reflect the supervisors' differential perceptions rather than the actual distribution of problem drinkers. Middle-class supervisors may be reluctant to associate deviant drinking with poor white-collar performance, while readily making this inference about poor work among lower-class subordinates. Thus the occupational concentration revealed in this study may be biased, filtered through the stereotypes of the middle class supervisor. The supervisory stereotypes of "good" white-collar workers and "bad" blue-collar workers are reinforced by the facts that white-collar, middle-class jobs are not subject to much supervision, that white-collar work tends to be less interdependent with the work of others, and that white-collar jobs afford many opportunities for "self-cover-up" of deviant behavior. Thus the deviance of these workers is less visible on the job than that of blue-collar workers.

Data using different identification sources suggest a random distribution across various occupational status levels. Straus and Bacon (1951), Wellman and associates (1957), Falkey and Schneyer (1957), Chodorkoff and his associates (1961), and Strayer (1957), using clinic or hospital patients, failed to find any concentration in a particular social stratum; nor was any such concentration found in a population of A.A. members (Trice, 1962). The likelihood of being identified as a deviant drinker by significant others in the work environment seems to be substantially greater for lower-class employees, even though most information shows an even distribution of deviant drinkers across status levels. If anything, problem drinking may be more frequent in higher-status occupations. Mulford (1964) found that a relatively high percentage of persons reporting troubles due to drinking were among the more educated and the higher-status occupations in his sample.

Similarly, research data show no definite concentration of deviant drinking in particular industries. When Straus and Bacon (1951) compared the distribution of clinic patients by type of industry with the same distribution in the general population, no unusual concentrations appeared. Chadorkoff and his associates (1961:107) in comparing the industrial distribution of deviant drinkers in six different studies concluded: ". . . [the type of industry distribution] demonstrates the ubiquitousness of the alcoholic. An industry or occupation may be absent or underrepresented in a particular sample of alcoholics, but the deficiency is apparently compensated in another."

Marihuana use, like alcohol, cuts across socio-economic lines. In this country marihuana use first became firmly established among low-status Mexican laborers around 1910 in the South and Southwest. The first urban concentration of lower-class marihuana users was allegedly in New Orleans; prohibition of alcohol in the 1920's is thought to have hastened its spread to low-status populations in other urban centers (Winick, 1965). Mayor LaGuardia's 1938 Committee on Marihuana reported that New York City marihuana use was concentrated among low-income minority groups (Schoenfeld, 1966). The low cost and easy cultivation of marihuana make it very attractive for low-income groups, but one of the many unanswered questions about this drug is why an increasing number of middle-class youth came to use it beginning in 1964-1965 (Harris Survey, 1968). The contacts between middle-class collegiate youth and minority group members during the civil rights movement of the mid-1960's may have led to sharing of drug experiences. The subsequent period has been marked by increasing interracial contacts among youth. During the same period the rejection of most facets of established society, including alcohol use, by the "hang loose" student subculture probably produced acceptance of marihuana among many middle-class youth as an alternative to alcohol.

A series of recent studies suggest that "the higher the social class and the higher the social class of one's parents, the greater the likelihood the individual will smoke marihuana" (Goode, 1970b:36). There was no significant difference by father's occupational background among high school users in Toronto, Canada (Addiction Research Foundation, 1969). Blumer (1967:78) concluded from his analysis of Oakland data that: "Youthful drug use is . . . lodged primarily in the lower strata but currently expanding into middle- and upper-class strata." The most frequently used drug in both Toronto and Oakland was marihuana. Douglas (1970:255) terms marihuana use "representative of the basic changes in attitude toward drugs among middle-class people in our society." Suchman (1968) and Mauss (1969) have also found increased adoption of marihuana among middle- and upper-middle-class youth, while Goode's (1969a) earlier data showed its continued use among youths in lower strata. Research has also indicated that the higher the academic reputation of a college, "the more likely that its students will smoke marihuana" (Goode, 1969a:111), while another study revealed increased adoption of drugs such as marihuana among working-class youth and a trend away from hard drugs (Klein and Phillips, 1968). Goode concludes that "today marihuana use is common in many social groups. A substantial minority of those in the arts and in the professional white-collar groups peripherally connected with the arts — journalism, market research, advertising, and publishing — have at least experimented with marihuana" (1969a:7). He also comments: "For the young adult who has begun working, and who has left his family of orientation, the higher is his education, income and occupational prestige, the greater are his chances of smoking marihuana" (Goode, 1970b:36). In sum, marihuana use is spread across the social spectrum, with perhaps a greater incidence of use among middle-class college students.

Worth further exploration is the subject of class differences between the use of marihuana and the use of other drugs in the middle and lower classes. For middle- and upper-middle-class youth, heavy use of marihuana apparently produces tendencies toward the use of hard psychedelics such as LSD or mescaline, rather than heroin (Goode, 1969c). For heavy marihuana users in lower socio-economic strata, however, regular marihuana use probably increases chances of using heroin rather than the psychedelics. Johnson (1971) found about a fifty percent probability that a marihuana user in New York City would try heroin if he were also a marihuana dealer and had intimate friends who had used heroin. Furthermore, Johnson found that the probability of heavy heroin using escalated with the amount of marihuana used and that this probability increased if one were a marihuana dealer. Snyder (1971), on the other hand, suggests there may be an inverse association between the use of marihuana and of heroin in certain circumstances, regardless of social class.

Regardless of middle-class experimentation and an unknown incidence of addiction, the highest prevalence of heroin use and addiction remains in the poorest and most deteriorated urban areas (Lindesmith, 1967). A few recent observers argue that the number of middle- and upper-middle-class narcotic users is increasing, especially in urban centers such as New York and Chicago (Joseph and Dole, 1970). Several studies suggest the heroin use is rejected by many middle-class student drug users, but Blum and his associates (1969b) have found a trend toward opiate use among a small minority of middle-class students. A trend toward more middle-class opiate use might be indicated by the incidence of narcotic addiction among physicians which tends to range from 30 to 100 times higher than that in the general population (Modlin and Montes, 1964). Apparently, such addiction may develop during the pressures and stresses of a professional career (Sherlock, 1967) rather than in medical school. Jazz musicians constitute another somewhat middle-class group with high incidence of opiate use. Among 357 jazz musicians studied in New York City, 53 percent had used heroin at least once, 24 percent had used it occasionally, and 16 percent were regular users (Winick, 1960). Although physicians and jazz musicians are outside the social class where heroin use predominates, their high rates probably do not reflect any trends toward middle-class heroin use, since these occupations have relatively unique opportunity structures for opiate uses which are not typical in other middle-class occupations. In sum, prevalence of opiate use and addiction remains highest in the bottom social strata.

Amphetamine use is probably a middle- and lower-middle-class phenomenon; research reports do not usually mention use among the lowest socio-economic classes. Amphetamine use appears to be highest among such diverse groups as moonlighters, professional athletes, long-haul truck drivers, entertainers, middle-class housewives, and college students during exam periods (Walsh, 1964; *Lancet,* 1964; Cox and Smart, 1970). Kalant (1966:65) summarizes that "people in the medical and para- medical and paramedical professions, and in recent years, married women or housewives are highly represented" in the series of cases she studied. Carey and Mandel (1968:171) focusing upon speed shooting, indicate "one unique feature of this development is its middle-class character." Despite these opinions and data, the expanding drug scene probably includes some use of amphetamines in the lowest social strata, especially among those who are competitive or upwardly mobile.

WORK EFFICIENCY: IMPACT OF DEVIANT DRINKING

Declining work performance and disruption of the activities of fellow workers and supervisors are the most direct effects of deviant drinking in work organizations. Evidence concerning work-role impairment of deviant drinkers comes from studies of Alcoholics Anonymous members, hospitalized alcoholics, and supervisors of deviants.

Two studies of A.A. respondents can be summarized as follows (Trice, 1962): Practically all respondents reported a substantial decrease in work effectiveness during the middle stages of their addiction; only one-tenth reported their work was unaffected. Fatigue, frequent mistakes, and uneven, frenzied work pace were reported as on-the-job symptoms. Those who reported no decline attributed this to opportunities to work "extra hard" at regular intervals which compensated for their otherwise poor performance. A work pace made up of temporary periods of increased effectiveness, followed by sharp declines was commonly described. Apparently these spurts assured the developing alcohol addict and those around him that his work was still acceptable.

Reports of decreased efficiency were found in all types of occupations. The data indicated, however, that the *manner* in which work efficiency declined varied markedly by occupational type. Professional, managerial, and other white-collar personnel tended to appear at work even when feeling unable to do an effective job, making them the classic "half-men" (Henderson and Bacon, 1953). Lower-status workers resorted to both absenteeism and further drinking when in this condition. Thus those in service, semiskilled, and unskilled jobs often described themselves as "periodics" whose records were marked by absenteeism and by sharp declines in work efficiency before and after absences. Lower-status problem drinkers reported they did a substantial day's work whenever they were on the job, if they were not coming off or going on a "spree."

Surprisingly, interview data revealed that the developing high-status alcoholic often achieved promotions during the middle stages of his addiction. This served to postpone his acceptance of the fact that he had lost control of his drinking. It may also indicate that compensatory performance is an effective means of preventing adverse managerial reaction, allowing for a normal succession of promotions. While these findings are limited by the fact that approximately 30 percent of the respondents in both studies reported no work standards against which to gauge their effectiveness, the similarity among the work histories where efficiency could be estimated makes it difficult to discredit the conclusions.

Studies of deviant drinkers who were not A.A. members, but patients in clinics and hospitals have revealed similar data. One study concluded that "impairment of functioning on the job as a result of drinking is evidenced by loss of time, drinking on the job, and difficulty in accepting supervision" (Strayer, 1957). A study by Maxwell (1960) revealed that "neglecting details formerly attended to," "lower quantity of work," and "lower quality of work" ranked among the first 18 on-the-job symptoms out of a list of 44 job-related impairments. Supervisors of alcoholics were consistently found to rate their job performance as "the worst" in comparison to the performance ratings of psychotics, neurotics, and normals (Trice, 1965a). Trice (1964) also asked supervisors to respond to the list of 44 early signs of developing alcoholism used in the Maxwell study cited above. Although "neglecting details formerly attended to" ranked thirty-eighth, "lower quality of work" and "lower quantity of work" ranked as the fifth and twelfth most significant symptoms respectively.

WORK EFFICIENCY: IMPACT OF THE NONOPIATE DRUGS

In Chapter Three we distinguished between four types of marihuana users: the experimenter, the social smoker, the heavy user, and the head, i.e. a person with an apparent psychological dependence on marihuana.

The latter two most concern us in regard to work efficiency. A study of marihuana use among military personnel in Vietnam concluded that 7.5 percent of the sample were heavy smokers (Roffman and Sapol, 1970). Goode (1969a) estimates that one-half the users in his study are experimenters, one-third social smokers, and only one percent true heads. (This leaves 16 percent in the heavy category, although Goode does not use this category.) Brenner and his associates (1970:38) comment that "measured against the large number of persons in the United States who smoke marihuana now and again without any impairment to their physical faculties or their ability to work or study, the number of pot heads — those who are psychologically dependent on marihuana — must be very small, at least at the present time." There is reason to assume the head is rarely employed in a regular fashion. The same observers comment that "psychological dependency is a chronic problem and therefore of a more serious nature than acute reactions. When a person smokes marihuana two or three times daily he accomplishes little else; there is just not enough time left for work" (Brenner *et al.,* 1970:38). Goode (1969a:110) states flatly that the committed "head" in the student population has "ceased to function in academic life."

Data on the association between drug use and academic performance have implications for those concerned with work efficiency. Suchman (1968), without distinguishing types of student users, reports that "drug use is more likely to occur among the poorer than the better students. Among those with an average grade of 3.0 or higher only 15.3 percent report the use of drugs as compared to 31.0 percent among those with an average of 2.5 or less." This grade difference, however, may be largely the result of the entire "hang loose" way of life that tends to surround drug users. A Canadian study has revealed a significant negative correlation between academic grades in junior and senior high school and orientation toward drugs (Addiction Research Foundation, 1969). Three other relevant findings come from studies by Blum and his associates (1969b): significantly less drug use is found among those rating their academic careers as "important"; students with the greatest number of "incomplete" grades rank highest in the use of hallucinogens, amphetamines, and opiates; and high rates of hallucinogen use were found among those who dropped out of school for reasons other than health. The trends in these data infer that regular use is accompanied by impairment of job performance.

Other observations of efficiency come from the Vietnam study where it was found that heavy marihuana smokers act in such a fashion as to obtain significantly more disciplinary actions (Roffman and Sapol,

1970). A psychiatrist states that "in studies on cases of prolonged use, subjects became indolent and non-productive and showed neglect of personal hygiene; they quickly lost interest in both assigned vocational tasks and recreational pursuits" (Jaffe, 1964:300). However, Goode (1969a:110) believes that the student who smokes from once a week to daily (thus corresponding to the heavy type) "may go to classes, do some of his studying, and generally operate in a 'high' state without those he encounters knowing it." This fits with the findings of Zinberg and Weil (1969:39) that the marihuana smoker can learn to compensate for the drug's adverse effects on performance. They report "users appear to be able to compensate 100 percent for the non-specific adverse effects of ordinary doses of marihuana on ordinary psychological performance (including driving)." Also, regular use of marihuana does not increase tolerance and so its abrupt withdrawal does not lead to physiological distress. Likewise it does not produce hangover. Murphy (1966) cites the work of Freedman and Rockmore who studied Army marihuana users. They could find no evidence of deteriorating effect on mind or body. Most of the users had been abstinent from the drug for long periods without any reduction in efficiency or need for medical help.

Murphy (1966), in his review of psychiatric literature, reports a consensual opinion that psychic habituation to marihuana is much weaker than similar habituation to alcohol or tobacco. Kalant and Kalant (1968:3), however, state that "despite the frequent statement that the drug creates no craving or severe psychic dependency, there are good case descriptions of persons who need to maintain a state of marihuana intoxication for most or all of their waking period, and whose social functioning is impaired by it." Kolansky and Moore (1971) describe clinical experiences that are similar. The generalizability of these clinical reports is unknown, and we have almost no idea of the "head" count.

Even though there may be definite job impairment associated with heavy marihuana use, it rarely approaches the progressive deterioration brought on by heavy alcohol use. The exception may be the true "head" who encounters the work world in only the most sporadic way. It must be noted that long-term effects of mild to moderate use of marihuana remain unknown and will continue to remain unknown until conclusive research replaces current social hysteria.

Probably none of the current "problem drugs" more appropriately fits the American work scene than the amphetamines, but little is known about this very American drug. The literature on its beneficial effects and abuses is "scanty and rather confusing" (Kalant, 1966:144). The drug clearly offers the ambitious, competitive, job-involved employee a source of increased energy and self-confidence. Likewise, amphetamines may produce "faster and more efficient thought and decision making, usually accompanied by a feeling of well being and even euphoria" (Kalant, 1966:5). While they have long been used by students preparing for exams (Becker, 1968), they have more recently been used for thrill seeking. Thus Goode (1969c:53) found that the amphetamines were "used by a large percentage of the sample to obtain a 'high.' " Forty-three percent of his student sample had used amphetamines, and many of the student respondents had *not* taken the drug for such "legitimate" reasons as examination pressures, but "did so for illicit reasons, reasons for which society would disapprove."

It seems probable that both students and workers may use amphetamines "for long periods of time without modification of dosage and without untoward results" (Kalant, 1966:36). Data do indicate, however, that repeated, heavy use may precipitate paranoid delusions, hallucinations, and violent excitement. Although these symptoms may fade rapidly upon withdrawal of the drug, in some instances amphetamines may precipitate schizophrenic-like symptoms (Kalant, 1966:76). In sum, we have the highly ambiguous situation in which a drug can materially improve work performance and participation in thousands of highly demanding job roles, but, in doing so, creates risks of temporary psychosis. A valid assessment of the dangers of amphetamines depends on the extent to which heavy use is an inevitable outcome of regular use. Addiction in the classic sense is a clear possibility, i.e. development of tolerance is common and physical dependency has been indicated by abnormal brain functioning upon amphetamine withdrawal; however, these addictive properties in no way approach those characterizing heroin. For most users, little immediate job impairment is to be expected, but the dependent user's work effectiveness may be sharply impaired by withdrawal distress with accompanying absences, emotional flare-ups on the job, and potentially high turnover.

Meager evidence suggests a trend toward greater amphetamine use among youth now entering the labor force. Carey and Mandel (1968) have provided a description of users of massive doses of speed whose behavior is clearly new on the youth scene. They suggest that a small portion of amphetamine users become addicted or experience psychotic behavior. Work organizations may encounter many experienced amphetamine users and some addicts whose job behavior, upon abstinence, will be disrupted in a pattern similar to opiate withdrawal. Because the amphetamines enhance job performance so neatly and are among the new drugs embraced by younger persons, they may become more of a drug problem for the work world than marihuana or the opiates. They may come to rival the martini and the cigarette as sources of major national health concern. As mentioned, however, this development should not be surprising in a competitive society where work organizations have long sanctioned the nearly unlimited use of stimulants on the job, viz. in the ubiquitous coffee break.

TURNOVER: IMPACT OF DEVIANT DRINKING

Data on job turnover among deviant-drinking employees indicates that the stereotype of them as "job hoppers" is inaccurate. More than half of the 1,438 clinic patients studied by Straus and Bacon (1951) had held their most recent job for at least three years and the majority of these had held it for five or more years. Strayer (1957) reports that 52 percent of 80 clinic cases held a single job for ten years or more; about 20 percent in this study showed high turnover rates. These high rates may be due to the low occupational level of his public-clinic patients among whom turnover is more frequent. Members of A.A. reported low rates of turnover (Trice, 1962); approximately 65 percent of the respondents reported four or fewer job shifts and almost 40 percent reported no changes at all.

Variations in both occupation and job freedom were associated with job changes in the A.A. study. There was less turnover among managers, while the service category had a high concentration of changes. Job change rates were high among those with the least job freedom. These data reflect turnover patterns similar to the labor force in general; apparently many deviant drinkers become addicted during only one or two job changes. Since job mobility is relatively low in occupations for which extensive training is required and substantially higher among operatives and laborers, the rates among the deviant drinkers studied are correspondingly "normal." Finally, these rates reflect the general decline in job change among the middle aged; the mean age of respondents was 44.8 years.

TURNOVER: IMPACT OF NONOPIATE DRUGS

The deviant drinker will typically continue to work at a full-time job through most of his developing addiction, despite poor performance and increased absenteeism. Frequently, this job is the same one he held before his problem drinking began. Out of a sample of 700 work histories of members of Alcoholics Anonymous, only four reported they did not work regularly during the middle phase of alcohol addiction (Trice, 1962).

We know much less about the occupational stability of deviant drug users or the prevalence of this behavior in the labor force. Several types of drugs would preclude a user's regular participation in the work force; for example, the economic demands of heroin addiction will probably at some point completely disrupt work-force participation for many addicts. On the other hand, long-term use of opiates can be associated with job stability, particularly among physicians and nurses (Sherlock, 1967; Winick, 1961). Considerable evidence indicates that short-term use of tranquilizers and amphetamines among many users may actually enhance and stabilize work preformance. It is, however, probably rare for heavy use of nonopiate drugs to be associated with long-term occupational tenure, although this does seem to hold true in many cases of heavy drinking. In any event the notion of a career or "progression of symptoms" such as in alcoholism is largely inapplicable for users of nonopiate drugs at the present time.

In considering the effect of drug use on job turnover, the physiological effects and potentially habituating features of the drugs have little relevance. The core of the issue is quantity of use. While true "heads" will only be sporadically employed, the possibility of relatively heavy turnover among moderate marihuana users is more significant for employers. Turnover in these instances may not be a direct result of drug use, but rather of social values that tend to be strongly associated with drug use. This "hang loose" ethic (Suchman, 1968) tends to be antiestablishment, to question deeply the value of career striving, and to call for work that is uniquely meaningful to the worker. Likewise, it calls for freedom to "do one's own thing." Turnover, especially among college-trained heavy marihuana users, may be quite high as they seek work situations compatible with their antiestablishment values.

There is no particular reason to expect that regular users of amphetamines will show exceptional turnover patterns. In fact, if the effects of the drug are in the desired direction, amphetamine users may well be long-term employees, as their work performance leads to upward mobility in the organization. The type of amphetamine user who is most prone to high turnover is the speed-freak who will probably not seek regular work. The paranoid reactions which may accompany heavy amphetamine use may include delusions that cause some users to leave employment. Amphetamine psychosis would likewise interrupt employment. Such occurrences are, however, genuinely rare at the present time. It is important to note that newer drug use is somewhat concentrated among the young and that young workers traditionally have higher turnover rates than other age groups. Thus young drug users will have higher turnover rates than the remainder of the work force; the extent to which these rates are a result of drug use remains to be determined by research.

COVER-UP: THE DEVIANT DRINKER

Two studies describe attempts of deviant drinkers to cover up their job-related drinking. A.A. members described three types of cover-up (Trice, 1962): First, the developing alcoholic himself would attempt a wide variety of stratagems to keep his drinking from becoming common knowledge. We refer to this as self-cover-up. Second, camouflage was provided by work associates: immediate supervisors, co-workers, and subordinates. Third were respondents who reported few attempts by themselves or others to conceal their deviance.

The two studies produced almost identical results regarding the frequency of the three patterns: 40 percent reported relying mainly on self-cover-up; 36 percent relied on cover-up by work associates (fellow workers accounted for 17 percent of the total; immediate supervisors, 12 percent; and subordinates, 7 percent); and 20 percent described few, if any, cover-up experiences (they typically felt that their drinking was common knowledge and that cover-up was unnecessary).

The relationship between the cover-up types and occupational types, job freedom, and off-the-job drinking experiences with fellow workers were also explored. In general, high-status alcoholics reported self-cover-up as the predominant type, probably because of their freedom from close supervision which made it easier to conceal their drinking problem by themselves. As would be expected, there were significant differences between types of cover-up and degree of job freedom. Self-cover-up, of course, was concentrated in those jobs with a maximum of freedom from both imposed work schedules and close supervision, rather than among lower-status workers where job freedom is relatively scarce. These latter individuals were either protected by work associates or not at all.

Practically all research subjects reported participating in off-the-job drinking with fellow workers, and again there was a cover-up difference between high- and low-status occupations. While high-status alcoholics participated in such activities, they were careful to drink normally, and waited until they had separated from work associates to drink heavily. While with associates they were inclined to drink small amounts and to avoid becoming the center of attention. The irony of this pattern of cover-up is subtle: by drinking "normally" with fellow workers, they could draw attention away from any cues of problem drinking; if they did not drink with co-workers at all, only the cues of deviance would be available, thus accelerating the identification and labeling process. In contrast, lower-status alcoholics were relatively uninhibited in their group drinking and often got drunk with co-workers. As a result, their excessive drinking and "loss of control" were easily observed by fellow workers.

Stamps (1965:79) also studied cover-up experiences in a sample of 400 alcoholics, some of whom were A.A. members. He similarly found that:

> A greater proportion of the high than the low status men used self-coverup methods. "Partial absenteeism," "lying," "avoidance of off-the-job social drinking," and "being careful to maintain normal drinking appearance" were self-coverup methods used by a higher percentage of the high status employees.

Stamps also found that occupational status was a factor in determining the type of cover-up help received. While a high percentage of high-status respondents received help from persons working under them, low-status workers received help from their supervisors and peers who made excuses for them or ignored their deviance altogether. Low-status employees also indicated that co-workers frequently did their work for them. Stamps (1965) found that respondents with much job freedom came to work and used cover-up methods on the job, avoiding "moving about" and other physical activity, whereas persons with little job freedom stayed away from the job until they were in better shape.

COVER-UP: USERS OF NONOPIATE DRUGS

The difference between alcohol use and the use of the so-called soft drugs is graphically illustrated by a consideration of on-the-job cover-up activities. Considerable time and energy is employed by the deviant drinker to cover up the facts of his deviance and project an image of normality. We believe, however, that most users of soft drugs spend only a tiny fraction of their energies in cover-up. This phenomenon seems to have four sources: the lower social visibility of the effects of drugs as compared with alcohol, the less disruptive effects of moderate drug use, the ability of few supervisors and co-workers to recognize drug use, and the lack of absolute norms of conduct in pluralistic American society. These factors appear to operate both singly and in concert to reduce the need for cover-up activities by users of these drugs.

Drugs such as tranquilizers, amphetamines, and barbiturates may have low visibility because they actually improve work performance. There is obviously little need to cover up an improvement in job performance unless it is visibly accompanied by some undesirable symptom such as loudness, excessive laughter, etc. In addition, marihuana users may not be socially visible since most users can control the effects of the drug, in part because of the possibility that the effects of this and other mild drugs on the central nervous system may be considerably less than parallel effects of alcohol (Goode, 1969a; Zinberg and Weil, 1969). Thus cover-up of use is easier than cover-up of alcohol use.

The knowledge-of-symptoms factor is very significant. First, most adult Americans feel competent to identify the symptoms of deviant alcohol use. Tell-tale odor, red eyes, a "bleary" appearance, slurred speech, and lessening of control over motor functions are almost universal results of deviant alcohol use that are difficult to hide. Most people have also experienced the results of alcohol use, if not personally then among their associates. While these symptoms of alcohol use are simply *familiar,* the symptoms of drug use are equally unfamiliar. Related to this difference is the "generation gap" with its alleged discrepancies in behavioral norms between older and younger generations. Expressiveness is a marked feature of youth-culture norms. By its nonconformist nature the youth ethic results in considerable blurring of everyday behavioral expectations held toward the young, with the possible consequence that drug-induced behaviors may be accepted by elders in the work place as the way "those kids" act.

With few widely known telltale effects, nonopiate drug use is not difficult to cover up, except that marihuana users must be careful where the drug is smoked. The visibility of the smoking and the distinctive odor of the smoke make cover-up necessary if the drug is used on the job, as is the case with the use of alcohol on the job. Since most other drugs are usually taken as pills, they are less obtrusive than alcohol or opiates.

Young work associates, especially those experienced with drugs, will undoubtedly cover up for other youthful workers. The whole youth culture is strongly against turning in one another for such deviance. This mutual protection appears more intense than that practiced by their elders.

ABSENTEEISM: IMPACT OF DEVIANT DRINKING

Combined with poor work, absenteeism accounts for most of the impact of alcohol use on work organizations. Much of this absenteeism stems from illness, brought about or exacerbated by heavy drinking. Compared with on-the-job accidents and turnover, these illnesses are more costly and are one of the main problems for supervisors who must deal with deviant-drinking employees (Trice, 1964; 1965b).

There are many opinions about the relation between hangover and absences. "Blue Monday" has been traditional for decades, but "we have no way of knowing how many employees come to work occasionally or frequently suffering from hangover" (*Quarterly Journal of Studies on Alcohol,* 1942). Slight (1948) believes that hangover in ordinary drinkers is debilitating after alcohol has left the body and that it leads to absenteeism. Hangover inefficiency, however, may derive from the indirect factors such as loss of sleep, oversmoking, and overactivity that accompany much social drinking (Karvinen, 1962; Takala *et al.,* 1958).

During World War II, studies of short absences for sickness in two large companies showed concentrations immediately before and after the weekend. Gastrointestinal disorders hit their peak during these periods indicating combinations of improper eating and drinking (Court, 1943; McGee and Cregor, 1942). A third war-time study showed three percent of the work force in a large steel mill absent one or more times because of excessive drinking (Stevenson, 1942). Two studies of disciplinary cases in the United States reach similar conclusions: one showed three times as many absences among heavy drinking cases (O'Brien, 1949); the other reported "excessive absences" (Stevenson, 1942). A Swedish report (Lingren, 1957) indicates a doubling of absenteeism among employees who had drinking problems following the abolition of liquor-rationing books in that country. Unfortunately, these reports do not describe the extent to which their samples are representative. Straus and Bacon (1951) found that heavy-drinking college students failed to meet obligations, such as conferences or classes, due to drinking or its results. This pattern appeared early among problem drinkers and preceded damaged friendships, accidents, or formal punishment.

Data about the job-absence patterns of alcohol addicts are more refined, and overall evidence indicates that eight to ten days lost per year is modal (Bureau of National Affairs, 1954; Covner, 1950). There are, however, wide variations around this model. Using this base for comparison, a study in a large public utility revealed twice as many sick days lost by alcoholic employees during the year prior to diagnosis in contrast to those lost by "normals" (Mann, 1952). The absenteeism rate among alcoholics in a Caribbean oil refinery was nearly three times the estimated average (Turfboer, 1959). Members of Alcoholics Anonymous estimated absences nearly four times the general average (Trice, 1962).

Studies which include comparison groups show similar results. Observer and Maxwell (1959) and Thorpe and Perrey (1950) reported that male alcoholics have nearly three times the sick absences of a matched control group. Godeau and Quentel (1958) found absenteeism among alcoholics in a French arsenal to be twice that of nonalcoholics, while Cavalie (1956) indicated that alcoholics' absences were nearly eight times those of other employees.

Data on those suffering from other behavior disorders indicate the deviant drinkers' absences are not unique. Two years before diagnosis, both alcoholic and mentally ill employees in a large utility had significantly greater incidence of sick days than others, and the rates for alcoholics were significantly higher than those for neurotics and psychotics (Trice, 1965b). During the single year before formal diagnosis, however, the rate for the mentally ill increased to a level significantly greater than that for the other employees. Following therapy, absenteeism dropped sharply among the mentally ill, but the treated alcoholics continued to show a higher rate of days absent.

"Partial absences" among deviant drinkers were first described by Franco (1954:456) as "unexplained disappearance from an assigned post during a tour of duty." Two studies on early signs of developing alcohol addiction showed leaving the post temporarily to be an early and frequent sign (Maxwell, 1960; Trice, 1964). Supervisors of alcoholic employees in one company also reported frequent partial absences (Trice, 1965b). A combination of hangovers, jitters, and drinking on the job can force the deviant drinker to abandon his work repeatedly.

Since no research provides an estimate of the actual amount of time lost through partial absenteeism, this type of absence may not be unique to alcoholics but could characterize other supervisory problems and may even be typical behavior of many normal employees. Both "partial" and "full" absenteeism vary with the occupational status of the alcoholic employee. In three studies (Trice, 1962; Maxwell and Wesson, 1963; Stamps, 1965), high-status employees showed more partial than stay-away absenteeism, while the converse was true for low-status persons. Since high-status positions typically have more freedom, their occupants may more easily engage in short-time departures from the job. Once at work, low-status alcoholics are less able to move about easily.

An absence pattern directly related to job inefficiency might be classified as "on-the-job absenteeism." High-status deviant drinkers are often in poor condition on the job, while lower-status alcoholics are inclined to do a substantial day of work when on the job and distribute their absences around these periods. Research reports by Trice (1965b) and by Warkov and his associates (1965) substantiate this pattern and show that supervisors of lower-status deviant drinkers are as concerned over absenteeism as alcoholism. According to Miller and Riessman (1961), the rhythm of life in the lower strata fluctuates between periods of relative routine and repetitive activity and "sought situations" of great emotional stimulation in which there may be heavy use of alcohol.

The role of job status in explaining variations in absenteeism among deviant drinkers was strikingly revealed by the work histories of Alcoholics Anonymous members (Trice, 1962). Professional and managerial deviant drinkers definitely tended to work while still feeling the ill effects of repeated excessive drinking. Among the high-status employees interviewed, a certified public accountant stated, "Whenever I felt I could possibly navigate and get down there without collapsing, I would go." A feature writer for a large newspaper said, "I rarely missed a day; I went to work if I could possibly stumble up the subway steps." Questionnaire data showed that the high-status group tended to report for work with fair regularity during the middle stages of their developing addiction. If they had to stay away, they returned to work after a very short absence. The lower-status group, by contrast, did not exhibit this kind of determination. Although they often came to work with hangovers, they showed an inclination to stay away altogether rather than to attempt work activities in an impaired condition. Large blocks of absences were obvious in their records. Tuesday absences were frequently added to Monday absences and unusual and bizarre excuses for absences were often used.

A sense of duty and responsibility was the reported major force compelling the high-status respondents to go to work despite the presence of hangover, excessive fatigue, and anxiety over blackouts about events accompanying the previous night's drinking. A district sales manager expressed this attitude, "I had an ingrained sense of duty and it would not be drowned in alcohol. In all my years of work I was conscientious about being on the job, so as badly as I would feel I would get up, shake it off, and go to work." A university professor stated that his "abhorrence of irresponsibility" did not leave him even when he became fully dependent on alcohol, while others spoke of maintaining high standards for themselves. Obviously these jobs provided opportunities for lower visibility and on-the-job absenteeism not available to lower-status workers.

This continued presence on the job helped convince the deviant employees that they were still normal. A production engineer rationalized this way: "As long as you appeared at places when you were expected to, and as long as you did some sort of skeleton thing, pretending to do your job . . . all these things meant that you did not have the problem you knew you really had . . . somehow, it was not getting the better of me . . . I could go to work."

This sense of responsibility was rarely mentioned by lower-status employees, many of whom indicated that their job involvement was based upon economic rewards. Going to work was frequently only an expedient for continued drinking. This low degree of job involvement probably does not reflect irresponsibility as much as it reflects differences in the inherent rewards available at different occupational levels (Liebow, 1967), as well as differential opportunities for on-the-job impairment. In other words, high-status occupations offer more than a paycheck; there are opportunities for self-expression and creativity and many opportunities for upward mobility. This is rarely the case in low-status occupations. Alcohol may thus provide a release from the routine and monotony of the job. A punch press operator reported that he "often had a few in a tavern across the street from the plant before going to work. Likely as not I could not make myself go to work and sweat it out, so I stayed where I was."

The interviews indicated that drinking and absenteeism were logical partners among low-status deviant drinkers. A waiter in a large restaurant commented, "Once you started on a drinking spree, you weren't expected back for a while." Drinking in groups made up of fellow workers which met during off-duty hours tended to sanction this assumption.

Crucial in accounting for the differences in absenteeism patterns between upper- and lower-status deviants are the opportunities for deviance on the job. Upper-status employees frequently came to the job and continued drinking, faked a job performance, or failed to perform at all. Their positions were only loosely interdependent on the work of others and usually they were not closely supervised. Their situation contrasts sharply with the interdependent work group and close supervision of lower-class jobs. The upper-status employees could often continue drinking during lunch time and often had the privacy to cover up some of their more blatant physical symptoms such as shakes and tremors. Furthermore, they were frequently free to move around the community or neighborhood. Sales executives and factory managers reported that opportunities to go out and "inspect" field activities gave them the opportunity to drink. Freedom of work hour scheduling also permitted such deviant activities. Significantly, low-status respondents who had jobs which required traveling in the community, such as delivery men, truck drivers, and garbage collectors, were more inclined to go to work and remain on the job, because their job activities usually facilitated cover-up and on-the-job drinking.

ABSENTEEISM: USERS OF NONOPIATE DRUGS

Absenteeism among users of nonopiate drugs may not be as severe as among problem drinkers. Hangovers of the alcohol type that produce physical distress do not appear. On the other hand, heavy use may be accompanied by various other ailments that would generate sick absences. Murphy (1966) reports on studies conducted in India (where the type of marihuana used is much stronger than that used in this country) that regular, heavy use is accompanied by insomnia, limited self-neglect, chronic bronchitis, some asthma, and disturbances of the large bowel. The Indian Hemp Drugs Commission Report, published in 1894 and focusing on the use of marihuana and related drugs in provinces of India, concluded the following about physical disorders associated with heavy use: "It may indirectly cause dysentery by weakening the constitution and it may cause bronchitis mainly through the action of the inhaled smoke on the bronchial tubes" (Mikuriya, 1968:269). Thus it seems reasonable to believe that heavy marihuana use can cause at least two conditions conducive to absenteeism: physical disorders that produce more than ordinary sick absences and commitment to a way of life in which work accomplishment is not valued, making absenteeism a likely form of behavior. One of the most common observations about marihuana is that its use is sociogenic, i.e. it takes place in small, intimate, compatible groups which develop strong bonds of cohesion (Goode, 1969c). The likelihood of marihuana use becoming a central part of spontaneous, informal work groups is thus relatively high, especially if young employees have already learned to smoke before coming to their jobs. Such groups would probably provide mutual protection and opportunities for higher-than-average absenteeism, including on-the-job and partial absenteeism. This protection would be especially expected in low-status situations where there were few rewards for individual performance or opportunities for mobility.

Many sources have indicated concern about the possibility of drug use among certain semi-skilled and clerical workers leading to both on-the-job and partial absenteeism. It is assumed that some jobs are so routinized that the worker could perform them while under the influence of marihuana with shoddy work and accidents as a result. No research data indicate the extent of on-the-job or partial absenteeism due to marihuana or other drug use. The findings of Weil and associates (1968) regarding successful compensatory behavior among experienced users indicates this behavior may well be prevalent but is probably difficult to detect.

No particular absenteeism pattern would necessarily be expected among users of other drugs such as amphetamines or tranquilizers, with the exception of those who use drugs excessively or experimentally to achieve highs. Among those dependent on amphetamines, for example, or among those combining different drugs for new thrills, considerable absenteeism and other forms of job impairment would be expected. Unlike deviant drinking, where absenteeism appears to be inevitable in the development of addiction, there is no reason to expect that absenteeism will constitute a job behavior cue to the presence of drug abuse.

Finally, the deleterious effects of tobacco smoking and heavy coffee drinking on work performance should be studied more closely. Our presently legal drugs may be as much a menace to job performance as the illegal drugs. For example, reliable data show that cigarette smokers, especially frequent users, have unusually high numbers of (1) days lost from work, i.e. days when they are absent because of illness or injury; (2) bed days, i.e. days when they are "sufficiently ill or disabled so as to spend all or most of the day in bed . . .; and (3) days of restricted activity, i.e. when a person cuts down his usual activities for most of a day because of an illness or an accident" (Horn, 1968:64). The National Health Survey as reported by Horn in 1965 found as follows:

(Days Lost from Work) — For those with a history of cigarette smoking, classified by heaviest amount smoked, the average number of days was 7 percent higher for men and 15 percent higher for women who had smoked less than 11 cigarettes per day; 33 percent higher for men and 60 percent higher for women who had smoked 11–20 cigarettes per day; 48 percent higher for men and 79 percent higher for women who had smoked 21–40 cigarettes per day; and 83 percent higher for men and 140 percent higher for women who had smoked more than 40 cigarettes per day. The relationships expressed by all three measures are somewhat higher among men aged 45–64 than among men aged 17–44, but lower among women aged 45–64 than among women aged 17–44. . . .

(Bed Days) — For those with a history of cigarette smoking, classified by heaviest amount smoked, the average number of days was 10 percent higher for men and 4 percent lower for women who had smoked less than 11 cigarette per day; 22 percent higher for men and 17 percent higher for women who had smoked 21–40 cigarettes per day; and 53 percent higher for men and 192 percent higher for women who had smoked more than 40 cigarettes per day. Relationships with smoking are higher for men than for women for all three measures except for age 17–44 in which the differences in morbidity rates between smokers and non-smokers are about the same. . . .

(Days of Restricted Activity) — For those with a history of cigarette smoking classified by heaviest amount smoked, the average number of days was 12 percent higher for men and 4 percent higher for women who had smoked 11–20 cigarettes per day; 30 percent higher for men and 48 percent higher for women who had smoked 21–40 cigarettes per day; and 81 percent higher for men and 146 percent higher for women who had smoked more than 40 cigarettes per day. Again rates are higher for men than for women in all three measures except for age group 17–44, in which differences in morbidity rates are higher for women (Horn, 1968: 64, 66).

Enterline (1968) reports the same absenteeism pattern. Since approximately 48 million Americans, from all social classes and diverse occupations smoked 524 billion cigarettes in 1967 (Kennedy, 1967), the cigarette smoker's job impairment is widespread and rivals that of alcohol. In addition, smokers as employees have poorer overall general health and suffer significantly higher rates of heart disease, lung cancer, emphysema, hypertension, and bronchitis. Practically no evidence is available on the effects of regular, heavy caffeine use, but observations indicate this drug also deserves further attention and attempts to assess its deleterious impacts.

ON-THE-JOB ACCIDENTS: IMPACT OF DEVIANT DRINKING

The belief that the deviant drinker's accident rate is higher than that of other workers is widespread. The evidence, however, does not support this belief except in the case of early-stage deviant drinkers. Jellinek's (1947) estimate that the rate of fatal accidents among inebriated workers was more than twice that of nonalcoholic laborers has often been used in references to on-the-job accidents. This figure, however, is misleading since it was based on all types of fatal accidents, only a third of which occurred at work. Two industrial physicians checking on-the-job accidents in a company of 1,800 employees found for 15 years no fatal injury directly or indirectly attributable to alcohol use. Their data showed only one injury that might be attributed to drinking, this one involving the worker's inattention coupled with his admission that he had had "a few drinks" the night before (Roberts and Russo, 1955). The work histories of A.A. members who were exposed to accidents also showed relatively few on-the-job accidents. The subjects of this study felt that the routine nature of many of their jobs, their own exceptional caution, protection from accidents by fellow workers, absenteeism when especially vulnerable to accidents, and their assignment by supervisors to less hazardous work were all responsible for their accident rate.

It is, however, logical to expect a deviant drinker to have more accidents than other workers. He would be less steady; his coordination, timing, motor responses, and sense of danger would be impaired. In addition, hangovers on the job could cause accidents. The evidence, however, does not support this logical assumption. About 20 percent of the A.A. members who were exposed to accidents reported at least one lost-time accident during the middle phase of addiction. When this proportion is translated into a frequency rate per million exposed-man-hours, it falls about halfway between high and low extremes for various types of industries. The rate is much higher than that found in typewriter assembly plants but much lower than the rates for logging, sawmills, and foundries. The tentative conclusion is that the lost-time accident rate reported by the A.A. respondents is not unusually high when compared with median rates. Furthermore, respondents in lower-status occupations (who were therefore most exposed to accidents) did not report a significantly greater amount of on-the-job accidents than those in higher-level jobs. Variations in job freedom showed no relationship to the number of accidents.

Respondents independently explained their safety record through five factors:

1. Extra caution that reduced quantity of work output but prevented accidents: Mulford (1964b) found a very similar attitude among nonalcoholic drinking drivers in Iowa.

2. This extra caution was especially manifest when a poor physical condition made accident risk higher than usual.

3. Absenteeism whenever hangover was severe: this is consistent with the findings on absenteeism among lower-status occupations. Interview evidence suggests that a supervisor often removed a deviant drinker from the job if he felt the worker might injure himself.

4. The repetitious nature of their jobs and their own routines for managing the effects of alcohol; together, these influences yielded a habitual work regularity that helped protect the drinkers from injury. Mulford's (1964b) findings on drinking drivers are in keeping with this point.

5. A substantial number of interviewees insisted they had had few accidents because they "steadied themselves" with alcohol during working hours: moderate drinking during the working day temporarily calmed hangover symptoms and allowed them to concentrate. These subjective results coincide with objective findings that moderate amounts of alcohol often tend to improve efficiency temporarily and may help the drinker present himself as being in a fairly integrated state (Straus, 1971).

In addition, deviant drinkers who drive as part of their jobs were not found to have higher accident rates. Extra caution and absenteeism were again offered as the explanations.

The data on work accidents are limited, however. For instance, the number of reported lost-time accidents tells us nothing about the seriousness of the accident nor the duration of lost time. Thus a minor accident with one work day lost is combined with a major one in which the loss may have been six months. Furthermore, some respondents may have been exposed to risk much longer than others and thus had a greater opportunity for accidents; there being no standardization for exposure in the data.

One research deficiency was eliminated with data developed from records of a large company which included adequate controls for comparisons between problem-drinking employees (identified by medical department records) and other workers (Observer and Maxwell, 1959). Problem drinkers accounted for more on-the-job accidents early in their disorder, but after their drinking problems had fully developed they were no more prone to on-the-job accidents than other employees. Apparently, early-stage alcoholics do not use preventive tactics such as extra caution, probably because a period of learning is necessary. Significantly, the alcoholic employees in this study had numerous off-the-job accidents, while the controls had none.

Similarly, Trice (1965b) compared accident data for nonalcoholics with that for labeled alcoholics, neurotics, and psychotics. On-the-job accident records provided three types of data: amount of lost time after accidents; number of accidents during an eight-year period before diagnosis and a one-year period after diagnosis; and data on cause, type, and location of accident and extent of injury. A fourth set of data came from personnel representatives who estimated the extent of accident risk in the employees' jobs on a four-point scale. Only one set of accident data showed any association with type of employee: alcoholics' jobs were described as significantly more exposed to accidents. Although not jobs of high danger, they nonetheless had more risk than others. Forty-five percent of alcoholics' jobs were in the "occasionally exposed" category, while 24 percent of the neurotics, 19 percent of the psychotics, and 18 percent of normals held such jobs.

Despite the differential exposure of the alcoholics, neither they nor any of the other diagnosed groups had on-the-job accident experience that differed significantly from that of each other or of the normals: 9 percent of the alcoholics, 6 percent of the psychotics, 4 percent of the neurotics, and 6 percent of the normal employees had one or more lost-time accidents during the eight-year period before formal diagnosis. Data for no-lost-time accidents were similar. In addition, none of the staff-collected data about accidents differed as to type of employee.

Thus, on the basis of formal accident data, no evidence of accident proneness emerged. Data for the eight-year period before diagnosis did, however, reveal that deviant drinkers were treated significantly more often
for contusions. Since the medical department treated off-the-job as well
as on-the-job injuries, such a finding suggests more minor off-the-job
injuries among deviant drinkers.

These results are supported by other data. An "early identification"
study carried out in the same company, with information supplied by
supervisors of the alcoholic employees, revealed accidents ranked the
lowest out of the 44 possible clues of developing alcoholism (Trice,
1964). This finding agrees with Maxwell's (1960) early identification
study in which approximately 400 alcoholics ranked accidents of both
types as the poorest clues to early-stage alcoholism.

These conclusions are also supported by a recent study of alcoholism
and fatal accidents. Brenner (1967) computed the rates of death by
fatal accidents in a sample of 1,343 persons who were patients in four
alcoholism rehabilitation clinics in San Francisco during 1954–57. Data
were collected from dates of admission through 1961, and specific death
rates by fatal accidents then were compared with the general Bay Area
statistics. Alcoholics were seven times as likely to have fatal accidents
as Bay Area residents of comparable age and sex. Of the 35 fatal accidents among the San Francisco alcoholics, however, only one was reported as occurring while at work. In addition, Brenner quotes Swedish
data indicating that, although alcoholics suffered almost twice as many
accidents as comparable counterparts, their injuries are typically leisure
time injuries, while those of the nonalcoholic controls were frequently
from accidents at work.

These data regarding on-the-job accidents dispel the myth of the
work-accident-prone deviant drinker, but also indicate that it is invalid
to assume similarity between on-the-job and off-the-job behavior. The
job typically contains opportunities for accident avoidance that are not
available in many nonwork settings. This finding provides further insight into features of the job which can cover up a variety of deviant
behaviors.

ACCIDENTS: EFFECTS OF NONOPIATE DRUG USE

No direct evidence about on-the-job accidents and drugs is available.
Certain findings do, however, permit the conclusion that employees who
are regular or even heavy users of marihuana will not be involved in
an abnormal number of on-the-job accidents. Goode (1970b:146) reports
a study of the effects of marihuana on simulated driving skills of ex-

perienced users: "The overall findings were that marihuana did not impair motor skills, that there were almost no differences driving high on marihuana and normal." The careful studies by Weil and associates (1968:1242) suggests that "regular users of marihuana do get high after smoking marihuana in a neutral setting, but do not show the same degree of impairment of performance on the tests [Continuous Performance Test, Digit Symbol Substitution Test, Continuous Performance with Strobe Light Distraction, Self-Rating Bipolar Mood Scale, and Pursuit Motor Test] as do the naive subjects." On the other hand, the Mayor's (La Guardia) Commission (1944) found that hand steadiness and complex reaction time may be adversely affected by both large and small doses of marihuana. Practically all studies also emphasize the wide variety of individual reactions, which further limits valid generalization. Goode (1970b:148), however, after reviewing the available data concludes ". . . the hypothesis that the marihuana high deteriorates motor skills far less than alcohol is, it may safely be said, firmly established."

Apparently the degree of experience with marihuana is the main determinant of possible personal control over behavior and, thereby, accident proneness. Becker (1967:167) concluded that "a novice marihuana user will find it difficult to drive while 'high,' but experienced users have no difficulty." Thus, the new on-the-job user of marihuana may be an accident risk. Regarding other drugs, the data are not clear about the development of compensatory behavior control. Other drugs may, however, be more dangerous than marihuana. Examining a group of heavy users of a wide range of psychoactive drugs in a Toronto clinic, Smart and associates (1969:70) found them "to have far more driving accidents than expected for their age, sex, and exposure in terms of miles driven." A summary of the studies on the effects of drug use on accidents concluded that eleven to fifteen percent of those involved in accidents had taken a psychotropic drug prior to the accident (Smart et al., 1969). Murphree has recently reported the detrimental effect on motor coordination and functioning of smoking nicotine cigarettes while drinking alcohol: "Thus we found in all our subjects who drank and then smoked cigarettes with a high nicotine content an additional impairment of coordination" (Recovery, 1971:1).

No research data lead us to expect any exceptional levels of accident rates among users of amphetamines and tranquilizers, with the exception of addicted or very heavy users. The stimulating effects of amphetamines may increase accident proneness, but evidence to support such a contention has not been reported. The vigilance against accidents among alcohol and marihuana users may also be the case among users of these drugs, possibly leading to an even lower-than-normal accident rate.

JOB BEHAVIORS AND THE CAREER OF THE OPIATE ADDICT

A troublesome feature of the current "drug hysteria" is the tendency to overgeneralize and ignore the wide range of human responses to drugs as well as the variety of dependencies on any particular drug. For example, we have noted various types of marihuana users; equally relevant are such questions as: What kind of marihuana was taken? How did it enter the body and in what amounts? With whom and for what purpose was it used? What was the emotional setting? What was the temperament of the user? All of these variables force us to modify any description of a "typical" effect on work behavior.

Much the same is true of the opiates and their impact on work behavior. The opiates are usually ranked among the most potent and "dangerous" of drugs. A good deal of popular imagery of the opiate user has prevented the diffusion of the facts. In this section we will outline the variations in the effects of the opiates and point out the range of users' job behaviors.

According to Chein and his associates (1964:359),

> There is no simple or single effect of opiates on work and productivity. Instead, a variety of behaviors vis-a-vis work may occur when a person is regularly using opiates. Whatever behavior we observe in a particular addict resulted not merely from opiates, but rather as a consequence of interactions between his needs and motives for addiction, his personality structure, and the neurophysiological effects of the drugs.

The stereotype of the opiate addict, however, shows scant regard for these variations, and Rubington (1967) shows that the "dope-fiend" stereotype pictures addicts as weak and ineffective in job and family roles, as immoral, and as eager to convert new addicts. The prolonged use of drugs allegedly wrecks their bodies, they become sexual menaces, they neglect work, and their condition is irreversible. Ausubel (1960:535) is much more explicit: "The typical drug-satiated addict is lethargic, semisomnolent, undependable, devoid of ambition, and preoccupied with grandiose fantasies. He loses all desire for socially productive work and exhibits little interest in food [and] sex . . . and lives mainly in the euphoric glow of his last dose and in anticipation of his next one." And, at another point, he flatly states, without citing evidence, that "it has been unequivocally demonstrated that opiate addiction, in the overwhelming majority of cases, interfered with the productivity of work, with the desire for real achievement, and with mature, responsible adjustment to problems of vocational . . . life" (Ausubel, 1960:535). In sharp contrast, Lindesmith and Gagnon (1964:178) insist that "there are substantial numbers of addicts who are responsible and productive members of society, who share the common frames of values, who have not abandoned the quest for success and are not immune to the frustrations involved in seeking it, and who are not overcome by defeatism, quietism and resignation."

Chein and his associates (1964:358) put these different viewpoints into perspective:

> But, in fact, the relationship between opiate addiction and work is quite complex. The number of professionally successful persons who were or are addicted to opiates is an indication that there is no necessary relationship between opiate use and an unproductive life. There are also a number of addicts who, indeed, never worked if they could help it, before they used drugs and who continue not to work, if they can possibly avoid it, after they became adicted. . . .
>
> There are many addicts we studied with sufficient industry and deportment to satisfy their employers. If, however, they were unable to satisfy their self-induced need for drugs before going to work, they might be too restless and irritable (early symptoms of the withdrawal syndrome) to work or be late or absent from work because of the many hours spent "making a connection." *If addicts lose their jobs, it is because they could not regularly obtain drugs, not because the opiates made their work unsatisfactory to their employers.* In our experience there are also a number of addicts who are able to work better when receiving drugs than when abstinent. Such a person is often preoccupied with obsessive doubts which inhibit him in the simplest tasks. When he uses opiates, he gets "drive," his obsessive doubts are suppressed and he is able to make decisions and act.
>
> The work habits of the few carefully observed patients who were readdicted in the research wards at the U.S. Public Health Service Hospital in Lexington were not sufficiently different from those of the other abstinent patients to provoke comment. These patients may have worked at a slower pace than some of their peers, but their efficiency and attentiveness were not otherwise impaired. [emphasis added]

In sum, there are opiate addicts whose work effectiveness is not adversely affected by their drug dependency, provided they have access to a sufficient supply to meet their tolerance for the drug. There are even those whose performance is improved with opiate use (Lindesmith and Gagnon, 1964). Finally, there are those whose performance is impaired, but the impairment is often to a large degree the result of social circumstances surrounding their addiction.

147

A classic instance of a secure supply of opiates is the physician-addict. Winick's (1961) data did not show that physician-addicts were less successful than nonaddict doctors. Pescor (1942:3) concludes that, due to the ready availability of opiates which keeps him out of the criminal subculture, the physician-addict typically has made a "comfortable-to-good economic adjustment even during the period of his addiction." His deviant drug use is socially invisible, and he is not socially stigmatized since he has not been isolated and processed by a formal labeling agency such as a court, hospital, or clinic. The addict may eventually come to official attention through identification by narcotic agents, but Pescor estimates that thirteen years of addiction is the norm. Thus the physician-addict apparently functions quite well in his professional role for a protracted period.

Opiate addiction is especially high among physicians in all Western nations and considerably higher than that of most other occupations in the United States (Simon and Lumry, 1969). Pescor (1942) reported the proportion of physicians among the drug addicts during his 1942 study was eight times greater than the proportion of physicians in a comparable general adult population. Wilner and Kassebaum (1965:162) report that during 1962 admission rates for physicians to the two federal drug-addiction hospitals (Fort Worth and Lexington) were "about ten times the proportion of physicians in the United States population." Similar but less pronounced rates are found for medically related occupations such as nursing (Barber, 1967).

An obvious explanation for this phenomenon is the unique availability of drugs for physicians, although some writers have raised the issues of professional role stresses and emotional predispositions (Sherlock, 1967; Jones, 1967; Modlin and Montes, 1964). Most significant for our concerns is that the absence of job impairment apparently stems from the fact that it is unnecessary for medical personnel to become involved in the criminal subculture to obtain their drugs. Addicts in other professions and occupations may, to a lesser degree, be able to develop go-betweens who essentially relieve them of involvement in the intricacies of the drug underworld. The fact of greatest significance here is that an addict can function in most situations provided he has his "fix," and it is then almost impossible for those in close contact with him to know he is on drugs. He can, it should be emphasized, need as many as four to five fixes a day (Salpukas, 1971).

Most opiate addicts, however, do not enjoy the protective advantages of affluence and cannot avoid involvement in the maze of connections, the theft, feelings of apprehension, anxieties, contact with other addicts, and the new self-image that comes from the addict subculture. *This necessary immersion in the deviant network of drug addicts brings about most of his job impairment, not the drug addiction itself.* The lower-class addict's life literally becomes drug-centered as he invests more and more of his energy in assuring his supply. There is some evidence that despite the fantastic cost per day needed to supply an addiction, some lower-status addicts have been regularly employed, but, even in these cases, involvement in the addict subculture will probably have negative effects on job performance. Absenteeism and turnover will likely be facets of this picture. In addition, the problem of employer security increases sharply due to the addict's need to maintain the drug supply. It should be underscored, however, that, if the addict has the amounts of the drug necessary to avoid withdrawal symptoms, he can often produce as well as other employees.

Withdrawal will almost inevitably bring about job impairment, especially if it occurs on the job. Between six and ten hours after his last fix, the addict will become restless, tense, unable to concentrate, hostile, depressed, cynical, and anxious. A few (two to four) hours later the physical symptoms begin: gastrointestinal, muscular, and nervous distress of severe proportions. This acute illness demonstrates physiological dependency, and, unless he gets a fix, he will soon experience sharp withdrawal distress. Obviously, he cannot perform adequately in such periods. After a few experiences with withdrawal distress, great efforts will be made to avoid it, leading to sporadic and partial absenteeism. When on the job, the addict's attention and faculties may be deeply preoccupied with avoiding the horrors of abstinence, leading to increased likelihood of accidents assuming he is clearly exposed to them. As he becomes more and more in need of the drug, he probably will not even give adequate attention to simple tasks, increasing work errors, and scrap rate.

A single fix will promptly reduce the symptoms brought on by the anticipated distress of abstinence (Clausen, 1961). As restlessness, nervousness, twitching, goose-flesh, and nausea subside, the addicted employee returns to his "cool," on-drug self, especially if he feels assured that he will not soon face the prospects of again being without his supply. Chein and associates (1964:362) has pointed out that a brief out-of-the-world period immediately follows administration of a fix, during which there is a lack of involvement in current experiences, which is followed by a "gradual return to a 'normal' state." For experienced addicts this is probably very short-lived. Although job impairment would be expected in this period, the employee will probably absent himself for a full experience of the sensation.

The level of ongoing anxiety and distress regarding supply and the fix is a function of how well socialized the addicted employee is in the addict subculture. Has he learned the skills necessary to procure, administer, and reach a high and, simultaneously, avoid exposure? Rubington (1967:16) provides the flavor of these skills necessary to "make out" in the addict subculture: "All the informal learning that goes into 'scoring,' 'making connections,' testing the quality of the 'stuff,' stashing the 'works,' using the 'outfit,' 'snorting,' 'skin popping,' 'main-lining,' 'tieing up,' in short, getting one's 'kicks' is acquired during the detached intimacy of addict social relations. In time skills for practicing deceit are learned as the need to obtain an illicit supply of drugs mounts."

The skills needed to "score" in the addict subculture carry with them certain beliefs that act against job involvement: "no set of obligations must take precedence over supporting one's habit. Outsiders are square and meant to be worked; insiders alone can be counted on to understand the drug mystique" (Rubington, 1967:16). An ethic of disengagement from "square" society pervades opiate subcultures, an ethic which reduces involvement considerably more than the "hang loose" ideology of the middle-class youth culture. Thus the very process of the lower-class addict's acquiring the knowledge to assure his supply will probably be accompanied by a loss of job interest and ambition and the growth of hostility toward typical work expectations. Obviously such norms support absenteeism and cover-up. Thus "junkies" tend to imitate middle-class dress styles and values in the work situation while in fact rejecting the basic norms of conventional society and its work orientation.

If the addict should be unable to "score," total job impairment is almost certain, for he must neglect work to search for narcotics. The more he fails in his search, the more the job is forgotten, and in 24 to 48 hours he has the most miserable withdrawal symptoms: constant chills, aching muscles, cramps, extreme perspiration, restlessness, sleeplessness, twitching ("kicking" the habit), nausea, and retching. These extreme discomforts rapidly reach a climax after about 48 hours of abstinence and then begin to taper off gradually. Five to seven days later the acute symptoms have subsided, but nervousness and weakness may go on for three or four weeks. The intensity of these withdrawal experiences explains the motivation for a fix. The addict who loses his supply or attempts "cold turkey" almost certainly will jeopardize his job security, and work performance would be very poor should he return to the job after three or four days of abstinence. A lesser but obvious degree of impairment would be present for as long as several weeks.

Thus, unless the addict has an extremely understanding employer, he risks losing his job *unless* he continues his addiction because of the intensity and duration of the symptoms of withdrawal. Even if he "kicks" the use of opiates, a physical and psychological desire that may compete with work involvement remains. The likelihood of such addicts returning to opiates or heroin is great.

The economic cost of addiction is also relevant to the work situation. The typical lower-class addict must spend from fifteen to seventy-five dollars a day, seven days a week, to maintain a source. Thus many addicts are pressured into moonlighting, borrowing, or stealing both on and off the job. Since stolen goods are sharply discounted, items worth a hundred to a hundred and fifty dollars are needed each day to pay for his opiates, and these needs constitute a genuine threat to his employer. That the addict may steal or embezzle or "borrow" cash, tools, and equipment is a security risk that cannot be ignored. Although less likely, moonlighting constitutes a problem for the employer since a second job will reduce work effectiveness for both employers.

So available data indicate that maintenance of the opiate habit probably produces more impediments to job stability and adequate performance than the direct effects of opiate ingestion. The social class of the opiate addict is a prime determinant of the degree to which he will be able to secure a steady supply of drugs, and obviously lower-class addicts are at a severe disadvantage. From this perspective it is tragic that opiate addiction has proven most attractive to the social class least able to "handle" it. We do not intend to imply that opiates are "harmless" as long as one can maintain a supply. Rather we are attempting to place the issue in perspective and at least partially reduce the stereotype that opiates turn the user into a demented "fiend." In this connection we can appropriately recall two of our earlier points: although infrequent, heroin experimentation without addiction does occur and there are heroin addicts who outgrow their addiction.

VI

Reactions of Supervisors to Deviant
Drinkers and Drug Users

FIRST-LINE supervision plays the most crucial role in programs to control deviant drinking and drug use in work organizations. The supervisor's position in the organization allows detection of developing deviance, and the closeness of first-line supervisors' relations with their charges sets the stage for effective actions toward the deviant. The supervisor's effectiveness is determined by five factors: his knowledge of the signs of deviant drinking and drug use, his knowledge of company policy regarding deviant drinkers and drug users, his willingness to implement those company policies, his firmness in implementing the policies, and his consistency in following through.

This chapter focuses on the reactions of supervisors in a large organization to the behaviors of alcoholic and mentally ill employees. The data indicate some of the job-related characteristics of deviants, but primarily cover the supervisor's perceptions of them. Supervisory reactions to alcoholic, neurotic, psychotic, and normal employees leads to a consideration of reactions to deviance in general (Erikson, 1962). A chronological presentation of the stages in the recognition process brings together data on supervisory reactions with information on job behavior of deviants discussed in the previous chapter.

Since the research study reported here does not include data on supervisory reactions to drug users, we can only speculate on the nature and sequence of those reactions. Given the similarity in job impairment patterns resulting from the overuse of alcohol and a mild drug like marihuana, many patterns of supervisory reaction will probably be similar.

Four major differences between alcohol and other drugs which are apt to be used in conjunction with work should be kept in mind, however, when generalizing from conclusions offered in this chapter:

1. The work behaviors associated with drug use are often less visible, less disruptive, and therefore less detectable than work behaviors associated with alcohol use.

2. The combination of certain drug use with certain work demands may produce enhanced concentration and work pace in contrast to the almost universally disruptive effects of alcohol. This may be especially true with regular use of amphetamines.

3. The use of certain drugs may not result in a progressive "accumulation" of deviant acts or progressively impaired behaviors. This would hold true for drugs such as marihuana and most tranquilizers.

4. Societal definitions and stereotypes of deviant drinkers and deviant drug users are very different. The strangeness of drug use may lead the supervisor to accept the "dope-fiend" stereotype. Thus a more rapid referral might be expected when supervisors become certain of deviant drug use; the ambivalence which characterizes supervisory reactions to the deviant drinker is the result of an empathy that the supervisor would probably not feel for the illegal drug user.

A STUDY OF SUPERVISORY REACTION

Supervisors' reactions to deviant employees constitute one example of behavioral labeling and social control, the dynamics of which are discussed in Chapter One. Because of the exchange relationship existing between the employer and the employee, the supervisor as the employer's agent becomes a significant other in the employee's life space: supervisors have legitimate grounds for expecting certain types of job performances from employees. To carry out his role, the supervisor typically can invoke both positive and negative sanctions. Whether or not these sanctions are activated depends on the quality of employee job performance relative to supervisory standards. The supervisor is, thus, able to define and react to inappropriate role performances among his subordinates; this reaction is a social index of deviance (Trice, 1965a).

Studies of deviance have overlooked work organizations in general and supervisor-subordinate relations in particular. With the exception of computing rates of deviance in different occupational levels, deviant behavior research has neglected the dynamics of the job. The fact that alcohol addicts are typically employed regularly during the development of their addiction has been established; however, their experiences on the job, the reactions they engender in peers and supervisors, and the effects of these experiences and reactions upon therapeutic response are largely unexplored. In order to understand these processes, we studied the specific factors affecting and associated with supervisors' reactions to deviant employees in their charge.

RESEARCH DESIGN

In this study (Trice, 1965a), deviants' immediate supervisors were the main sources of data. Using cases identified through the medical department records of a large public utility, the study traced the reactions of immediate supervisors to the behavior of deviant employees and assessed the manner in which the reactions themselves helped define these workers as deviants.

The specific research questions were

1. What indicators of deviant behavior were visible to the supervisor before the employee's diagnosis?

2. How did the supervisor's reactions reflect the fact of employee deviance?

3. What factors directed the supervisor to use the company medical department after he had defined his subordinate's behavior as deviant?

4. What effect did the supervisor's attitude toward use of the medical department have on the employee's subsequent response to therapy?

The size of the studied organization yielded many different patterns of work activities, so the results may be applicable to many organizations. This organization was relatively unique, however, since a program designed to manage deviant drinking was already in effect when the research was conducted. In this program line supervisors were the primary policy agents; therefore, the data reveal the obstacles that must be overcome in implementing a deviance-management program which is integrated into everyday organizational life.

For the study, a list of all employees diagnosed as behavioral deviants from 1958 through 1961 was developed from medical records. These 577 cases were grouped into alcoholic, neurotic, and psychotic categories, and two systematic samples were drawn from this population. First was a 20 percent sample of the 189 cases diagnosed in 1961. The research team then located the 37 employees who had been the immediate supervisors of these deviants at the time of formal diagnosis. The results of an exploratory study of these supervisors formed the basis for a structured interview schedule.

The second systematic sample was comprised of half of the 388 cases diagnosed from 1958 through 1960. Thirty-seven percent of the sample were alcoholics, 20 percent were psychotics, and 43 percent were neurotic. The supervisor at the time of each formal diagnosis was located for an interview, and these managerial personnel were subjects for the central study. A one percent systematic sample of 204 employees served as a comparison group of normals, and their supervisors were likewise interviewed.

To construct the central interview, the supervisors in the pilot study were asked open-ended questions such as: "Tell me what it was like to be boss of (employee)?" "What makes an employee a 'problem' for you?" "Was (employee) one?" "How would you rate his work?" Responses suggested that reactions to the four types of employees (alcoholic, psychotic, neurotic, and normals) varied substantially. Indecision on the part of supervisors was prominent. Regarding their action toward problem cases, supervisors used such phrases as "I see-sawed back and forth about him," or "I was torn both ways." At the same time, they had felt pressure to do something. The factors found to encourage or discourage action by pilot-study supervisors toward problem employees provided items for the central study. These factors are summarized in Table 1.

The interview schedule called for all supervisors to provide the following data:

1. Rating of the employee's work performance relative to the best or worst employee under his supervision (a) during the year of the employee's diagnosis, and (b) during the two years previous to diagnosis;

2. Classifying the employee as to whether he was a recurrent supervisory problem during the two years before the diagnosis;

3. A self-classification of the supervisor during the same period regarding his indecision about the problem employee;

4. A self-classification of the supervisor as (a) inclined toward referral to the medical department, (b) split between referral and non-referral, or (c) not inclined toward referral.

The interview also included a choice of as many as four of the factors which appear in Table 1. The factors chosen were to comprise the most accurate description of a supervisor's reaction to the diagnosed employee.

Personnel department representatives also provided estimates of job-role change and social visibility experienced by the diagnosed employees during the three years before diagnosis. These data included:

1. Number of supervisory changes;

2. Extent of task changes in the job;

3. Extent to which the employee was visible to his supervisor and fellow workers;

4. Extent to which his job was interdependent with the work activities of other employees;

5. Extent to which he was free to arrange the order of his tasks; and

6. Extent to which the employee's off-the-job behavior influenced on-the-job ratings.

Table 1: Factors Influencing Supervisory Action

Discouraging Factors	Encouraging Factors
1. He might be "bugged."	1. He was often surly, arrogant and even defiant.
2. He was often an able worker.	2. He put me in a "bad light."
3. Referral would hurt his family.	3. It would help out his family if I took action.
4. He was well liked and popular.	4. He had a bad effect on fellow workers.
5. I had come up through the ranks with him.	5. I had to watch him more closely.
6. Referral would mean his separation from the company.	6. He wasn't getting work out.
7. It was my duty to handle the problem.	7. He was out a good deal.
8. He would soon be shifted to another job.	8. I never knew what to expect.
9. He "snapped out of it" frequently.	9. He was lacking in self-respect.
10. Referral would get me mixed up with the union.	10. He was a safety risk.
11. Referral would involve me in inconvenience.	11. My boss would back me up.
12. I felt "in between" employees and management.	12. I needed to do something as soon as possible.
	13. I wanted to replace him.

156

RESEARCH RESULTS

Change Experiences. Analysis of these data indicates that diagnosed employees, with the exception of psychotics, tended to experience relatively few supervisory or task changes before diagnosis. This analysis suggests stability in supervisor-employee relations and implies a clear-cut and substantial basis for observing changes in behavior. Data on psychotics suggest that adjustment to technical and supervisory changes might precipitate a psychosis or at least reveal its nature so that diagnosis becomes more probable; of course, it is also possible that bizarre behavior has led management to change an individual's work role or supervision.

Social Visibility. The diagnosed employees clearly differ from the normals in social visibility. Overall, their work-role assignments were significantly more interdependent with the work of fellow employees and they were less free to arrange the order of their work. Alcoholics were rated highest on social visibility. These findings imply concentration of diagnosed cases in lower-status jobs and are consistent with other research. Blau (1955), for example, found that supervisors in a state employment agency felt free to interrupt the work of their subordinates, but the supervisors of more highly skilled federal investigators were more cautious. Jaques (1956) found that a good measure of job status was the length of time an employee had free to arrange his approaches to his various tasks.

More interestingly, these data indicate that diagnosis of alcoholism or mental illness may in part result from social visibility. Less freedom to arrange work implies closer supervisory scrutiny. Furthermore, having one's work "tied-in" closely with the work of others means exposure of one's behavior to fellow workers. Therefore deviation should become more noticeable and cover-up less easy.

Absenteeism under these visibility conditions would be especially conspicuous. Unusual absences were frequently found to be the reason for an initial examination and diagnosis of an employee by the medical department. Absence rates for all the diagnosed types of employees rose sharply as the year of diagnosis approached. In short, the process of being labeled alcoholic or mentally ill in this company depended in part on overall social visibility on the job.

Job Performance. Supervisory ratings of the job performances of deviant drinkers and psychotics grouped around "closer to worst," with alcoholics rated in this manner significantly more than psychotics. Conversely, the ratings of neurotics and normals grouped about "closer to best." Thus deviant drinking and psychoses impaired job performance, while the job performances of neurotics pleased their supervisors. Neurotics were frequently described by supervisors as "one of the best I have" or "he is my best worker." Since many of the neuroses were anxiety states or obsessive-compulsive in content, they probably were expressed as an inordinate concern about work. Other researchers have commented on the social acceptability of neuroses. Leavy and Freedman (1956:60) conclude that "cultural evaluation of work may provide a screen of acceptability for compulsive overactivity," while Bradley (1961) described a specific work-related neurotic syndrome of "work addiction" discussed in Chapter Four.

The supervisors' classification of their workers as supervisory problems revealed a similar pattern. All supervisors of alcoholics classified these employees as problems, as did 65 percent of the supervisors of psychotics. Supervisors of neurotics saw 37 percent of these employees as problems while supervisors of normals (used as a baseline) classified 17 percent of their charges this way.

Supervisory Decisiveness.   Having perceived the employee as a problem, how decisive was the supervisor in taking some kind of action? Given the consistency in labeling the deviant drinker as a "poor worker" and a "problem," it would appear logical that their supervisors would not hesitate to take some kind of action.

The data, however, indicate that such supervisors saw themselves as more indecisive than did the other supervisors. By contrast, supervisors of "problem" neurotics and "problem" normals described themselves as decisive is not taking action. Interview data suggest they tolerated the "problem" behavior, allowing these employees to play the eccentric role. As mentioned, much of this behavior may have been highly productive.

Supervisors of "problem" psychotics classified themselves as relatively decisive in terms of formal action. This decision was generally triggered by some dramatic antisocial episode which, combined with absenteeism, convinced them a definite illness was present and outside help was needed.

Referral to the Medical Department.   A similar pattern of supervisory reaction was revealed when the supervisors classified themselves regarding their tendency to refer problem cases to the medical department. While supervisors of alcoholics described themselves as ambivalent about this type of action, the psychotics' supervisors were strongly inclined to refer their subordinates to staff physicians, but few of the supervisors of problem neurotics and problem normals were willing to do so.

Tables 2 and 3 present the encouraging and discouraging factors which supervisors reported as affecting their referral decisions (Trice, 1965). Associations between each factor and the type of deviant employee are also shown. Among the factors encouraging referral shown in Table 2, two were common to all supervisors: "I had to watch him more closely," and "He was out a great deal." Apparently a problem employee takes an inordinate amount of the supervisor's time and causes the problems concomitant with absenteeism. The beliefs that the employee lacked self-respect and that the supervisor's own superior would back him up were encouraging to supervisors of all types, but were regarded as major factors in less than ten percent of the cases.

Table 2: Patterns of Association Between Factors Encouraging Supervisors to Use Medical Department and Type of Employee

Encouraging Factor	Association with Type of Employee
I had to watch him more closely.	
He was out a great deal.	Associated with All Types
He was lacking in self-respect.	
My boss would back me up.	
I never knew what to expect.	
He was a safety risk.	
I needed to do something as soon as possible.	Associated with Supervisors of Alcoholics
It would help out his family if I took action.	
He had a bad effect on fellow workers.	Associated with Supervisors of Alcoholics and Psychotics
He wasn't getting work out.	
He put me in a bad light.	Associated with Supervisors of Alcoholics and Neurotics
I wanted to replace him.	
He was often surly, arrogant and defiant.	Associated with Supervisors of Neurotics and Psychotics

Table 3: Patterns of Association Between Factors Discouraging
Supervisors to Use Medical Department and Type of Employee

Discouraging Factors	Association With Type of Employee
It was my duty to handle the problem.	
He was often an able worker.	
Referral would mean his separation from the company.	
I felt "in between" employees and management.	Associated with All Types
Referral would hurt his family.	
He might be "bugged."	
Referral would involve me in inconvenience.	
Referral would get me mixed up with the union.	
He "snapped out of it" frequently.	Associated with Supervisors of Alcoholics
I had come up through the ranks with him.	Associated with Supervisors of Alcoholics and Psychotics
He was well liked and popular.	Associated with Supervisors of Neurotics and Psychotics
He would soon be shifted to another job.	Associated with Supervisors of Psychotics

Four of the encouraging factors were associated solely with supervisors of alcoholics. Of these, "I never knew what to expect" had the
greatest potency while the other three had only mild force. Deviant
drinkers appear to frustrate their supervisors by engaging in unpredictable behavior. Although safety concerns are associated solely with alcoholics, they were mentioned as factors in less than ten percent of these
cases.

Supervisors of psychotics and alcoholics believed these employees adversely affected fellow workers. Supervisors of neurotics and alcoholics shared a cluster of encouraging factors centering on poor work which reflected the supervisor's problems in completing the tasks of the work group, leading to a desire to replace the employee or to consider referral to the medical department. The alcoholics' supervisors did *not* report one factor reported by the other supervisors of problem employees: "He was often surly, arrogant, and defiant." Statistically, this was a strong predisposing factor for supervisors of nonalcoholics, but alcoholic employees, either by choice or temperament, are apparently not as unpleasant or outwardly hostile as other problem employees. Interview responses suggested the alcoholic employee was frequently meek and self-critical, especially when directly confronted with the facts of his drinking. This may be a manipulatory strategy to keep the problem between himself and his supervisor, thereby avoiding referral.

Turning to the factors discouraging referral shown in Table 3, we find they were fewer but more potent. A block to medical department referral shared by all types of supervisors was: "It was my duty to handle the problem." Statistically, this was by far the strongest of the entire set of positive and negative factors. The supervisor apparently saw both management and treatment of problem employees as part of his supervisory role. This belief was reinforced by two less influential factors: "referral would mean his separation from the company" and "he had often been a capable worker." Statistically weaker factors of damaging the family, being caught between workers and management, and personal inconvenience backed up this cluster of discouraging factors.

Supervisors of alcoholics experienced a unique discouraging factor which complements the encouraging factor of "I never knew what to expect." By performing well for a short but obvious period of time, the deviant drinker both pleased and confounded his supervisor, leaving him unable to predict the next phase of behavior.

Supervisors of alcoholics shared with psychotics' supervisors a block in the form of personal friendship: "I had come up through the ranks with him." The deviant's popularity mildly deterred supervisors of neurotics and psychotics from referral, but did not influence the supervisors of alcoholics. Supervisors of psychotics were deterred from action by the belief that the employee's transfer was imminent.

Supervisory Attitudes and Therapeutic Response. Was a favorable supervisory attitude toward medical department referrals associated with favorable response to therapy by the employee? In all instances in this company, diagnosed employees experienced some kind of therapy, usually company-supplied. Alcoholics as a group showed the poorest response to therapy, based on the physician's estimate of progress, with 41 percent showing success. Half of the psychotics were therapeutic successes, as were 73 percent of the neurotics.

There was no association between favorable supervisory attitudes toward referral and favorable responses to therapy. The supervisors' *ambivalent* attitude toward referral was, however, associated with poor therapeutic responses of both alcoholics and psychotics. Among these two types, most of those who responded to therapy had supervisors who had described themselves as *inclined toward not* referring the employee to the medical department. While this appears to indicate that a supervisory inclination toward referral was of little value in supporting therapeutic responses, an ambivalent attitude toward referral held by the supervisors of those who did not respond to therapy suggests that *indecision* about referral may have worked against therapeutic response. Firmness of *supervisory attitude* is the important dimension, even though the firmness may be originally opposed to referral. The main point lies in the detrimental effect of indecision on therapeutic response.

The beneficial effects of decisiveness may be indirectly illustrated by the neurotics' therapeutic response patterns. Lack of response to therapy was significantly associated with supervisors who did not see the neurotics as supervisory problems, but neurotics whose supervisors saw them as definite problems tended to show more therapeutic success. To a degree, these findings coincide with the research of Stanton and Schwartz (1954): when a patient in a private mental hospital was subject to subtle staff disagreements, he became less responsive; once the disagreements were resolved, his responsiveness increased.

BARRIERS TO SUPERVISORY ACTION

Our data clearly imply that being labeled and receiving medical treatment depend in part upon social visibility. In a practical sense, this indicates many deviant employees may escape labeling because of low job visibility. As we discussed in Chapter Four deviant drinkers may be hidden more by the nature of the job than by the calculated efforts of the individual himself, his associates, or his boss. Social visibility, however, may do more than expose the individual to diagnostic processes; it may also contribute to etiology. The combination of continual close interaction with work associates and the lack of job freedom might be stressful for some individuals, making them more vulnerable to the use of alcohol and drugs as well as to emotional disturbances. Such customary rigidity may also lead to undue stress when supervisory or task changes occur.

Importantly, only psychotics were felt to be fully deviant by their supervisors. In contrast, supervisors defined neurotics as desirable conformists who were effectively carrying out their jobs. Deviant drinkers were "half-way" deviants; their supervisors saw them as deviant in role performance but were ambivalent about taking action. There may be a relation between the supervisor's indecision and the deviant drinker's penchant for manipulating those around him. By "snapping out of it" at appropriate times and by readily admitting his poor work if directly confronted, such an employee can add to his supervisor's indecision and thereby protect himself. The combination of this manipulative skill with the vacillations of the deviant drinker's supervisor may, over time, facilitate full-blown alcohol addiction.

From this mosaic of reluctances, it is easier to understand the reactions of line supervisors to company medical programs which deal with alcoholism and mental illness. *The extent to which line supervisors are willing to refer employees to such programs and to "back up" the referral are crucial to a program's success, however.* Consequently, blocks to referral should be closely examined, especially the prevalent and defeating supervisory idea that: "It is my duty to handle the problem." A few quotes from the research interviews amplify this sentiment: "It is a part of a supervisor's job to help out and understand his men rather than turn them over to someone else." "It is a matter of doing my duty as a boss and helping him overcome his problems before I turn to formalities." These expressions indicate three facets of supervisory secondary gain obtained through "independence": an opportunity to enhance the supervisory role, a reluctance to communicate across organizational lines, (especially to staff personnel), and self-reliance consistent with the cultural value of autonomy and personal willpower. Supervisors see in their problem employees an opportunity to seize upon a valued aspect of their jobs, understanding and helping workers. Since supervisors are commonly indoctrinated in the human relations aspect of their jobs, it is no surprise to find them incorporating into their role perceptions a helping, "do it myself" note. The supervisors insist they must "help the problem employee help himself," and this attitude may reflect the training they have received.

Curtailment of the supervisor's power and influence in recent years may have added to this need for role enhancement. Many of their former functions have been transferred to staff personnel such as personnel officers, industrial engineers, and industrial relations specialists; supervisors are sensitive to further encroachments. Deviant drinkers and other problem employees may serve to revive lost authority and to sustain the supervisor's self-image. Deviant employees may thus help first-line supervisors legitimize their roles in the company.

These self-concepts may also mesh with the sentiments of subordinates. Whyte, for example, concludes that "subordinates value highly a boss who works out criticisms directly with them and does not pass them on to other levels. . . . 'This problem is just between you and me; let's work it out together, and no one else has to hear about it!'" (Whyte, 1961:400). Backing up this combination is the frequent belief that referral to staff facilities will result in separation from the company.

Communication patterns may also support these deterrents. Supervisors typically restrict consultations across formal lines, especially line-staff boundaries (Blau and Scott, 1962). Instead, they are apt to rely on informal discussions with peers. Here they may find additional reinforcement for going it alone with a problem employee. Finally, one of the major values of American life, self-reliance, supports supervisors in their resolve to manage the deviant employees themselves (Williams, 1970). Staff services may deprive the supervisor of his right to "help" as well as preventing the problem employee from helping himself.

SOCIAL PROCESSES IN RECOGNIZING DEVIANTS

The past two chapters have included data and discussion on deviant behavior in the work place and the reactions of the supervisors. An outline of the progression through which the deviance recognition process passes will now be used to integrate these two groups of information.

We have no data and few reported observations of the process of recognizing a deviant drug user. Knowledge of deviant drug use will usually trigger the "dope-fiend" stereotype so that referral rapidly follows recognition. It is intriguing to speculate on how this reaction might be altered when current youth move into supervisory posts. As outlined in Chapter Five, however, deviant drug use has few of the clear-cut on-the-job clues that characterize deviant drinking. This lack may not only reduce the overall probability of recognition of the deviance, but may also increase the chance of drug use occurring on the job over a long period of time. This, in turn, implies that the deviant drug user could become well integrated into the work group before his deviance is detected. While the extent to which this would create supervisory reluctance to take action is unknown, it is conceivable that friendship and work group camaraderie may reduce the potency of the "dope-fiend" stereotype and lead to the same delayed recognition that occurs with the deviant drinker. In any event, empirical comparisons of the recognition process for drinkers and drug users are necessary to answer these questions.

A combination of "hard" and "soft" research data has led us to the formulation of a four-stage recognition sequence:

1. *Disrupted-but-Normal:* A period during which intermittent disruption of job performance occurs. Although these behaviors deviate from expectations, they are neither frequent nor disruptive enough to indicate "abnormality."

2. *Blocked Awareness:* Significant others link the employee's behavior with alcohol use, but recognition of the existence of a "drinking problem" strikes numerous barriers. While deviance may increase, in amount and degree, the employee remains "normal" because of these blocks in recognition.

3. *See-Saw:* As the impairment of job behavior increases, significant others become indecisive about whether to define the behavior as a deviant-drinking problem or to leave it within the "normal" zone.

4. *Decision to Recognize:* The accumulation of deviance finally tips indecision toward recognizing the behaviors as abnormal. The appropriateness of referral to some treatment facility is recognized.

The "Disrupted-but-Normal" Stage. The first phase has been described in two research studies. In the first it was observed, "the general ignorance about alcoholism and the failure to recognize the significance of the early symptoms add to the difficulty of identification" (Trice, 1957a:532); and, in the second, "it is one thing to notice that an employee's behavior is 'different,' but to define it for what it may well become — serious alcoholism — is quite another" (Trice, 1964:8).

This first stage is long, lasting several years. This length is related to the fact that alcohol addiction is progressive, often taking ten to fifteen years to develop. *There are no dramatic symptoms in the early phases.* The loss of control that signals well developed addiction comes on almost imperceptibly in most instances. The supervisor is only vaguely aware of numerous subjective signs such as minor hand tremors, increased nervousness, hangovers on the job, avoidance of boss and work associates, and morning drinking before work. All of these signs have been reported by deviant drinkers themselves as early clues (Maxwell, 1960). The supervisor and work associates also begin to note overt behaviors such as leaving the work post temporarily, unusual excuses for half-day and whole-day absences, lower quality of work, mood changes after lunch, and bleary eyes. The supervisor may get a general impression of job impairment, but it is not severe enough to be regarded as abnormal. It is one thing for significant others to notice these signs; it is quite another for them to accumulate in amounts sufficient to trigger recognition of a serious behavior problem. In sum, this stage is a period of "primary" deviation during which the employee integrates deviance into his "normal" work role (Lemert, 1967).

The "Blocked Awareness" Stage. The second phase consists of two parts: (1) a growing awareness that deviance is linked with drinking, but (2) the emergence of numerous barriers that continue to define behavior within normal parameters. Deviant job behaviors such as absenteeism and poor work quality accumulate, but significant others typically tend to tolerate rather than recognize the deviancy.

The awareness that the deviant behavior is alcohol-linked varies with occupational status. As pointed out in Chapter Four, developing alcoholics in high-status professional and managerial jobs enjoy enough freedom from supervision to conceal their drinking problems for long periods. Most other occupations are visible and relatively scheduled so that excessive drinking behavior is known. The widely held belief that the deviant drinker is "hidden" is certainly untrue. He may be hidden so that staff people and upper management do not know about him, but work associates generally recognize a definite connection between his deviant actions and his drinking. To some extent this is due to new kinds of on-the-job behaviors that emerge in this phase. The deviant can no longer camouflage his hangovers and the quantity and quality of his work declines. What work he does do is spasmodic.

This new linkage between drinking and impaired job performance does not typically lead to action. Significant others are typically reluctant to alter their social definitions of a person even though he has engaged in unfamiliar and puzzling behavior. There are three barriers to action:

1. Low visibility of the employee which removes from view disruptive work behaviors: For example, jobs that take the employee away from a central work place allow numerous opportunities for cover-up that would otherwise be unavailable (Trice, 1962).

2. The status level of the deviant drinker: Since power varies directly with position in the formal organization, higher status positions create numerous barriers to early recognition. Their visibility goes down and opportunities for self-concealment go up. In addition, work associates are increasingly unwilling to connect poor job performance with

alcoholism as the status of the employee increases (Warkov and Bacon, 1965). Thus, those in lower-status jobs are much more visible and are more vulnerable to identification and labeling.

3. A substantial degree of tolerance for the deviant drinker: A.A. members have reported that significant others in their environment were slow to express serious concern about their drinking (Bailey and Leach, 1965). Probably the chief reason for this is a lack of social distance between significant others and the deviant drinker. Often he and his supervisor have come up through the ranks together and are friends away from the job. The deviant drinker has also often been a good worker and may be difficult to replace. Within the company the supervisor often feels that any action he might take based on his recognition of deviant drinking may be suspect "upstairs" and put him in a bad light. All these rationalizations reflect a general discomfort in accepting what is becoming obvious: the subordinate has a drinking problem, but it is difficult for the immediate supervisor to admit that this is the case.

Various procedures within unionized companies which are designed to protect workers from arbitrary actions may also discredit the growing awareness of a drinking problem. A supervisor faces the possibility of being discredited by union representatives if he moves too quickly to refer a deviant drinker to the personnel or medical departments. Organizations such as the federal civil service have specific procedures whereby a superior officer reviews action taken toward a subordinate. Such reviews may reverse or in some way contradict the conclusions of the immediate supervisor. These prospects can block action.

The "See-Saw" Stage. Recognition might never occur except for the steady accumulation of behaviors that aggravate work associates and impair job performance. Supervisors report a tendency for the deviant drinker to eventually begin drinking at lunch time, show sharp personality changes after lunch, engage in loud talking, and manifest quite obvious hand tremors. In addition, the earlier deviant behaviors have now become more frequent and noticeable: partial absenteeism, absence excuses that border on blatant lying, bleary eyes, lower quality and quantity of work, and hangovers on the job.

The accumulation of these deviant behaviors tends to counteract the numerous blocking forces. Consequently this is a period of indecision and vacillation during which the significant other is pulled both ways, i.e. toward definitely defining the employee as a deviant and toward "balancing out" the untoward behavior with compensating features

167

("when he works, he really works") and continuing to regard him as still normal.

The need to supervise the deviant more closely, his amassed absences, his unpredictable work performance, his adverse effect on fellow workers, all compete with the blocking factors and press for a redefinition of the employee as abnormal. At the same time, the deviant drinker, attempting to manipulate the situation in his own behalf, "snaps out of it" temporarily and makes a valiant effort to return to his normal standing. As a result, the supervisor vacillates. When the employee appears normal the supervisor believes matters to be improving; but, as the increased disruptions return and threaten operations and reputations within the work group, the supervisor again classifies the behavior as deviant. He is, in effect, on the verge of recognition.

Two major obstacles to recognition are not yet overcome: the supervisor's concern that taking some kind of formal action will bring about referral to a treatment facility and his belief that such referral may produce rejection by fellow workers and friends. Supporting this fear is the aforementioned belief of supervisors that it is their responsibility to manage the deviant employee without using labels.

"Decision to Recognize" Stage. Accumulated deviant behaviors eventually overcome these blocks to recognition. By this time the developing addict begins to drink during working hours and his absenteeism is aggravated by minor illnesses such as bronchitis and other upper respiratory diseases. Flushed face and red eyes now join the overt symptoms of hangover. The entire array of problems created by the deviant drinker becomes intolerable for those who work with him. They lose empathy with him and begin to accept the appropriateness of labels such as "different," and "abnormal." "I just can't understand him any more." A well defined social category called "alcoholic" is readily available to them. The social distance between the deviant drinker and his significant others widens. As this occurs, they recognize him as not only one who is different, but one toward whom they must act differently than they have in the past.

CONCLUSION

It should be evident that the problems of deviant drinking, and possibly those of deviant drug use, would be reduced through earlier recognition of, and action toward, the deviant employee. Supervisors and work associates apparently go to considerable lengths to "normalize" behaviors that are clearly inappropriate and disruptive. This type of reaction, or absence of reaction, is common throughout social life because accusing others of deviancy risks considerable disruption of interpersonal relationships (Roman and Trice, 1971b). Not only may the accused successfully discredit the accuser, but the potency of the accusation of deviance may permanently change the tone of interaction. The intimacy of work groups often prevents this.

Earlier recognition is possible, however. In the succeeding chapters we detail strategies for reducing the potency and risks inherent in confrontation, for making confrontation of deviants the responsibility rather than the choice of the supervisor, and for increasing the support of unions behind a deviance-management program.

VII

The Strategy of Constructive Confrontation

DESPITE the immediate supervisor's ambivalence about taking action toward the deviant employee, he is in a much better position to intervene than others who are close to the deviant. In contrast to the deviant's wife, clergyman, or family physician, the supervisor has legitimate and explicit expectations for his employees to perform their roles without impairment. While the supervisor's personal sentiments often color his performance expectations, these norms are definitely based in the employment contract. In contrast, the deviant's wife and his personal friends are enmeshed in diffuse, emotionally charged relations with the deviant; their attempts at intervention are usually manipulated by the deviant because they typically lack authority to make effective demands for behavior change. As William George (1971:3) has pointed out: "It may be possible to convince a relative or friend that one's drinking is under control. But it is quite another thing to explain away a work record."

Several factors pressure the supervisor to take action. His own performance is judged by his success at getting the work out, and this limits his tolerance of nonperformance. Other employees and union representatives expect the supervisor to relieve them of the burdens created by absenteeism, shoddy performance, and accident risks. Finally, with proper training emphasizing principles of supervision, the supervisor can learn that confrontation of deviants is an explicit and important part of his role.

The likelihood of supervisors' successful confrontation of abusers of alcohol and other drugs increases if they feel supported by their own supervisors, who in turn should have clear-cut policy guidelines from top management. Equally important is the assurance that the supervisor will have the support of the union when he must confront a deviant union member. Expectations for these kinds of support are based on the most fundamental aspects of work life: workers at all levels and in all occupations within an organization are expected to perform adequately. If they do not, supervisors have both the right and the duty to confront them with the facts of their poor performance and to urge them to improve. Dealing with poor performance is a basic responsibility of a supervisor; and this responsibility is especially important in cases where work performance has declined, as is usually the case with the deviant drinker. There is no doubt that evidence of alcohol or drug abuse will typically become obvious in impaired performance one way or another, calling upon the supervisor to use his proper authority. Such intervention represents one of the few legitimate avenues, save police power, for entering the deviant's life and motivating him to alter his behavior. It is not necessary for the supervisor to be a skilled diagnostician; he needs only to be alert to the signs of impaired performance and to be equipped to deal effectively and realistically with it. In sum, there is a high potential for success at prevention and rehabilitation implicit in the supervisor's role, once an organization has formulated a clear-cut alcohol- and drug-abuse policy which emphasizes early and effective confrontation and which receives consistent support from all levels of both management and the union.

The policy of constructive confrontation which we recommend is built upon the basic features of work organizations; in most organizations policy implementation will not require developing new managerial skills or other complex procedures. It does, however, call for basic policy guidelines: (1) Drug dependency behaviors produce unacceptable job performance and these behaviors are likely to become health problems; (2) since these are potential health problems, with physiological and psychiatric consequences, the organization will provide typical health coverage similar to that for other disorders; (3) unless job performance returns to an acceptable level, however, a crisis precipitation strategy will be implemented. Apart from legal questions, the parallels between drinking and drug use allow for the development of a single program to deal with both. For illustrative purposes, however, we will use alcohol abuse as an example. Alcohol-dependent employees often use the fact that they are still employed as evidence that nothing is wrong with their drinking. This fact partly explains their normal on-the-job accident rate; they become overly cautious so that an accident will not "spotlight" them, and this caution hampers performance. Claiming that their jobs are unaffected lies at the center of a strong, elaborate network of rationalizations and deceptions that justifies their drinking.

Alcohol-dependent employees are skilled at manipulating and maneuvering those around them so they can continue drinking. Alcohol is an emotional necessity of the first order. As the middle stage of addiction approaches they must drink more to get the relief wanted. Money problems are a tangible sign; three times as many garnishments and twice as many levies and legal assignments as among average employees were found among alcoholics in one large company (Trice, 1964). Nonetheless, the problem drinker is skillful in manipulating significant others; he "snaps out of it" when supervision becomes aggravated. When he is a union member he can be adroit at playing management against the union.

CONSTRUCTIVE CONFRONTATION AND CRISIS PRECIPITATION

The constructive confrontation strategy includes that part of a company's policy that calls for a series of confrontations based on poor performance and, if necessary, for bringing about a job-related crisis in the deviant drinker's life while he still holds a job. Equally important in the policy are the definition of alcohol addiction as a health problem and the provision of typical treatment care for it. If he does not respond to confrontation, crisis precipitation is crucial since his denial and manipulation system must be weakened. Thus his supervisors or steward can weaken his defenses merely by confronting him about his poor job performance. If crisis precipitation is a part of policy, and the union supports it, the supervisor has a potent technique. Without ever mentioning alcoholism he can confront the deviant drinker on the basis of impaired work, *emphasizing* that constructive help without stigma is available to the employee if he chooses to accept it. A second confrontation, based on accurate records documenting continuing job impairment and again offering the health benefits of the company, is a natural part of a supervisor's role. Usually such confrontations are timed so they do not coincide with routine performance appraisals. Should performance remain impaired, the third confrontation would introduce a crisis and, it is hoped, a medical representative — often an industrial nurse is effective (Trice and Belasco, 1965) — would suggest that alcohol may be the problem. The supervisor, using the company policy, describes what could happen if job performance does not return to normal. Examples of potential disciplinary action include: lay-offs without pay, reduction in grade, loss of a portion of seniority, and even termination. The medical representative would introduce the *possibility* of alcohol addiction and very explicitly tell him what health benefits and services are available. Finally, should his work continue to be impaired, a crisis would be precipitated by supervision in the presence of a union representative, and the threat of disciplinary action would be carried through (the Christopher D. Smithers Foundation, Inc., 1969).

Substantial opinion and results support this strategy (Lemere, 1958; Gerard, 1962; Tiebout, 1965). Representative is the position of Fox, a psychiatrist specializing in alcoholism: "No patient will even consider giving up alcohol until the suffering it causes him is greater than the pleasure it gives him. He must lose something important to him, or at least be threatened with such a loss" (Fox, 1958:805). Results of rehabilitation efforts which have used this work-based strategy appear to be better than those of efforts under others conditions (Pfeffer and Feldman, 1956; Kuhn, 1961; Franco, 1960). Describing his extensive experience in Consolidated Edison Company of New York, Dr. Franco in 1965 reported:

> We can say that, over the years, we have rehabilitated about half of the people that we recognize as alcoholics. The figure runs a little closer to 60 percent who retained their jobs since certain people can continue to work and really have quite a drinking problem (Franco, 1965:2).

Other evidence suggests that state hospital programs average around 20 percent success at rehabilitation (Belasco and Trice, 1968), while efforts directed at police court inebriates can expect around 10 percent (Myerson, 1956).

The constructive confrontation strategy specifically assumes that social control, in some form, is necessary in human behavior (Simmel, 1950); that since society fails to produce clear sanctions about alcohol use, developing alcohol addicts never face consistent sanctions — a situation which produces feeble internal controls (Inkeles, 1968) — and that enforced cooperation relieves the deviant drinker of the burden of developing motivation for himself. The strategy activates and uses social controls *within* the system rather than assigning the drinker to a deviant role that removes him from the system. There are also deficiencies in the strategy: high-status deviant drinkers are difficult to confront; a true crisis is difficult to precipitate in low-status jobs; impaired job performance may be difficult to detect and document; and the initial constructive theme of rehabilitative help may be passed over too quickly and the crisis part overdone. Such improper emphasis raises the possibility of triggering suicide: "Some authorities say the alcoholic must 'hit bottom.' This period of crisis is frequently associated with suicidal action, so that for any group of alcoholics, about 5 percent may be expected sooner or later to commit suicide" (Litman, 1970:302).

This strategy is labeled "constructive" because such a confrontation serves the long-range interests of the employee, his union, and the

173

employer. With the approach we have outlined, immediate disciplinary action is not necessary. While confrontations may be repeated, supervisory demands that the employee change his behavior cannot go on endlessly or they will soon be recognized as meaningless gestures. Organizations should develop clear-cut policy statements — based on professional prognosis if possible — on the number of chances an employee is given before a definite disciplinary action is taken. The constructive dimension of this strategy is lost if disciplinary action is taken on the first or second confrontation.

The basic assumptions of constructive confrontation are that alcohol and drugs have no place in work organizations and that work organizations may legitimately expect unimpaired performances from their employees. Help through the medical department, Alcoholics Anonymous, or such specialized agencies as methadone clinics should be offered to those employees who cannot alter their behavior without outside help. The essence of constructive confrontation, however, is that it defines the use of alcohol and drugs in conjunction with the job as inappropriate behavior rather than as "sick" behavior. As outlined in Chapter One, the application of the disease label to those who can control their behavior with adequate motivation may have the undesirable side effect of relieving individuals from responsibility for their behavior. Such an excuse can then serve to justify further deviance. Persons dependent on alcohol or drugs may simply be left with a label, and an excuse, a situation in which no effective treatment is available.

Some work organizations have modeled deviant-drinking programs upon the disease concept of alcoholism, assuming that such labels will prevent undue disciplinary action and lead to humanitarian and effective management of problem behavior. In such situations, all drinkers and drug users are referred to the medical department and required to follow its recommendations. While such an approach may be humanitarian, it makes it difficult to motivate the deviant to alter his own behavior. Since the sick label implies that the undesired behavior is out of the individual's control, he often cannot respond to the demand that he alter his behavior. While the medical department and its various therapeutic recommendations are of great value to those who are unable to control their drinking or drug use, constructive confrontation avoids using disease labels as much as possible. Based as it is on the legitimate relationship between the employer and the employee, confrontation can be based on the existence of inappropriate behavior without attributing disease. Medical labeling and treatment is the last step, used when it is evident that the deviance is out of the individual's control, that a genuine sickness exists, and that he is unable to respond to confrontation. It is essential to note that the medical department may be successful in offering counseling and other help without imputing disease, although the very nature of such a referral can subtly connote that the deviance is out of the individual's control.

Supervisors, at all levels, can make or break the effectiveness of constructive confrontation. They alone are in a position to identify impairment and such identification is clearly part of their normal scope of responsibility. The supervisor who fails to take appropriate action toward deviant employees may be subject to disciplinary action himself. Conceivably a chain of confrontations could move up the organizational hierarchy when tolerance for deviant drinking or drug abuse is evident.

CONSTRUCTIVE CONFRONTATION AND OTHER
PREVENTIVE STRATEGIES

Preventing deviant behavior has been advocated as the goal of organizational policy programs dealing with social problems since it is very difficult to break up firmly established patterns of deviance (Caplan, 1964; Kandel and Williams, 1964). The prevention of any given type of deviant behavior remains, however, largely unrealized. An examination of a range of preventive strategies and their assumptions may yield some understanding of why prevention has typically failed. Likewise, an outline of these strategies and their applicability to work organizations may clarify the usefulness of the constructive confrontation strategy. Strategies we have delineated overlap somewhat with each other, while any given program frequently has combined elements of several of these strategies.

Differential Risks. A strategy originally developed by public health workers calls for locating those persons who bear high risk for the development of a particular pattern of deviant behavior. Once such persons are located they are closely watched for developing signs of deviance, or treated in some way to reduce their susceptibility. Use of this strategy in public health includes tests to check infants for risks of mental retardation and diet supplementation for persons susceptible to vitamin deficiency diseases.

This strategy currently is inapplicable to the prevention of deviant drinking and drug use since we lack clear-cut evidence of the characteristics which lead to these types of deviations. While we are able to describe the "typical" deviant drinker or drug user, most people with these social characteristics are not deviant. Even if we were able to locate a susceptible group, there is little knowledge of what procedures might keep them from becoming deviant.

Social Inoculation. This strategy calls for immunizing an entire population to a particular pattern of deviant behavior through uniform intervention which keeps persons from reacting to stressors which may lead to the deviance. Mass inoculation and vaccination for the prevention of devastating diseases are public health examples of this strategy. Also representative are programs which have attempted to "fortify" young children from poverty subcultures for coping with stress experiences (Kellam and Scheiff, 1967; Visotsky, 1967).

Plaut (1963:66) advocates using a form of this strategy to reduce deviant drinking. He argues that "since alcoholism can be viewed as a maladaptive means of dealing with personal problems of tension, its rate would be reduced, if, generally speaking, the psychological functioning of persons could be improved." He cites successful examples of such prevention in the preparation of Peace Corps trainees and surgical patients, but does not specify tactics for "improving psychological functioning" that would be effective for curbing deviant drinking. The same argument has been advanced by Chafetz and Demone (1962), but again without specifying effective patterns of inoculation. Thus, while inoculation against deviant drinking and drug abuse might be desirable in work organizations, the means for implementing such a strategy are lacking.

Replication of "Immune" Circumstances. A third strategy calls for locating populations "immune" to certain patterns of deviant behavior (Cumming, 1963), developing explanations for such low incidence, and then using these explanations as a basis for preventive programs in susceptible populations. For example, very low rates of alcohol addiction are found among the Orthodox Jewish (Snyder, 1958), Cantonese Chinese (Barnett, 1955), Italian (Lolli *et al.,* 1958), and Laotian (Westermeyer, 1971) populations. In Orthodox Jewish subcultures, alcohol typically has a ritual and religious connotation because of its early introduction to children in family-based religious observances. Allegedly, this leads to less tolerance for alcohol abuse in the subculture. Lolli and his associates (1958) have concluded that Italian populations use alcohol primarily in the family setting as a food (in contrast to the cocktail hour) and that this connotation has likewise created a set of attitudes which reduces tolerance for alcohol abuse. Westermeyer (1971) observed little tolerance for excessive drinking in the Meos subculture of Laos even though drinking occasions were regular. The drinker who became boisterous through intoxication was quickly excluded from the drinking group.

These observations have led some to advocate that all children be introduced to alcohol at an early age in order to reduce the risk of subsequent addiction (Chafetz, 1967). It has also been urged that alcohol use be primarily associated with meals so that individuals come to view it as a food used within the family setting (Plaut, 1967). The means by which such strategies could be implemented on a significant scale in American society so that they would affect abusive drinking in work organizations has not been specified.

Normative Change. This strategy is based on the observation that in some situations no action regarding deviance is taken until the behavior becomes a fully established pattern. For example, observers have argued that drunkenness is tolerated within American society, that the abstinent are frequently ridiculed and pressured to "conform," that alcohol is widely seen as a tranquilizer and as a means of relief for personal problems (Plaut, 1967), and that alcohol use is frequently a means for asserting masculinity (Maddox and McCall, 1964).

The advocates of the normative change preventive strategy argue that these patterns should be changed: drunkenness should not be tolerated, but abstinence should; alcohol should not be used as a means of personal relief; and no attachment of masculinity should accompany adolescent use of alcohol (Plaut, 1967). While this strategy might apply to work organizations in that alcohol or drug use might be rewarded in some work groups, the means for bringing about widespread normative change either in a work organization or in a society are not easily specified. The changes that have been advocated would be difficult to bring about; they include the assumption of "greater responsibility" by alcoholic beverage producers and distributors in their advertising and promotion, less idealization of alcoholic beverages in the mass media, and greater effort by hosts to discourage inappropriate use of alcohol when serving it to family or friends (Plaut, 1967).

Reduction of Stress This strategy attempts to change the social circumstances surrounding those who might develop deviant behavior. Instead of increasing resources for individuals to cope with stress, this strategy calls for reducing risks by eliminating stressors. Public health examples of this strategy include closed sewage systems, the eradication of disease-carrying animals and insects, and the provision of improved living conditions.

Like social inoculation, this strategy assumes knowledge of the types of stresses which lead to deviance. While such recommendations as "improving the community" to reduce the incidence of alcohol abuse (McGavran, 1963) sound credible, the lack of specific knowledge of what sorts of improvements should be attempted generally preclude successful implementation. This strategy may have some applicability in work organizations, however, as described in Chapter Four. Management may try to eliminate stressful working conditions as well as work situations marked by low visibility, thus reducing the possibility that full-blown patterns of deviance may develop before they are detected.

Prohibition. The strategy of prohibition may be applicable to alcohol and drug use since their abuse requires ingestion of the respective substances. This strategy assumes that control mechanisms can be developed which will fully eliminate the manufacture and use of these substances. The American experience with national prohibition of alcohol (Sinclair, 1962) and current attempts at prohibiting the sale and use of marihuana, opiates, and other drugs illustrate this approach. The natural occurrence of alcohol and several of the illegal drugs prevents such schemes from being effective; control networks cannot possibly ferret out all incidents of use of such natural substances. Furthermore, the moralistic bases of prohibition can make the prohibited substances an exciting symbol of rebellion among those who doubt the validity of the prohibition. The existence of organized crime illustrates the fact that illegal items will be available when a market demand exists (Cressey, 1969).

Selective prohibition does, however, seem possible. The effectiveness of the constructive confrontation strategy may be enhanced if the use of alcohol and drugs in conjunction with job performance is specifically forbidden. Such prohibition may not entail the difficulties involved in national prohibition since these norms do not attempt to encompass the alcohol or drug use that may occur during off-the-job hours.

Severe Sanctions. This preventive strategy is similar to prohibition but does not assume that control of the manufacture, sale, or use of deviance-producing substances will be effective. Instead, the use of prohibited substances is so severely sanctioned that potential deviants will find the cost of deviation too high. Severe sanctions might also be used to create examples of the consequences of deviance so that nondeviants will avoid such behavior. Examples of this preventive approach are criminal punishments for public drunkenness, immediate suspension of a drunk driver's operator's license, and, in several European countries, imprisonment of the drinking driver.

An element of severe sanctions is found in the constructive confrontation strategy. The sanctions, however, do not stem from a moralistic view, but rather are a legitimate part of the employer-employee contract. Furthermore, sanctions are not brought to bear upon the deviant until he refuses to respond to repeated confrontations and to accept assistance in dealing with his problem.

Early Identification. Rather than attempting to prevent the initial occurrence of a deviant behavior pattern, the early identification strategy locates persons and intervenes before the deviant pattern is fully developed. The instances in which this strategy has been employed have typically used medical definitions of deviance, assuming a disease will get worse if it is not treated (Bordua, 1967). Early identification has been advocated for dealing with many types of psychiatric disorders and deviant behaviors, including alcohol and drug abuse.

When it is based on the disease model, early identification assumes the existence of physiological, psychological, or behavioral indices of deviancy. Successful early identification must include an effective follow-up program if intervention is to be successful over the long term. The constructive confrontation strategy definitely incorporates a portion of the early identification strategy, but explicitly avoids the necessity of searching out signs of developing "disease." The cue for early identification is impaired job performance.

Education. The education model of prevention calls for teaching people about particular types of deviant behavior, their causes, and the signs of their occurrence (Plaut, 1967). "Education for positive mental health" (Cumming and Cumming, 1963), "Education for child rearing" (Brim, 1960; Visotsky, 1967), and sex education are examples of the use of this preventive approach.

In the prevention of alcohol and drug abuse, education tries to change attitudes regarding the appropriate and inappropriate uses of alcohol and drugs. While drug education is primarily oriented toward abstinence, some programs include information on the appropriate use of legal drugs. A work organization might conceivably initiate an education program attempting to deter workers from the abuse of alcohol or drugs. One of the few reported evaluations of an alcohol education effort, however, indicated little success in altering drinking patterns over a one-year period, although desired changes apparently endured for a month after the education ended (Williams *et al.*, 1968). Another study found that, if the prevention of drug use was desired, mass media programs were the most effective; the behavior of experienced users, on the other hand, would be more effectively altered through some program involving personal contact rather than through large-scale educational efforts (Fejer *et al.,*

1971). While education may not be effective in curbing individual incidents of abuse, it may be useful in educating significant others in the appropriate means of reacting to events of observed deviance. Such education for line supervisors is an explicit part of the constructive confrontation strategy as we further discuss below.

This inventory of preventive approaches is not intended to be exhaustive and does not include description of such strategies as the development of functional substitutes for undesirable drugs or the prevention of deviance through altering societal definitions, a strategy reflected in the current efforts of homosexuals to gain societal acceptance for their sexual behavior. The constructive confrontation strategy embodies aspects of several of the more traditional strategies we have outlined; its design, however, attempts to avoid some of the impractical aspects of these traditional strategies. Constructive confrontation involves the early identification of deviation through the cue of impaired job performance. It attempts to employ normative change by creating an atmosphere in the organization which discourages the use of alcohol and drugs. The severe sanctions strategy is employed as a last resort if the deviant employee refuses to respond to the threat of job disruption. Education is a part of the constructive confrontation strategy in that supervisors must be aware of the appropriate steps in policy implementation.

PREPARING FOR POLICY IMPLEMENTATION

Successful implementation of constructive confrontation depends first upon successful preparation. Two types of preparation are discussed in depth in subsequent chapters: the means for securing effective cooperation between labor organizations and management is discussed in Chapter Eight and availability and proper use of treatment and rehabilitation resources for individuals who become addicted to alcohol or drugs is discussed in Chapter Nine. The remainder of this chapter will deal with various steps necessary for successful policy implementation as well as barriers to successful implementation which may arise in certain local situations.

Written Policy. The determination to implement the program to deal with alcohol and drug abuse should be accompanied by a written policy statement which is circulated throughout the organization (Presnall, 1967). Such a written policy serves three purposes:

First, circulation of procedural statements fully informs employees of the consequences of using alcohol or drugs in conjunction with job performance. Such policy statements can easily be provided to new employees along with other materials describing fringe benefits and other company rules.

Second, a written policy spells out the distribution of authority and responsibility involved in policy implementation. Such clarity should minimize potential line-staff conflicts. For example, the manner in which the personnel and medical departments are to be called in by line personnel can be clearly articulated. Likewise such statements can clearly spell out the scope of the immediate supervisor's responsibility.

Third, a written policy eliminates the possibility of ambiguity or favoritism. The supervisory ambivalences described in Chapter Six stemmed at least in part from a feeling that each case of deviance should be evaluated on the basis of the employee's seniority, his past performance, and his relations with the supervisor. A written policy makes it clear that recognition and confrontation are the responsibilities of the supervisor, regardless of organizational level or personal characteristics of the employee.

Backup Support. Organizational support is essential to successful constructive confrontation. While the initial recognition of job impairment and confrontation of the deviant is the duty of the supervisor, he must have the backup support of his own supervisor if the strategy is to be effective. If several confrontations are necessary, each additional confrontation should involve representatives of higher levels of management, as well as medical or personnel department representatives. Illustrations of the lack of backup support include situations where higher-level supervisors or staff personnel contradict the substance of the initial confrontation, or deal directly with the deviant employee without consulting his immediate supervisor.

The first-line supervisor is "the beginning edge" of management and is frequently ambivalent about his loyalty to management and labor. He has frequently come up through the ranks and may empathize strongly with the personal problems of his charges, some of whom he may have worked with for many years. If he is left to carry out repeated confrontations without the support of higher management, pressures may lead him to take the side of his subordinate. Involving others in the confrontation avoids this potential problem and clear-cut procedures for backup support should be spelled out in the written policy.

Organization-Wide Programs. Partly because of the influence of the Skid Row and dope-fiend stereotypes, there is a tendency for management to concentrate on detecting alcohol and drug abuse in the lower echelon of the work force. While research evidence clearly indicates that alcohol or drug abuse may occur at any organizational level, many organizations tend to implement deviance-control policies selectively, excluding those in middle- and upper-managerial positions from policy coverage. Such discrimination is often reflected by restrictions against the use of alcohol in the company cafeteria while drinks are available in the executive dining room. In many other circumstances middle- and upper-management personnel are allowed or even encouraged to consume alcohol during working hours as a part of lunch or of entertaining clients. While some evidence indicates that there is a very small group of highly anxious individuals whose performance is enhanced by the calming effects of alcohol (Straus, 1971), the bulk of research indicates that alcohol does not enhance work performance at any status level. It is doubtful that many of the management personnel who drink at lunch time actually believe that they are enhancing their job performance; rather lunch time drinking is a subtle but highly symbolic prerogative of high status in the organization.

Policy programs on deviant drinking and drug use must be uniform across all levels of the organization for two reasons. First, there is little to counteract the argument that on-the-job drinking serves no useful function for any employee. Some may argue that relaxation is necessary in the face of executive stress, that lunch time drinking is a helpful catalyst in successful bargaining with clients, or that one cannot possibly enjoy a lunchtime sandwich without a couple of beers. Research clearly indicates that alcohol creates the risk of impaired job performance, whether that performance involves assembly line production or managerial decision making. Organizations which have prohibited alcohol in their executive dining rooms have not reported any consequent loss of clients or other types of organizational failure. The unfortunate custom of noontime drinking receives societal support in many instances from eating places which encourage noontime drinking or which only serve lunch at the bar. The custom continues because it is painless, makes a profit for the bar, and in many instances provides short-time emotional rewards to participants.

A second and perhaps more important reason for a company-wide policy is the issue of discrimination. Any control program will definitely disturb company peace if it is administered with favoritism. Line employees who are subject to the restrictions of the policy will have a legitimate basis for grievance if such a policy does not apply to upper-echelon employees. While some organizations will attempt to initiate control policies while maintaining opportunities for drinking by management personnel, programs with such exclusive focus invite failure. While toleration of beer drinking at lunch may appear harmless to some program designers, such tolerance introduces ambiguity into the policy program, leading to arbitrary decisions about what constitutes "acceptable drinking"; in this way it undermines the written policy.

Small-Company Policy and Program. Most employees do not work for large corporations — nearly one out of every two persons employed in the United States is an owner, manager, or worker in a small business. The nation's production takes place in small- and middle-sized companies. Furthermore, "in the future the large corporation is likely to be overshadowed by the hospitals, universities, research institutes, government agencies and professional organizations that are the hallmark of a service economy" (Fuchs, 1968:10). These work organizations vary by extent of supervisory levels between employees and owner-managers, by the number of personnel staff available, by the possible tightness or looseness of control by a parent organization, by the strength of trade associations to which they may belong. In sum, the small company probably does not have such internal facilities as full-time medical and industrial relations personnel. Some may have ties with a parent company that provides a degree of help, but not on an immediate basis. The industrial nurse is probably the employee who could most readily work into a program. In addition, there is often a half-time personnel man who could easily become aware of and administer a program. Another difference lies in the less formal organization of small companies. A "family" atmosphere is more prevalent, and there is less emphasis on formal authority as such. The personalities of the men who own and manage small firms often give them individual qualities. Their leadership and guidance determine policy and its effectiveness. Sanctions such as crisis precipitation are thus more individualized, more informal. For a variety of reasons, such as fewer staff people to screen and to select new employees in smaller companies, "it seems probable that the alcoholic employee is present in at least equal if not greater numbers in small companies as in large" (Smithers Foundation, 1969:62).

Because of these differences from large companies the general strategy of a deviant-drinking program needs to be fitted to small business. All the basic ingredients of a company program must be used, but altered somewhat for a smaller firm. Thus policy must have the same "basics" — recognition as a health problem, provision of treatment help, and crisis precipitation if reasonable progress is not forthcoming — but these can be individualized. It need not be a highly formal statement but can be recognized policy among management. Such a policy is easier to write in a small company for there are fewer segments to object to and delay a policy decision. Many small companies can quickly and easily form, communicate, and carry out such a policy without too much concern over communication, coordination, or "lip service." Management is close to all phases of an operation and can immediately see that a policy is carried out — for example, in thousands of small companies, management and ownership are in the hands of the same person. At the same time, there is apt to be more reluctance to use constructive confrontation, because of the more personalized nature of policy, less medical personnel to set clear prognosis, and the greater tolerance of smaller companies, this vital part of a policy may easily be watered down. It may even be forgotten entirely if a union is present. So where policy is concerned the small company must be more concerned with follow-through, setting the possible point of crisis as realistically and fairly as possible.

The tolerance of small companies can seriously weaken a policy. This is as much a matter of top management's attitude as of the supervisor's attitude. To a sharp degree the greatest problem a small company faces in putting a policy into use is the tendency of the manager-owner to give the deviant drinker many "last chances." In other words, small companies, especially their top management, are more prone to be overly lenient on the job threat part of a policy. Actually, the small company, compared with the large one, can truly precipitate a crisis. It also probably has a better chance to coordinate its policy with the reaction of the spouse because of personalized relationships both off and on the job. In no other place in the work world does an employer have a better chance to bring a drinking problem clearly into the open and deal with it directly. The weak point, however, remains the tolerance of manager-owners of small businesses. All the advantages of the small company may easily be lost because management will not resort to crisis precipitation after reasonable therapy. If the deviant drinker discovers this to be the case the opportunity to motivate him will be lost.

What are some ways a small company can maintain a policy and program? First, small companies can develop a program through their trade associations. Second, they can develop a policy for problem employees in general, with the approach to deviant drinking as a part of it. Both of these possibilities exist in many types of small business. Thus a trade association with many affiliated small businesses often helps its members with personnel administration techniques and employee health hints. Such trade groups could summarize and circulate the experiences of small companies which operate alcohol-abuse programs. This could be done anonymously, although there is a tendency today for companies with programs to allow the use of their names. There are, of course, groups of small employers who operate joint health programs made up of both treatment of health problems and training of supervisors about them. Such a group could include alcohol abuse as a prominent health problem. Among the cooperating companies a common policy could be worked out and a program of training and treatment operated through the association for each member company. In this way there would be a substantial number of cases and a program could be used enough to get it into working order.

Probably more practical, but less effective, is a broad policy on problem employees with the deviant drinker as a prominent example. Rare is the small company that does not encounter the employee whose job performance is, or becomes, impaired. Some guidelines must be developed toward such employees, and the problem-employee approach is a viable one.

Finally, many small companies — for example, in the building and needle trades — have been organized by the same labor union. Since these unions bargain and work with most of the small companies of their industries, they have a special opportunity to stimulate owners and managers to initiate and develop industry-wide policies in their health programs. Chapter Eight includes a discussion of exclusive union action.

Legal Drug Use and the Medical Department. The company medical department may confuse a control program through its policies in prescribing legal psychoactive drugs. Medicine's increased reliance on drugs and the treatment of emotional problems (Lennard *et al.*, 1971) may be reflected in many company medical departments. A broader range of "life problems" are seen as deserving professional attention by many medical practitioners, e.g. anxieties accompanying a change experience and feelings of depression associated with disruption or loss.

Thus it is possible that while most employees are working under programs which forbid and control alcohol and drug abuse, the medical department may offer other employees legal drugs to alleviate symptoms of stress. Such practices could conceivably undermine an organizational control program in three ways: First, the undesirable effects of drug use may impair work roles regardless of the legitimacy of the drug's source. Second, this inconsistency may become obvious to those in the work force, constituting a potential means for undermining the program. Thus a clear line is drawn between appropriate and inappropriate drug use. Third, the availability of mood-altering drugs through legitimate channels in the organization may simply change the avenues by which employees desirous of mood alteration acquire the means for such experiences.

There are no simple solutions for this potential problem which clearly offers opportunities for intraorganizational conflict. The medical department will rarely tolerate any attempted control of medical practices by others in the organization. Many of the criticisms of the trends towards increased drug usage and broader definitions of medical-psychiatric problems, however, come from within the medical profession itself. All physicians may become increasingly aware of these problems and take them into consideration in modification of their own practices. This issue may be considered in the initial development of an alcohol and illegal drug control program, in which the medical department should be deeply involved. The result may be to design prescription practices that minimize potential problems of legal drug-related impairment and prevent opportunities for illegal distribution of legal drugs.

"Witch Hunt". As discussed in Chapters One and Two, various branches of the problem industry have attempted to create widespread fear and overreactions to the problems of drug deviance in the work place. The creation of such hysteria may threaten the successful implementation of constructive confrontation. The strategy may be enthusiastically adopted with an overemphasis on the confrontation aspect and neglect of the constructive dimension (Murray, 1971). In other words, irrational fears can trigger witch-hunts in some organizations. This reaction may become particularly acute when management adopts the attitude that the majority of employees who are members of minority groups are probably drug addicts and institutes mechanisms to catch such individuals and remove them from the organization. Such overenthusiasm for confrontation can be avoided by clear-cut statements of the rationale for the policy used as a preamble to written procedures. The constructive confrontation strategy is not designed to make the employer a policing agency for the rest of society, but is rather designed to help the organization achieve its intended production goals.

Absence of Supervisory Authority. Constructive confrontation assumes that the deviant individual will be responsible to a supervisor. There are several instances in which such supervisory authority may be absent or partially absent.

First, as outlined in Chapter Four, professional and technical specialists whose skills are unique to their position and loosely related to other organizational functions may be difficult to supervise. Without clear criteria of job performance, job impairment becomes difficult to detect. Related to this are persons whose job duties result in low visibility from supervision. While performance criteria may be clear-cut in these circumstances, the supervisor often has little knowledge of the actual on-the-job behavior of the employee. These risks should be recognized in the organization and steps taken to minimize their occurrence.

Second, implementation of constructive confrontation may be extremely difficult in the case of top-level executives. If such executives develop obvious patterns of role impairment, their subordinates could bring this behavior to the attention of the board of directors who, in turn, may be able to take charge of confrontation. On the other hand, this action could be ineffective or even disastrous to the subordinate attempting such an intervention. Such a dilemma should only occur in the case of the top executive who has developed deviant patterns, the probability of which is obviously low in any single organization.

A third potential barrier to effective confrontation occurs when supervisory personnel themselves develop deviant patterns. While confrontation by subordinates is again possible, it may clearly place them in jeopardy. When constructive confrontation is, however, implemented consistently across the organization, responsibility for confrontation moves up to the next level of supervision. Thus deviance by supervisors themselves will be problematic only in those situations where they are at the top of the hierarchy or where a policy is exclusively focused on the nonmanagerial segment of the work force.

Supervisory Training for Constructive Confrontation. The potential for rehabilitation, and even prevention, present in constructive confrontation lies chiefly among middle management, lower-level supervision, union shop stewards, and local union officials. What training strategies will help to develop this potential into concrete action? A recent series of evaluation studies of supervisory training about alcoholic employees found some positive and hopeful suggestions (Trice and Belasco, 1968; Belasco and Trice, 1969). Altogether there were three series in the study as it unfolded: first, the study evaluated a direct, intense training that focused exclusively on alcoholism and alcoholic employees; second, because of experiences and results in the first series, the study evaluated a "problem employee" approach in which a variety of emotionally disturbed employees, including alcoholics, were the focus of attention; finally it evaluated a "general supervision" approach in which the main emphasis was on the nature of general supervision, but with a focus on difficult problem employee cases — alcoholics, depressives, and compulsive workers — who were used to examine the supervisory process. In each series the study used a Solomon four-way design (Solomon, 1949) for separating training effect from the effect of the evaluative research itself on the trainees. In order to measure the effects of this contamination, the Solomon design adds two more trainee groups to the two making up the traditional experimental before-after design (Chapin, 1947). One of these additional groups did not fill out the initial scales but experienced the training and filled out the post-training scales. The second additional group only filled out the post-training scales and questionnaires and did not participate in the training. Use of this four-way design thus allowed for the assessment of the effects of training and of the contaminating effects of responding to written scales and instruments. A semantic differential scale (Osgood *et al.,* 1965) measured attitude toward various types of problem employees and an action questionnaire measured the extent to which individual supervisors in a large upstate New York organization would act to confront a specific problem employee.

The training program used the conference leadership discussion pattern, with each session based upon case studies reflecting that particular series. For example, the problem employee series used such cases as a female accounting clerk who had been poorly placed in her job and who was now facing retirement and a maintenance mechanic in the middle phase of alcohol addiction whose productivity had begun to decline. The basic guiding questions considered by the participants were "What would you do?" "Why would you do it?" "What would be the consequences of each action?" The case content did not include materials on other drug abuse, but the format could easily be broadened to do so.

The sessions focused on factual information about problem drinkers and problem employees, on the reluctance of supervisors to take action toward deviant employees, and on the potentials of various rehabilitation alternatives. The final sessions reviewed additional cases in an effort to apply the ideas already discussed. In the general-supervision approach, trainees were asked to write their own cases and apply to those cases principles and procedures discussed in the training; role playing illustrated the importance of listening skills in confronting and handling problem drinkers and problem employees in all series.

Data analysis revealed a surprising conclusion: completion of the scales alone, without the training experience, resulted in consistent and statistically significant changes in knowledge about deviant drinkers and problem employees, changes in attitudes toward them, and changes in predispositions toward action. The discovery of this dramatic research effect was incidental to the main goal of the investigation. The primary concern was with changes brought about by the training itself. The overall findings were that changes associated with the training were moderate, but clear-cut; that attitudes toward deviant-drinking employees and those toward other kinds of problem employees are closely related; and that negative attitudes toward deviant drinkers and problem employees are directly related to stronger propensities to confront and take action toward these employees. The training experience led to greater knowledge of problem employees, to less favorable attitudes toward them, and to greater propensities to confront them and refer them to appropriate agents. These changes were most pronounced in the general supervision series and least pronounced in the exclusive alcoholism series. The results encourage companies to expand programs to include deviant drug users. The data indicated that a supervisor's feelings about a deviant drinker and his mode of confronting such an employee were very similar to his feelings and action predispositions toward a frequently absent, overly aggressive, or mentally ill employee. We believe that such propensities would carry over to confrontation of the drug-using employee — perhaps even more so since social distance between supervisors and deviant drug users is already present and therefore easily stimulated.

The training material had been developed on the assumptions that it was desirable to induce more favorable attitudes toward deviant employees and that intolerance toward them constituted a major deterrent to early supervisory confrontation. The evidence revealed, however, that the lower the tolerance of the supervisor for deviant behavior, the greater his willingness to engage in realistic confrontation and referral. An unexpected set of data indicated that the overall stigma presumed to be attached to deviant employees in the work place was not revealed: this population of supervisors was mildly positive toward problem employees before the training experience. If this group's attitudes are similar to those in other supervisory populations, a major task of training may be to create *intolerance* toward deviant drinkers and drug users.

There is a possible explanation for the relation between negative attitudes toward deviants and the willingness to take constructive action toward them. As shown in Chapter Six, supervisors tend to tolerate and absorb the disruptive behavior of the deviant employee for long periods. Some have attributed this inaction to the stigma of the alcoholic label and the supervisor's unwillingness to attach such a label to a fellow employee. These data, however, suggest that this is not the case, but, rather, that the supervisor's reluctance to exert sanctions against the deviant is based on favorable attitudes toward him. This reflects the process of normalization discussed earlier.

All of the supervisors in this study had direct, face-to-face contact with their charges and were similar to them in terms of social class, education, and work experience. Many of them had been promoted from the ranks and had at one time worked alongside their present subordinates. Many supervisors are friendly with employees who become chronically deviant, and the disruptiveness of the deviant does not immediately destroy this camaraderie. Furthermore, the professional's image of the deviant as disruptive and socially undesirable may be an exaggeration of the stereotypes held by the layman. Thus the educational problem is to create social distance between the supervisor and the drug-abusing employee, producing a willingness to confront the employee as a means of helping him (Goffman, 1963). Surprisingly, these relations between attitudes and action held across organizational levels of supervision. Lower-level supervisors had consistently more favorable attitudes toward deviant employees, but these differences were not statistically significant.

Some specific suggestions for future training and its improvement come from the body of data. Most supervisory training assumes that the same technique and training content are equally effective in changing behavior across an entire population of supervisors. These populations consists of individuals with a range of personalities, social backgrounds, and different supervisory demands. The assumption that a single training experience is equally relevant and effective across the board may be wrong. It is somewhat the same as assuming that any person could do any job. Just as job success may improve when job demands are matched with individual characteristics, certain training experiences which are matched with certain individuals may greatly improve training success rates. In retrospect, we feel that if it had been possible to identify the characteristics of the trainee who would change in the desired direction before we had initiated the training the likelihood of training success could have been improved by 31 percent (Trice and Belasco, 1968). Thus, if training programs for the management of deviant drinking and drug abuse are seriously undertaken, a battery of training techniques, each geared to a different supervisory subpopulation, could be developed.

Several other practical suggestions arise from this research. The relationship between unfavorable attitudes toward deviant employees and positive orientations toward action cannot be overemphasized. The mental health model promulgated in many quarters seems to argue for an increase in the acceptance and toleration of the deviant employee's behavior (rather than emphasizing the problems that he causes for those in the work place and for his family). The more desirable course of action, at least in the work place, seems to be to lower the tolerance level of significant others surrounding a deviant individual. At the same time it is critical that such "symptoms" be kept in perspective; only behaviors disruptive to job performance should be the concern of management. These data suggest that scales and questionnaires used before training would also be helpful. Filling out the questionnaire sensitizes the trainee to the essential aspects in the material which will be communicated.

Finally, a very important recommendation to emerge from these data is the necessity of making training content relevant for the trainees and increasing their stake in behavior change. Supervisory training can be placed in the context of learning supervisory skills and abilities. In other words, the supervisor who is reluctant to identify and confront deviant-drinking and drug-using employees may have all the problems discussed previously, but his reluctance is also symptomatic of his ineptitude as a management representative. The supervisor who tolerates a semiproductive drinker or drug user may also tolerate other partially productive employees. Thus, by focusing on such factors as costs, waste, and absenteeism the point may be clearly made to trainees that the supervisor who cannot manage deviant drinkers and drug users may be a poor supervisor in other ways. This training strategy may precipitate a crisis for the first-level supervisor, making earlier identification of these deviants less of a personal choice. Furthermore, deviant-drinking or drug-using employees provide excellent cases for magnifying the nature of the supervisory role so that its expectations are clearly outlined. Practically speaking, this merely calls for the use of cases involving deviant-drinking and drug-using employees in conjunction with other problem employee cases in general supervisory training. Not only is this tactic salient for practical-minded supervisors who may never have a deviant employee, it also provides them with information about alcohol and drug abuse without concentrating exclusively on it.

Maximum training success seems to result when policies designed to deal with deviant drinkers and other types of problem employees are a central part of supervisory role expectations. Likewise, the extent to which the effective management of deviants is seen as an essential facet of effective supervision may increase the success of both supervisory training and actual supervisory practices. The integration of this type of training and these role expectations into the socialization of both new and old supervisors is essential to the long-run effectiveness of a deviant-drinking and drug-use management program.

POTENTIAL FAILURES OF CONSTRUCTIVE CONFRONTATION

A policy of constructive confrontation will inevitably meet with some failures. Among the potential failures are those employees who view drinking or drug use as more rewarding than their job security. If they refuse to alter their behavior or to seek the help that the employer offers, the employer has no alternative but to dismiss the employee after a set number of confrontations has occurred. This may be extremely painful in some circumstances, particularly where the employee's skills are unique and highly valued by the organization, but the effectiveness of any policy lies in its consistent implementation. If exceptions are made and certain deviants are allowed to continue on the job because their performances are regarded as indispensable or because their personal relationships with their supervisors prevent meaningful confrontation, the entire program will be undermined in the eyes of the rest of the work force. Should such exceptions occur, the stage will be set for legitimate grievances when the policy is fully implemented in other circumstances.

Employers will undoubtedly encounter employees whose commitment to the job is so weak that confrontation will have little meaning. This situation may occur in low-status occupations where the employee sees the job as yielding few rewards and the threat of job disruption is inadequate to precipitate a crisis. Failures may also occur with short-tenured employees who have few investments in a particular position or organization. Such low job commitment might be particularly prevalent among the youthful excessive users of illegal drugs who are oriented to the hang loose ethic. Low commitment may also characterize the street addict category of opiate users. Failure to respond to confrontation of offers of treatment among such employees leaves the employer with little choice but dismissal. It should be emphasized, however, that regularized excessive drinking does not usually begin until the mid-years of an occupational career, a point at which most individuals have heavy investments in a particular organization and position. Thus most problem-drinking employees should be responsive to constructive confrontation.

Constructive confrontation may also be ineffective when an employer has inadvertently hired an individual already addicted to alcohol or drugs. In these instances the issue of employer responsibility is a significant consideration. Work organizations are established to accomplish a given set of tasks rather than to provide a haven for the solution of personal problems. On the other hand, some employers may feel a social responsibility to offer help to the newly hired, addicted employee under company auspices. Commitment to constructive confrontation may require the dismissal of the employees who are established deviants, if they refuse to alter their behavior or to enter the treatment programs that might be offered by the employer.

POLICIES ON OTHER DRUGS

Although an alcohol abuse policy sets the background for other drug policies, it does not specifically spell out such guidelines. Even though written policies that do this are few, the outlines of different types of other drug policies have appeared. Probably most frequent in our experience is the treat-each-case-individually approach, such as advocated by Kiev (1970:19), ". . . it should be emphasized that blanket disciplinary measures for drug abuse are often inappropriate. It is more desirable to consider each case of drug abuse and violation on the individual merits." Rush and Brown (1971) also found the individual case approach to be prominent among companies who formally described themselves as without a policy on drugs. This approach appears to seek a way to avoid legal labeling, to use constructive confrontation, but to resort to police action in cases that seem flagrant or unresponsive. Formalized, this approach tends to see drug dependency among employees as behavior leading to poor performance and to health problems and calling for help from rehabilitatory and counseling specialists. At the same time, it directs that a crisis may be precipitated in that drug use can become a permanent entry in an employee's personnel file and applicants who admit to the use of drugs will not be employed (Rush and Brown, 1971). Some policies of this type distinguish between the drug-dependent employee and the employee pusher. Usually the latter is immediately discharged if a solid case can be made, and he is reported to appropriate police agencies.

Another type of policy seems to be roughly equal in numbers (Sohn, considered dangerous or illegal by the U.S. Department of Justice . . . are prohibited on company property . . . any employee who carries onto 1970), but it calls for discharge of users. An airline directs that "drugs company property, has in his possession on company property or reports to work under the influence of any of these substances is subject to discharge" (Rush and Brown, 1971:12). Murray (1971) believes that most companies are taking a hard line on drug use and describes a company which uses undercover agents to detect users and then applies their policy of dismissal only. Kurtis (1971:24) describes a bank whose policy extends to off-the-job behavior: ". . . it is the policy of the company that possession or sale of dangerous drugs [such as heroin, LSD, barbiturates, amphetamines, marihuana, etc.] by an employee off the premises will make the employee subject to release for the first such offense." Kurtis (1971:23) describes "still others [which] see themselves as an intricate part of the community make-up and know that they have to expand their existing health services to meet changing social demands." Apparently a large public utility described by Rush and Brown (1971:14) takes this as their basic theme. After stating that the illegal sale, use, possession, or transfer of drugs while on company business is prohibited and that any employee who engages in any of these acts is "subject to disciplinary action up to and including dismissal," the statement goes on to say that "it is company policy to attempt rehabilitaion whenever appropriate." More explicitly:

> The disciplinary action to be taken will be determined by consideration of all circumstances. Efforts toward rehabilitation should be made where there is a likelihood of success. Consultation with Personnel, Labor Relations, Benefit, Medical, and Legal people is often warranted before final determination of rehabilitative or disciplinary action (Rush and Brown, 1971:14).

The implementation of this policy calls for specific supervisor action: he should inform his own supervisors and representatives of the personnel department, consult with the medical department, confront the employee with specifics about his poor job performance, absences, and lateness, but make no mention of drug abuse. After referral to medical personnel and their decision about rehabilitation possibilities, the supervisor explains "exactly what improvement in performance and behavior is expected, ascertaining that the employee understands that improvement is necessary if he is to continue on the job." The policy, however, explicitly cautions the supervisor not to engage in counseling efforts. Finally, if performance does not improve, supervision introduces the likelihood of further disciplinary action — suspension or dismissal — and follows through if necessary.

We have noted two practical problems in many of these policies. They seem first to focus operationally almost exclusively on heroin dependency and second to neglect the need for legal caution in identification.

As we have shown, legal drugs other than alcohol (often illegally secured) such as barbiturates and amphetamines can be a greater problem for the work place both in numbers and impact than heroin — despite forces operating to increase heroin's use. Consequently, exclusive focus on heroin neglects these other important drug problems. This, however, is not confined to work-world people. According to Irwin (1971), who is a pharmacologist, law enforcement personnel ranked heroin as having the greatest hazards for society while they rated alcohol low. In contrast, he had ranked alcohol highest. Furthermore, the legal problems of accusing an employee of illegal drug use can be considerable, and management — even medical personnel — should emphasize impaired job performance since this is industry's rightful domain. "A high standard of proof must be met to sustain the discharge of an employee for the possession, use, or sale of drugs and the company must clearly meet that standard. The proof of guilt should go beyond a mere preponderance of the evidence. The proof of guilt should be clear and convincing" (Willig, 1971:9). Costs involved in securing such evidence suggests the wisdom of a policy that takes a confrontation position based primarily upon on-the-job performance without direct drug-use accusations. Even when an employer uses urine tests as a device to determine continued employment, there can be legal problems such as "the difficulty in evaluating the degree and extent of psychopathology . . ." (Willig, 1971:57). As in alcoholism cases, disciplinary or dismissal action will probably be more readily accepted by arbitrators and courts if the employer has sincerely attempted to provide rehabilitation opportunities for the drug-dependent employee (Trice and Belasco, 1966a).

SUMMARY

The constructive confrontation strategy is based upon recognition of impaired performance. Such performance breeches the employment contract and legitimately may lead to a series of confrontations which demand that the employee either alter his behavior or face penalties — even dismissal. Rigorous implementation of the strategy, with the responsibility for the recognition of job impairment vested in immediate supervision, will result in a confrontation of most deviants at a point where their behavior is still under their personal control. Assuming job commitment and personal investment in job security, confrontation at this point in the development of a deviant pattern should produce adequate motivation for behavior change. The implementation of the strategy requires numerous preparatory steps, some of which may be difficult in small organizations. There are clearly types of employees who will be so unresponsive to confrontation that dismissal will be the only alternative. While consistency in policy implementation may appear painful in the short run, the long-term gains of a respected program uniformly applied to all should not be understated.

Most observations, research, and experiences on which these recommendations are based have focused on the deviant-drinking employee. While much more remains to be learned about the occasional drug abuser who appears in the work place, there is no reason why constructive confrontation cannot be employed with those drug abusers who do appear. At present many employers seem to believe that discovery of drug abuse should lead to immediate dismissal. Such an attitude overlooks the basic nature of the relationship between the employer and the employee and may place the employer in an undesirable policing role. While there is no promise that any employee will be responsive to constructive confrontation, it appears that much will be gained if such an opportunity for behavior change is provided to the deviant employee, regardless of whether his deviance stems from alcohol or other drugs.

The potential Achilles' Heel of any alcohol- and drug-control program is the reaction of the union or other employee organizations. We now consider the problems of union-management cooperation.

VIII

Union-Management Cooperation and Conflict

AN established fact of industrial relations is that management programs involving employee welfare must have the full consent and cooperation of the labor union or other employee organizations if they are to be effective and durable (Belasco *et al.*, 1969). This is especially true of programs designed to deal with deviant drinking and drug use. Union-management cooperation and mutual support are essential to the line supervisors' effectiveness in such programs when he is confronted with a deviant drinker or drug user. Indeed, the absence of union cooperation may destroy the best designed programs for the management of deviance.

Portions of this chapter are based on research dealing with successful union-management cooperation in the implementation of deviance control and related programs. Research interviews were conducted in work organizations throughout the Northeastern United States with union and management representatives who had played key roles in the evolution and implementation of particular programs.* For comparison, data were gathered on a variety of cooperative programs dealing with general employee welfare as well as with deviant drinking and alcoholism. At the time of the study, no formal programs specifically designed to deal with drug use were known to the researchers.

In this chapter we first examine the structural features of unions which discourage or encourage participation in management-based programs. Second, we look at the status of the union shop steward and the parallels that exist between the problems of his role and those of the first-line supervisor. We then assess the relations between different patterns of program development and different degrees of union-man-

---

* Parts of these data were collected and initially analyzed by Dr. George Ritzer, currently associate professor of sociology at the University of Kansas.

agement cooperation. Descriptions of several programs are given, together with a series of suggestions for improving union-management cooperation in alcohol- and drug-abuse programs.

THE BASIS FOR UNION-MANAGEMENT COOPERATION

Developed as a defense in a hostile industrial world, unions by definition are often conflictual rather than cooperating organizations. But a conflictual relationship need not completely prevent cooperative relations. Conflict and cooperation are "two sides of the same coin, alternative expressions of the same forces" (Stagner, 1956:13), ". . . they are not separate things, but phases of one process which always involves some of both" (Coser, 1956:39). Thus, "unions can engage in conflictual relations with management in the sense of vigorous pursuit of bargaining demands or the prosecution of grievances, while performing more 'positive' functions for the enterprise at the same time" (Tannenbaum, 1965:720).

Informal cooperation creeps into even the most rigid contract and reduces disputes (Kuhn, 1961; Dalton, 1959). Formal cooperation with management occurs in the Scanlon Plan and among locals of the Amalgamated Clothing Workers Union which have helped weak, unionized firms compete with nonunionized shops. Some specialists detect a trend toward increased accommodation and cooperation (Walton and McKersie, 1965). Forces creating this trend include federal laws legitimizing unions, technological changes which raise problems calling for joint solutions, and increases in the numbers of union and management experts who speak the same language.

The major motivation of unions remains the protection of members' job interests (Derber *et al.,* 1961). This indicates that cooperation may be more likely on issues such as safety, health, and other matters well removed from financial issues. Three factors are needed to move toward cooperation: union and management each accepting the legitimacy of the other; concern for *mutual interests* other than wages, hours, and working conditions; and full respect for the other's function (Walton and McKersie, 1965). Mutual interests in safety, health, and retirement lead directly to the possibility of joint programs on alcohol and drug abuse even though there may be conflict over grievances. If both sides realize the potential loss such deviance causes to both the worker and the organization, they would be more likely to recognize their common interest in the emotional and physical well being of union members. In sum, both sides can easily share a goal, making cooperation more likely (Stagner, 1956:60). As Leo Perlis (1971:1), director of the AFL-CIO's Department of Community Services, expresses it: "Industrial programs for the rehabilitation of alcoholic employees are neither pro-management nor pro-labor, but simply pro-people." Labor's concern about other drug abuse appeared in the New York City Central Labor Council's seminar on drug addiction control in early 1971 *(Industrial Bulletin,* 1971).

Historically, labor unions have been reluctant to accept management programs dealing with employee welfare without full assurance that union members are protected from arbitrary management action. This reluctance may be particularly potent where the authority to label an individual as a deviant lies with the company medical department. This staff agency may be viewed by the union as comprised exclusively of "management representatives." A union welfare specialist recently pointed out that "labor is generally suspicious of management's interest in the mental health of its employees. Too often such interest has been used as a guise for anti-employee practices, whether by design or by unintended consequence" (Weiner, 1967:196). Illustrative is a study of the way unions in New York City, which were part of a larger study of how various organizations conceived of the problem, responded to a question concerning the allocation of resources for alcoholism rehabilitation:

> Responses indicate that virtually all of those replying felt that such a program should be run by outside community agencies, or, more prefer-ably, by the union's community services committee, or by some combination of these two. This finding may be taken as some indication of the basic distrust with which union members regard any efforts of a business organization to deal constructively with problem drinking, and should certainly be considered when planning any alcoholism program for business (D. Holmes, 1963:138) .

To many blue-collar employees, "mental health" may appear as a middle-class definition of conformity and good behavior. According to analyses presented by Offer and Sabshin (1966), this impression may be correct. Union leaders who are especially aware of the social class differences between the union and management may feel very negative toward deviant-drinking and drug-use programs. In other words, there may be a suspicion that norms defining deviance will be more strictly enforced among blue-collar and lower-status workers. Furthermore, it is possible that "deviant behavior" may appear to union leaders as a vague and mysterious concept; their reaction to this ambiguity may be rejection and retreat. Support of an alcohol and drug program may appear to give management a blank check to label union members. Instead of taking an active interest in a particular management-based program, unions may adopt an attitude of apathy and disinterest, coupled with a vague threat to disrupt any program which might "injure" a union member.

One essential fact cannot be overemphasized: the representatives of the union or other employee organization must be made explicitly aware of the assumptions underlying deviant-drinking and drug-use programs. Definitions and the reasoning behind preventive actions must be shared by both groups. All parties must understand that such programs will yield long-range benefits for employees who may be permanently damaging themselves with alcohol or drugs. As pointed out in Chapter Seven, the employee will certainly benefit in the long run if his status in the work organization is maintained through a period of difficulty with alcohol or drugs. The probability of the employee's resuming normal behavior will be increased and the problems of re-entering an occupational role after a period of isolated treatment for a behavior disorder will be avoided. Despite considerable research, progress has been very slow in successfully rehabilitating or "delabeling," chronic deviants, particularly in cases of emotional disorders (Sussman, 1966). Early identification, in connection with supportive action, will clearly benefit all involved.

Both the work organization and the union benefit if a deviant-drinking and drug-use program results in the retention of good employees and makes the hiring and training of replacements unnecessary. In sum, the basis for union-management cooperation is simply logical (Smithers Foundation, 1970). Certainly, it can hardly be argued by either labor or management that the use of alcohol or drugs in a way which impairs job performance is a "good thing" or that employees should feel free to engage in such behavior.

In addition, union and management representatives should be equally aware of the difficulties surrounding the handling of an alcoholic or drug-using employee; his bizarre excuses for absences and his potentially disruptive on-the-job behavior present problems to both union and management representatives. A recognition of the *need for consensus* in confronting and handling such an employee is essential for a successful program.

A frequently ignored factor which often indirectly determines the success or failure of union-management cooperation in a deviant-drinking and drug-use program is the extent to which management adopts a *company-wide policy* toward deviant drinking and drug use. A successful program to deal with this problem cannot be directed solely at union members or blue-collar employees; the rules and procedures must apply to all individuals in the organization. Unions feel a justifiable reluctance to cooperate in a program which sets guidelines for behavior which, in effect, apply only to union members. For example, a production union may resent a no-drinking rule if alcohol is available to management personnel in the executive dining room at lunch time or otherwise used among white-collar employees without management sanctions. Especially difficult is the situation where specific knowledge of the deviant drinking or drug use of certain management personnel is widespread in a company work force. Programs applied only to nonsupervisory or blue-collar employees are frequently seen by the union as being "against" union members — and this may indeed be the case. Company-wide policy is therefore essential; otherwise, the union can effectively argue that the program is discriminatory.

DOUBLE BINDS FOR THE SHOP STEWARD

The union shop steward is essential to the success of a program. In the same way as the supervisor, he can observe first hand impaired performance due to deviant behavior among individuals with whom he is personally acquainted.

The steward's role does, however, contain ambiguities regarding the handling of the deviant drinker and drug user. He may see the damage the deviant is doing to himself, his job, and his family. Furthermore, having often known the employee perhaps for years, he may feel he intimately understands the problems which underlie the individual's deviance. The steward's exposure to this personal deterioration, combined with his conception of his own role as an *aid* to union members, is likely to create pressure for him to act. On the other hand, he may know full well that even if he pressures the deviant into treatment, he may subsequently have to represent the employee if he uses the grievance procedure. Because of their positions in the organization, stewards usually do not know how to act, and these cross-pressures may leave them feeling powerless (Whyte, 1969).

Initially, the steward may excuse the behavior, justifying it on the basis of the deviant's life problems. He may have seen the individual previously engage in deviance but subsequently shape up. These rationalizations may lead the steward to cover up the deviance as a way of relieving some of the pressures on the deviant. The usual consequence of this protective strategy is the continuation and possible accentuation of the deviant behavior. The steward at this point may realize that his effort is doomed to failure and that he is placed in a double bind: he sees equally undesirable consequences from doing nothing and from taking action.

An essential ingredient of the dilemma of the shop steward is the fact that he, together with most union officials, is elected to his position. This mode of status achievement forces him into a political atmosphere where he must respond to the needs and desires of his electorate. When faced with the obligation to confront a deviant employee, the political nature of his position frequently prevents such action.

By engaging in some form of referral or confrontation the steward risks alienating a portion of his electorate and, as a result, losing the next election. By taking action toward the deviant employee, the steward may appear to other union members as an agent of management. Furthermore, the deviant may be a popular and well liked member of the work group, another factor which works against the steward taking action without damaging his political position. Finally, in terms of his perception of the protective function of the union, the steward may see the act of turning in or confronting the deviant as a definite contradiction of his role expectations. There are clear-cut pressures in such situations to "keep it among the boys" and avoid collusion with management.

There is also pressure on the steward to take action, as he comes to recognize that the deviant employee is causing difficulty for his supervisor and fellow workers. Certain of the deviant's fellow employees may actually pressure the union official to take action toward the disruptive worker, thus facing the steward with loss of political influence if he fails to respond to the desires of his electorate. Part of the work group may see him as a traitor if he does anything about the deviant, while another part may see him as irresponsible if he fails to take action. Thus the cross-currents put him in a position where he may suffer regardless of the action he takes.

UNION STRUCTURE AND POSSIBLE COOPERATION

Basic structural characteristics of labor unions may affect their cooperation with programs designed to deal with deviant drinking and drug use. The first characteristic is the union's division into two operating levels, one made up of those who actively conduct collective bargaining locally and the other of those who transact union business at the regional or national level. Local officials are usually elected for relatively short terms, while regional officials are either appointed or elected for long terms. Thus the local official is typically member oriented. He is less concerned with overall organizational problems of the union than are the regional officials. This difference in focus creates a gap within the union to such an extent that individual stewards may experience a good deal of frustration when they attempt to deal with high-level union officials. This becomes apparent where problems of deviant employees are under consideration. Lack of consensus between different union levels is a source of further ambivalence for the local official. Several stewards interviewed in our study described instances where regional representatives accepted the disciplining or discharging of a deviant-drinking employee in exchange for management concessions on other grievances, much to the chagrin of local shop stewards.

A source of positive union attitudes is its various staff officials, particularly community service officers. This source may, however, be offset by a basic fact of bureaucratic life: the attitude of "line" officials toward the suggestions of those in staff positions may be very skeptical (Blau and Scott, 1962). This skepticism may particularly be found where line officials have achieved their positions by election from the rank and file while the staff personnel have been hired on the basis of their professional or semiprofessional backgrounds.

These characteristics of the labor union — the philosophy of protecting members, the political nature of first-line officials, and the possible frictions among union functionaries — may be obstacles to effectively involving the union in the development and implementation of programs which deal with deviant drinking and drug use. On the other hand these binds might actually be catalysts to union participation if they are seen in their context. The union is committed to the protection and aid of all its members, but typically has no effective way of handling the deviant employee so his problems can be controlled and resolved. Recognition of the double binds produced when union officials face a deviant employee may possibly motivate joint union-management participation in such programs. Such shared understanding, of course, requires opening communication channels that may be blocked with distrust. The overall tone of cooperation between union and management in a local situation is probably an excellent predictor of success or failure in this specific endeavor.

There are several further reasons for optimism. Our field experiences and those of others have revealed a "dual loyalty" among union members. In the early 1950's both Rose (1952) and Purcell (1953) found union members to have an attitude of reasonableness toward management. Overall, unions attract members who are neither vehemently pro-union or promanagement (Miller and Rosen, 1957). Whyte, reviewing twelve studies on dual loyalty, concluded, "As the collective bargaining relationship becomes established, it is more likely to be accompanied by dual than by divided loyalty. This is perhaps the most thoroughly demonstrated proposition that we have on human relations in industry" (Whyte, 1969:472). Moreover, Whyte observes that where the union is well established, dual loyalty appears even among management people: "These men tend to accept the union organization as part of the whole institutional system and recognize an obligation to union leaders in their positions as leaders, in much the same way they feel obligation toward fellow members of management" (Whyte, 1969:475).

Such findings suggest receptivity and support for alcohol and drug programs among the rank and file. Effective support for such programs can begin "at the bottom" (Sayles and Strauss, 1967; Kuhn, 1961). Informal relations set a potential for formal joint action; and, even if it is stymied by widespread conflicts elsewhere, joint informal understanding about effective help for alcoholic employees can emerge where it matters most, among stewards and first-line supervisors. Our fieldwork disclosed three types of concern about the alcoholic that emerged among supervisors and stewards: (1) "he was drinking himself to death"; (2) the belief both union and management would benefit because he was a big "headache" for both; (3) his fellow workers' concern with lower productivity, high absenteeism, and accident risk. Although an official policy and program is an eventual necessity, the "native" sources of support in the rank and file assure more rapid overall success for the program.

EXCLUSIVE MANAGEMENT ACTION

Turning to different patterns of cooperation, we can examine a program dealing with deviant drinking in a large upstate New York manufacturing company, familiar to the authors. This program is handled exclusively by management, despite cooperation with the union in most other areas of employee welfare. The management representative who spots a deviant drinker refers him to the supervisor of the recreation department who is a recovered alcoholic. The recreation director then talks with the deviant drinker and acts as an informal counselor. On the basis of his judgment, he either regards his own counseling as adequate or refers the employee to the company physician, a psychiatrist, a clinic, or Alcoholics Anonymous. The only union involvement in this program is defensive or protective intervention following disciplinary action brought against a deviant drinker by the company; at that time the union will defend the man should he file a grievance. Interviews with union officials indicate they are satisfied with this limited role and feel they have no other part to play.

A second example of nearly exclusive management action is found in a large Midwestern public utility. This organization has no specific policy toward deviant drinkers, although most supervisors deal with them through disciplinary procedures. Supervisors are informally urged to send deviant drinkers to the personnel department for advice and counseling. The personnel manager may than refer the deviant drinker to any of a number of different agencies, including the company medical department, a psychiatrist, a clergyman, a hospital, Alcoholics Anonymous, or the community service representative of the AFL-CIO. The union is kept informed about the action being taken with each deviant drinker, but it is not expected to become involved. Interviews with union leaders indicated they were "happy to have management do it" because deviant drinking is as big a burden to them as it is to management.

Although relations between union and management were amiable in these two settings, a more negative union role is possible, e.g. active opposition to a program where management and labor are viewed as "two contenders in a prize ring." More likely is a passive, suspicious union attitude where each case of management action is evaluated singly. Sometimes this yields consensus while on other occasions grievances and even arbitration may be precipitated.

Although permitting management to take the full responsibility for managing deviants is seen as probably the easiest way out for many locals, lack of action by the union has its problems. First, although fighting disciplinary decisions is the safest course for union leadership at the national or international level, this may create considerable discomfort for local stewards. They may be involuntarily committed to the undesirable position of excusing and defending obviously disruptive employees as well as having to oppose the actions of line supervisors in already complicated situations. Second, internal union conflict may develop as a reaction to a "do-nothing" international policy, particularly when it concerns such an emotionally charged subject as alcohol and drug use. Third, progressive managers are likely to be troubled by a union which will not take any positive action. This may develop or strengthen feelings of alienation between union and management which in turn may spread into other areas of joint concern.

Perhaps the most adverse consequence of a unilateral management policy is the potential loss suffered by the deviant employee. He may be held in limbo while union and management haggle over whether the disciplinary action taken toward him was justified. During this time he might well react to the stress by additional use of alcohol or drugs. The focus of the conflict usually is not upon *his* problem but upon the union-management relation, a situation in sharp contrast to the union goal of employee protection. Thus, although in many ways the simplest form of action, the absence of union involvement may also be the least desirable.

EXCLUSIVE UNION ACTION

Our data indicate the usual precursor of the development of a program exclusively based in the union is ineffective handling of deviants by management. For example, a program which was originally a joint union-management effort between a large steel company and the steelworkers' union evolved into a program almost exclusively union-based. Union leaders claim that the company did not follow through with its initial agreement: the company policy instead resulted in discharges for nearly all deviant drinkers. The organization had followed a policy of three days' suspension following the first incident, five days for the second, and discharge following the third. Frequently the union was not told of the problem until the deviant drinker had been disciplined or fired. Recognizing the difficulties of long and complex arbitration, the union undertook to deal with the deviant drinker by counseling him and his family and by trying to get him into treatment. The typical procedure which emerged was an initial interview of the deviant by a union official, after which the deviant drinker is referred to a clinic, psychiatrist, or Alcoholics Anonymous. The union has not set up any treatment facilities of its own, leaving this responsibility to community agencies.

Three relatively small locals of a large international union took responsibility for handling deviant drinkers where management had refused to take any such responsibility. The union's procedure which emerged is as follows: If a case of deviant drinking is revealed, usually by decreased productivity and increased absenteeism, the company personnel department notifies the union. The union's program is not particularly well organized and is limited primarily to counseling, with occasional informal referral. Because of the few available resources and the consequent lack of organization, the union does not intensively follow up the cases it handles. A similar pattern was revealed in another organization where the first-line union officials generally refer deviant drinkers to the union community service representative, who in turn refers the individual to a psychiatrist or other community facility.

UNION-MANAGEMENT COOPERATION AND CONFLICT

Obviously, the union local as an organization usually does not have adequate funds or facilities to manage deviance effectively. Additionally, the officials of the union typically do not have adequate training or experience to handle the problems of a deviant drinker or drug user effectively. If they are unpaid officials, they are burdened with working with deviants on their own time.

These makeshift efforts may lead to internal conflict in a union local. Rank-and-file union members tend to look to the leadership for policy, assistance, and guidance. A steward who requests help with a deviant from the union and receives ad hoc or ineffective assistance is likely to become disillusioned with the union program. Likewise, when emphasis is placed on managing deviance in a full-scale manner at the expense of other union activities, the typical union member tends to feel he is being ignored. Finally, placing the union in a role of conducting employee welfare programs may disrupt the whole fabric of union-management relations since this type of activity is customarily management-based. Thus a program designed to deal with deviant drinking and drug use which is primarily union-based is probably better than nothing, but it may disrupt the union's organization and membership goals.

JOINT UNION-MANAGEMENT ACTION

Despite the apparent logic and value of joint union-management cooperation, there are relatively few successful cooperative programs for controlling alcohol and drug abuse. However, AFL–CIO Community Services are currently very active in exploring means for cooperative agreements in a range of trades and industries (Andrus, 1971).

In one instance we found the joint nature of the program rested on the fact that the initial confrontation with the deviant drinker involved both the line supervisor and the shop steward. If this effort failed, the two referred the problem to the grievance committee, and the union business agent then conferred with management in a relatively ad hoc fashion for each deviant drinker. Union officials stated that no deviant drinkers had been helped by this program.

Another joint effort also had very limited union involvement. The program included the following possible steps: suspension of a deviant drinker with a classification of "unfit for duty"; an interview with the individual by the district division head, with a union representative present if requested; treatment by the company physician or in a community facility; and, finally, a meeting with representatives of the personnel department, the individual's department, and the medical department at which some decision regarding the continued employment of the individual was reached. The medical department representative was said to be the most influential participant in this last meeting. The only joint aspect of this policy is the possible presence of the union representative at the initial referral interview.

A third instance is a thoroughly successful program carried out by a city government agency in a large Eastern city. The success appears due to the presence of a counselor who is an ex-union member and a former alcoholic. He is employed by management, but his background apparently makes him sympathetic to union interests. The union in this organization had a history of losing cases involving deviant drinkers at arbitration and thus welcomed some alternative program. The union was squarely behind the counselor and actively supported the use of his services.

A final example of a joint union-management effort directed toward the control of deviant drinking is by far the most successful one revealed in the survey. At the urging of the local Community Council on Alcoholism, a joint committee on alcoholism was set up at an automotive parts plant. A joint union-management committee with equal representation from both parties was eventually formed. The program operates in this manner:

1. A deviant drinker is referred to the joint committee by his foreman, his shop steward, or the personnel department.

2. At a meeting with the joint committee, the drinker is directly confronted with the facts of his deviance and is asked to admit that he is a developing alcoholic. He continues to return to the committee after each additional "transgression" until he accepts the label of alcoholic.

3. After this admission and labeling, the joint committee offers the man help. They refer him to local treatment agencies and place him on sick leave if residential treatment is required. If he fails to seek or continue treatment, the joint committee disciplines him. This had only been necessary in one case at the time the research interviews were conducted.

4. The joint committee follows his progress, visiting him and his family, helping to smooth the transition back to work.

At first, the union was reluctant to go along with this program, feeling that it interfered too much in the employees' personal lives. Also it was felt that the union members' reaction would result in political suicide for any leader involved. These predictions were not borne out, since union officials were reelected on every occasion between the committee's inception and the time of the research interviews. This program might be criticized for its rather casual use of the "sick" label without any evidence of the presence of illness. Experimentation with the use of the poor performer label rather than the "sick" label in the confrontations might improve the program's effectiveness.

Interviews with union officials involved in these joints efforts clearly indicated ambivalence toward this type of cooperation with management. On the one hand, they saw the program as a great help in managing a previously difficult problem. They felt that this form of joint effort was a legitimate partnership with management; it gave union officials a "status boost" and offered hope for cooperation in other areas. On the negative side, however, there was a definite feeling that cooperation with management might lead to charges of collusion from the rank and file and then to political defeat for the leaders. For example, in one situation local officials charged that an international representative who worked closely with management on several joint programs had "sold out" to the company.

Thus, although joint union-management cooperation in programs designed to handle deviant drinkers and drug users can be most effective, this pattern has not yet been widely accepted. In many organizations drinking and drug use do not appear to be major problems, either because of organizational size or because of the composition of the work force. In these instances, deviant employees can be handled in an ad hoc fashion with some consensus between union and management.

Another barrier to wider acceptance stems from traditional union attitudes toward employee protection. The union may see only one course of action when a member has been disciplined because of deviant behavior: arbitration. Arbitrators tend to favor management's disciplinary rights where off-job behavior destroys employee efficiency (Sussman, 1964). However, in more than 50 percent of the published arbitration cases dealing with discharge of deviant drinkers the arbitrator called for reinstatement (Trice and Belasco, 1966a). A follow-up of these reinstated employees, however, indicated that three out of four were no longer employed at the same company, half of them having been discharged for a recurrence of the same offense. Thus, just as the "corrective" discipline of discharge may be ineffective in the long run for management, likewise the action of arbitration may be ineffective for the union. It is extremely difficult, however, to communicate these facts to union officials in work settings where cases involving alcohol and drug abuse are infrequent.

The notion of union involvement with management in programs dealing with employee welfare is relatively new and is generally met with pessimism, given a tradition of sporadic hostility or temporary peaceful co-existence with management in certain locals. When this tradition is combined with relative ignorance of the effective management of deviant drinking and drug use in a work organization, the small number of extant successful union-management programs is not surprising. The structure of the union-management relationship, however, does not necessarily prevent effective cooperative programs. As deviant drinking and drug use become more visible in work organizations and as knowledge of the potential gains to be achieved by cooperative efforts is diffused, we would predict the evolution of more joint programs.

The ideal program would combine union-management cooperation with constructive confrontation. Since this strategy requires the union to forego to some extent a deviant union member's rights, union cooperation in such a program is doubtful *unless* the union is fully aware of the assumptions underlying constructive confrontation and of the long-run gains. The definitive nature of the strategy may be attractive to union officials bothered by the definitional ambiguity of most programs. In any event, frank communication between union and management during program development is essential to success.

INITIATING UNION-MANAGEMENT COOPERATION

It appears that the cooperative *potential* is great enough that the future will see an increase in the number of joint programs. The Director of the AFL-CIO Community Services has said: "For in our passion for fair play . . . we are eager to participate in any program that attempts to treat this problem fairly" (Perlis, 1958:536). He has recently voiced similar sentiments about drug dependency in general (Perlis, 1970). Pat Greathouse, vice-president of the United Automobile, Aerospace and Agricultural Implement Workers of America, is a specific example of a union leader showing interest and willingness to explore cooperative efforts (Greathouse, 1969). We have encountered managements who are equally willing. In many instances, however, neither side seems to have thought of making a simple gesture toward the other.

Joint explorations with alcohol and drug-abuse organizations about what can be done are open to both management and labor. A pattern for such exploratory talks formed when business agents of the Amalgamated Clothing Workers engaged in regular dialogues with the staff of a mental health center (Weiner, 1967). Company medical departments, the National Council on Alcoholism, and the AFL–CIO Community Services Department are also readily available for assistance. *Early* involvement of both sides cannot be overemphasized. "A sharing of responsibilities does not necessarily mean that management must have the full concurrence of the union. . . . No new action, however, is taken by management without a thorough discussion with the key union people" (Whyte, 1969:520).

"Dual loyalty" provides a base for education within the union about why the union cooperates with management. We have observed such educational programs in a large international union and have seen the extent to which suspicions of collusion were sharply reduced. Finally, both sides can influence community agencies to provide effective rehabilitation services.

Successfully influencing management and union officials calls for a mixture of intuition, luck, and flexible preparation. However, our research group's observations provide a model for attempting such influence. Since union opposition can be the Achilles' heel of a company program, the strategy calls for first "stacking the cards" in favor of approaching those situations with the highest likelihood of joint union-management cooperation, demonstrating alcohol and drug abuse to be problems in which each has a stake. Chances for success increase if the industry is large and uniform as opposed to one dominated by many small shops or contractors. The fit increases more if a management does not have a history of paternalism and if the union lacks a militant history. Similarly, opportunity increases if the two sides previously resolved critical events jointly (e.g. job transfers following automation). Chances are likewise better if union leadership rejects the notion that labor relations should be one of conflict and if top management does *not* see its prerogatives as sacred. A stable union, operating without divisive internal politics, adds to the likelihood of success. So does a collectively bargained national contract that includes provisions for joint union-management committees. The ability of both union and management to obtain support of lower-level personnel moves toward the cooperative ideal, especially if the union is a professional or a clerical one, and if neither of the two sides is too powerful or too weak vis-a-vis the other. The ideal model is complete if there are close personal relations between members of both sides. "Stacking the deck" in attempting to assure success with the first company may also produce a "snowball" effect on other companies in the community, e.g. a model of success may simply induce other trials.

In closing, we offer several suggestions for union officers in different types of structural situations. Where there is no formal program in a work organization, union officials can familiarize themselves with community facilities, private physicians who treat deviant drinkers and drug users, clinics, and Alcoholics Anonymous groups. The AFL–CIO Community Services has initiated and actively supports a Union Counsellor Training Program, available in many areas (Andrus, 1971).

Where an exclusively management-based program is in operation, the union can make its greatest contribution through its shop stewards. Because of the close relations of stewards with the rank and file, they can recognize deviant drinking and drug use, support the supervisor in the confrontation of the employee, and encourage the employee to seek treatment if necessary.

Unions which try to carry out their own programs have several community facilities available to them in the form of local alcoholism and drug-abuse councils, mental health councils, or local medical societies. The union can enlist the aid of these agencies and obtain help and advice at no cost. A union program might benefit from the leadership of formerly deviant union members. These individuals are in excellent positions to understand the problems of deviant drinkers and drug users.

Increased communication and education are the key elements determining the success of joint union-management programs. Such joint efforts show great promise, but they also have many potential problems. Thus general education about alcohol and drug problems and their control is essential and can be appropriately included in typical training. Likewise, as much understanding as possible could be injected into the use of disciplinary and grievance procedures, should these become necessary. Employee welfare should remain the primary consideration.

IX

Therapeutic Alternatives for
Deviant Drinkers and Drug Users

WHEN the constructive confrontation strategy is implemented early and used effectively, referral to "formal" therapy is often unnecessary; but some individuals will be unresponsive to constructive confrontation for a variety of reasons: continued deviance and cover-up after confrontation, physical addiction at the time of employment, or failure in early identification so that the employee is heavily dependent upon alcohol or drugs before attention is drawn to his deviance. In such circumstances referral to a treatment program may be necessary to return the employee to effective functioning.

In this chapter we focus on two therapeutic alternatives which minimize discontinuity in the job role: Alcoholics Anonymous for the addicted drinker and methadone-maintenance for the heroin addict. Both of these methods show promise of reducing disruptive impact and permanent impairment of the employee's life. We also consider very briefly other possible strategies to be used should these methods prove unfeasible. We pay little attention to a range of other therapies which seem unrealistic in light of the greater availability and practicality of the methods which allow the worker to stay on the job. Finally, we briefly consider the therapeutic alternatives in the instances of amphetamine and barbiturate addiction.

TREATMENT OF THE DEVIANT DRINKER:
ALCOHOLICS ANONYMOUS

Alcoholics Anonymous is the single most effective form of "therapy" for the chronic deviant drinker. It is available in nearly every locality; involves simple and straightforward referral of deviant drinkers; and is a type of therapeutic activity which illustrates some of the basic sociological principles considered throughout this book. Because of its unique features, the structure and function of Alcoholics Anonymous must be described in a detail which also highlights its advantages and disadvantages in producing and maintaining abstinence* in developed or developing alcohol addicts (Trice, 1958; Gellman, 1964).

A.A. is a fellowship of compulsive adult drinkers who have joined together to abstain from alcohol use. The organization was formed by problem drinkers and does not involve professional therapists. Despite this lay leadership, it has apparently achieved a success rate which surpasses those of professional therapies (Trice, *et al.*, 1969). The interaction between members of A.A. takes place at both open public meetings and closed meetings which are strictly for members. Members frankly narrate their experiences with alcohol and the severe problems which they developed. They explain how the A.A. program helped them to achieve sobriety, with the goal that this sharing of experiences will encourage others to attempt abstinence. Essential to the group's functioning is its web of close interaction. In addition to regular meetings, informal contacts between members often occur over lunch, after work, or at informal social activities. Contacts between members are available around the clock.

A.A. contradicts most traditional models of organizational functioning. For example, because of the intense member interaction, one would expect strong "boundary maintenance" (efforts to differentiate insiders from outsiders), but this is not the case. Membership in A.A. depends solely upon whether a deviant drinker says that he is a member. One would expect such "closeness" to call for a high degree of organization; however, A.A. has no officers, no hierarchy, and no dues. Local secretaries are necessary, but their tenure is usually short.

As an organization, A.A. has a single purpose: to help problem drinkers stay away from alcohol. Continual efforts are necessary to prevent the organization from embracing any other cause, and this emphasis has kept A.A. apart from temperance or political movements. The A.A. method may be demonstrated through a description of a typical open meeting.

> On a Friday night in a small midwestern city, members gather at a large suburban brick house which is the A.A. clubhouse. Some are wearing casual sport clothes, while others are dressed more conservatively. A group of people still in work clothes walk from the bus stop toward the house

---

* A.A. members typically use the term "sobriety" rather than abstinence, implying that successful affiliation involves more than not using alcohol. This terminology does, however, draw attention away from the fact that abstinence is an absolute requisite of being a successful A.A. member.

for the 8 p.m. meeting. However, as one member put it, "We never start them; we have to do some coffee klatching first."

In the meeting room people stand around and talk in small groups. One man describes his reaction to telling his "story" last week to patients at a mental hospital: "I saw myself as I used to be, sitting right there in the front row." In another group a woman is recapitulating last Saturday night's party saying, "We had a hilarious time and all of it without any booze."

Approximately sixty persons have assembled when a man at the speaker's stand calls for a moment of silence to be used as each person sees fit. He then begins, "My name is Jim P. and I am an alcoholic," going on to explain the general nature of the fellowship. As chairman of the "meeting," Jim has invited two members of a new group in a nearby community to speak.

"My name is Dave L. and I am an alcoholic," begins the first. His anecdotes are embellished with frank humor, and laughter from the group interrupts him frequently. In becoming addicted to alcohol he had gone from being manager of a chain grocery store to working as an itinerant laborer. His family had forsaken him, and numerous times he had heard himself branded as hopeless by a hospital ward physician. Twice he had almost died from delirium tremens (D.T.'s), but he did not "hit bottom" and feel a need to reform until his third attack.

Dave had previously scorned the idea of A.A., thinking that the various members who had talked to him during his hospital days were merely "shooting angles." He finally went to a meeting and was surprised to learn that as an alcoholic he was "sick" but could still be respectable. Dave stated that he had finally, with difficulty, accepted the idea of a "higher power" and finishes his story dramatically, telling the group that he had found in A.A. a "bunch of real friends — twice as good as my drinking buddies who pumped me for every cent I had."

Dave is followed by a female speaker who tells a similar story of downward social progression as her control over alcohol use decreased. She said she had had no difficulty in accepting the program once she had admitted to herself that her drinking had defeated her.

After her story is finished, the chairman concludes with remarks concerning anonymity. A.A., he explains, makes every effort to protect the names of its members and insists on anonymity at all times and places. After these remarks, he asks everyone to stand and together they repeat the Lord's Prayer. The formal meeting is over and once again the coffee klatching resumes, lasting far into the night for some (Trice, 1958:109).

The format at closed meetings generally involves a more informal, very frank discussion of how the program works. At these meetings members frequently discuss their more intimate personal problems, a shared experience which increases the intensity of the fellowship.

One of the few formalized aspects of A.A. is a written set of "Twelve Steps" which set forth the goals of the organization and of its individual members. These Steps are suggestions for progressive abstinence. The suggestions were formulated by early A.A. members who attempted to assess the specific steps they had taken to reach sobriety within the context of fellowship. The Twelve Steps are as follows:

1. We admitted we were powerless over alcohol — that our lives had become unmanageable.

2. We came to believe that a Power greater than ourselves could restore us to sanity.

3. We made a decision to turn our will and our lives over to the care of God as we understood Him.

4. We made a searching and fearless moral inventory of ourselves.

5. We admitted to God, to ourselves, and to another human being the exact nature of our wrongs.

6. We were entirely ready to have God remove all these defects of character.

7. We humbly asked Him to remove our shortcomings.

8. We made a list of all persons we had harmed and become willing to make amends to them all.

9. We directed amends to such people wherever possible, except when to do so would injure them or others.

10. We continued to take personal inventory and when we were wrong promptly admitted it.

11. We sought through prayer and meditation to improve our conscious contact with God, as we understood him, praying only for knowledge of His Will for us and the power to carry that out.

12. Having had a spiritual awakening as the result of these steps we tried to carry this message to alcoholics and practice these principles in all our affairs.

One of the most bitterly debated points in the development of the Twelve Steps was their spiritual reference. Atheist and agnostic members challenged the concept of God and lodged objections to the doctrinal implications of certain of the steps. Slowly the debate was resolved through the use of the phrases "a Power greater than ourselves" and "God, as we understand Him." Thus, the organization definitely has a spiritual base, although relatively unspecified.

According to A.A., these Steps parallel the psychological changes which the deviant drinker undergoes as he moves toward sobriety. The First Step relieves the deviant drinker from needing to demonstrate that he can drink like others. Instead of grudgingly complying to abstinence, he completely surrenders. This surrender is followed, in the next two Steps, by the realization that some form of outside help is needed to maintain abstinence. In the Fourth Step the deviant drinker tries to understand the web of rationalizations that he created in order to justify his deviant drinking. The next Steps may lead to anxiety reduction through the sharing of emotional difficulties with others and to the reduction of guilt by restitution to those he has injured through his excessive drinking.

The final Step is regarded as the zenith of A.A. activity. Only through willingness to help others can the organization reach its goals while maintaining an interpersonal fellowship. Through "Twelfth Step Work" the A.A. member makes himself available to the novice as a consultant and a companion and thereby renews his own spiritual experiences.

The authors of the Twelve Steps clearly assumed that deviant drinkers resist pressure and authority in any form. Thus the Steps were labeled "suggestions." This permissive tone has come to pervade A.A. as an organization, and the Steps are phrased in terms of "we did" rather than "you must." On the other hand, conformity to the "authority" of the Steps is necessary for success in A.A.

A.A.'s strategy stems from the earlier established Oxford Groups, a semireligious movement which emphasized confessions, interpersonal sharing of emotional problems, unselfishness, and prayer to a Supreme Being as conceived by the individual. In 1934, Bill W., a New York stockbroker and alcohol addict, was introduced to an Oxford Group by a friend who had found that he could stay away from alcohol by attending these meetings and following the Group's precepts. Bill W. attended these meetings and found that he also could remain sober after experiencing what he termed a spiritual awakening.

Bill promptly tried to bring other problem drinkers into the Oxford Group, but failed because of what he later called "too much preaching." His doctor advised altering his methods by first convincing deviant drinkers that they suffered from a physical allergy to alcohol as well as a psychological obsession with it, reserving the treatment's spiritual aspects for later. Early in 1935, Bill tried this modified approach with an addicted physician, Dr. Bob S., and was successful. The two then employed these tactics with others and the first A.A. group emerged from their efforts.

As part of a drive to diffuse the A.A. concept and attract a potential membership, the early members published their "stories" in a book entitled *Alcoholics Anonymous* which created much interest in the organization. After a national magazine published a favorable article in 1941, groups of deviant drinkers across the country acquired the book and began to hold meetings.

Since the founders wished to avoid bureaucracy, A.A. had no organizational mechanics to guide this sudden membership expansion. From 1942 to 1946. policies evolved through trial and error and the co-founders became concerned about linking the various member groups, by this time located throughout the world. Thus the Board of Trustees (composed of both alcoholics and nonalcoholics and formed in the late 1930's as a single formal mechanism for guidance) authorized a General Service Conference, an annual international meeting of elected representatives.

This conference has proved successful. It does not have authority over local groups, but the viewpoints about policy problems which are debated are communicated to local groups, which then accept or ignore them. Thus the central leadership is strictly "by suggestion" in a pattern similar to the Twelve Steps.

Since A.A. successfully developed within American society, it is helpful to examine its incorporation of important American value orientations (Williams, 1970). First, the organization and its program are totally pragmatic. The organization and its members pay little attention to scientific theories about deviant drinking and alcoholism and in this respect mirror the American emphasis on practicality and efficiency, as well as the cultural emphasis on action rather than contemplation. This pragmatism is also reflected in the simplified approach to spiritual experiences, a pattern comparable to the behavior of many Americans who seek such experiences outside formal religious groups (e.g. various fraternal orders with religious overtones). American society likewise is oriented to humanitarianism and to giving transgressors a second chance. This is precisely A.A.'s goal as outlined in the Twelve Steps. From pre-Revolutionary days, American society has been suspicious of established authority. Such suspicion remains today in the negative connotations of the term "bureaucracy." A.A.'s traditional and continuing efforts to resist the creation of hierarchies, central coordination, or other forms of formal organization tap into this American value. The American values of individualism and personal autonomy are reflected in the nature of the Twelve Steps and by the fact that recommendations from the Board of Trustees are suggestions rather than directives.

Finally, and perhaps most significantly, A.A.'s pattern directly taps overlapping American values of achievement and self-control. Through exemplifying these values, the A.A. member is able to employ his past in such a way that his social standing may eventually be regained and even enhanced. This is the process of A.A. delabeling and relabeling which calls for a somewhat detailed explanation (Trice and Roman, 1970b).

THERAPEUTIC ALTERNATIVES

As discussed in Chapter One, the labeled deviant may undergo such changes in self-concept and patterns of association that he comes to play the societal role assigned to a particular type of deviant. The performance of this role may eventually become socially embedded as his own and other's adaptations to the deviant behavior continue. This adaptation in turn increases the consensus of those around him that he indeed *is* a deviant. The .more widely he is labeled as deviant, the more stigmatized he becomes, continually decreasing his acceptance in normal society. Most treatment agencies try to reverse the process so that the person who ceases his deviant actions becomes reaccepted as normal. Regardless of treatment success, most of these delabeling attempts, except for A.A.'s, are unsuccessful. Other efforts neither remove the stigmatic label nor replace it with one that is socially acceptable.

A.A.'s successful "delabeling" is intimately tied to the pattern of public confession in the A.A. "stories." It would appear that someone who publicly admits that he was at one time "a sidewalk drunk" and "down and out" is being extremely brave and courageous — or extremely stupid by risking his future reputation with such admissions. This type of performance, however, taps directly into two essential American values: self-control and the achievement of upward social mobility. The A.A. member admits that he once lost his self-control, but his successful affiliation with A.A. indicates that he regained it. Furthermore, his exercise of self-control appears to exceed the level of most people's similar accomplishments. To have achieved control over the use of a substance which he previously found extremely rewarding is seen by others as reflective of superior strength and decency, despite the fact that at other times in his life he had apparently lost every vestige of self-control.

Many A.A. members incidentally achieve upward social mobility along with achieving abstinence. Unlike most people, who have not experienced great downward or upward mobility, the A.A. member went to "the bottom" and "lost everything" in a social sense, but regained it by being a successful A.A. affiliate. Not only has he returned to respectability, but he has done so without the aid of alcohol, which a large number of normals regard as a necessary aid to maintaining their own stability. Seen in this light, it seems plausible that A.A. encourages affiliates to create stories of an earlier life sharply different from their present status; thus, in some instances A.A. "stories" may be exaggerations of the truth. It would be quite ineffective to report to the fellowship that one had lost control of his drinking and had to stay away from his job a few days a week for several years, but had never lost his job, was never in jail, was never on Skid Row, was never hospitalized, was never deserted by his family, and never had the DT's. The extent to which the member can lengthen his mobility trip is directly related to the social approval he obtains when his story becomes known. Prestige may be obtained both within A.A. and in the community. These processes are most subtle, and occur in spite of the fact that the typical A.A. member appears to be labeling himself as *once* being weak and helpless.

The A.A. member may also gain social approval because his behavior represents powerful testimony for the middle-class way of life. By reporting experiences of "hedonistic debilitation," the individual is saying he experienced a way of life totally contrary to dominant middle-class orientations. The fact that the individual who joined A.A. chooses to forsake this way of life for sobriety and respectability is strongly supportive of community values. Unlike almost everyone else, the A.A. member has been "to the other side" and tasted the life of hedonism and irresponsibility. He reports a "trip" into what is essentially the underworld of sin and degradation; but by the fact of his return he shows he prefers the life of diligence and respectability.

This tapping of cherished community values appears to allow the A.A. member to divest himself to the negative connotation of his previously deviant label. Not only is he delabeled as an "alcoholic" but he is re-labeled as a successful A.A. member. Empirical data are lacking on the actual extent to which A.A. members are destigmatized in terms of community reactions, but this type of affiliation apparently allows one to regain the social status and trust enjoyed by nondeviants. The observed willingness with which successful A.A. members inform others of this membership (often without any solicitation) supports this argument.

Such delabeling is exceptional when contrasted with the careers of other types of deviants (Miller, 1964; Roth and Eddy, 1967; Goffman, 1963; Edgerton, 1967). In cases of other behavior disorders, it appears almost impossible to divest oneself of the deviant label once it has been obtained and once the community becomes aware of its existence. Whereas deviant drinkers may be able to make a "round trip" into and out of a deviant status, other types of labels may be only one-way tickets. For former mental patients, membership in organizations such as Recovery, Incorporated, has been typically ineffective for destigmatization (Wechsler, 1960; Sagarin, 1969). The only sure way the former mental patient can hope to escape stigma is to cover up the fact that he was once labeled. Cover-up, however, does not affect the deviant's self-concept, and his acceptance of negative attributions from others often continues to occur. The inability of former mental patients to destigmatize themselves should not be overlooked as a factor accounting for the high rates of readmission of mental patients.

The visibility of deviant alcohol use is another important factor in A.A.'s successful delabeling. If a deviant drinker claims that he is "off the bottle," there are outward signs that this is the case; he can hardly say that he is not drunk and at the same time be intoxicated. Since most people have experienced and viewed the effects of alcohol, they feel competent to judge the legitimacy of the "dry alcoholic's" claims. The mental patient, however, cannot so easily display the signs of non-deviancy simply because these signs are not clear. His malady was in large part confined "within his head" and there is no outward and visible sign that this disorder has been cured other than the fact of his discharge from the hospital. Such discharges are invariably accompanied by the description "improved" rather than "cured." Thus, the former mental patient may carry with him the possibility of unpredictable and potentially dangerous behavior. Whereas discharge from the hospital could conceivably serve to delabel mental patients, the publicity that accompanies crimes and other deviant acts committed by former mental patients has made it ineffective (Scheff, 1966). By contrast, regular A.A. membership is an effective means for societal readmission.

Effective as A.A. may be, it is not without shortcomings which make it inappropriate for some deviant drinkers. Obviously, some find affiliation very difficult. It may be argued that a new self-concept and even a new life organization are necessary for a long-term deviant drinker to re-adapt successfully to society without the use of alcohol. This change in self-concept may be expedited by A.A. through guilt reduction, accomplished partly by the deviant's adopting the attitude that alcohol abuse is an illness rather than immoral behavior. Self-concept changes are also affected by the group solidarity which pervades A.A. and by participation in "Twelfth Step Work" in which the individual actually tries to help others. Thus the individual who successfully enters the organization finds himself within a network of mutual obligations; he can share emotional problems and assistance so that his need for alcohol as an aid to adaptation may be permanently reduced or eliminated. The benefits of these structural supports, however, are not available until affiliation occurs.

Research on affiliation with A.A. has revealed that successful affiliates regard themselves as persons who can easily share their basic emotional reactions with others and adapt to the casual "give and take" that occurs both before and after A.A. meetings (Trice, 1957b). The unsuccessful affiliates rated significantly lower on these characteristics. Apparently a portion of these interpersonal skills are learned, since successful affiliates were found to have had considerable previous experience participating in informal groups; however, stable psychological factors are probably also involved. Another analysis revealed that successful affiliates showed a significantly stronger emotional need for affiliation as indicated by projective tests (Trice, 1959). A substantial degree of affiliative concern in the personality of a deviant drinker may increase his potential for group affiliations, particularly with a group which emphasizes a tight web of interpersonal relationships.

A before-and-after study of the effectiveness of hospital-based therapy for alcohol addicts included consideration of successful A.A. affiliation after release (Trice and Roman, 1970a). The successful affiliates showed friendliness, geniality, and outgoingness, characteristics which mesh well with the emphasis upon interaction predominant in A.A. They also were significantly more introspective and guilt-prone than those who did not affiliate, a trait which may be appropriate to the frequent public confessions that are prevalent in A.A. meetings. Finally, successful affiliates had a higher degree of physical stability at the time of their affiliation attempt, indicating a minimal level of physical functioning was necessary for successful A.A. participation.

The data from these studies also indicate that the successful affiliates felt greater emotional conflict about their drinking behavior and had definitely perceived it as a threat to status in the family, occupation, and community. Nonaffiliates associated the "pleasures of living" with their heavy drinking experiences. They did not perceive blackouts, tremors, or, in some cases, even delirium tremens as indications of illness, but rather as the price for a good time. They saw their drinking behavior as a source of prestige and status among their peers. The variations in attitudes revealed in these data, collected after the affiliation experience, may be, at least in part, an artifact of the attitude changes accompanying A.A. membership. Aside from this, the eventually successful A.A. affiliates appear to have had ambivalences toward alcohol use at the time of the affiliation attempts.

An earlier research study indicated that progression into the middle state of alcohol addiction is usually necessary for successful A.A. affiliation (Trice and Wahl, 1958). This finding emphasizes the frequent irrelevancy of A.A. for the typical "deviant drinker." Our later study also showed that extensive experiences with labeling agents, indicated by numerous hospitalizations, were more apt to characterize the successful affiliates (Trice and Roman, 1970a).

We also included consideration of the different experiences which had accompanied the affiliation attempts of those who were successful and unsuccessful. The unsuccessful affiliates, significantly, reported having friends and relatives who had stopped drinking of their own volition. Having such willpower models, these individuals apparently saw imitation of this behavior as more desirable than affiliation with an unknown group. The successful affiliates did not report acquaintance with such models.

Among other obstacles to affiliation reported by the unsuccessful affiliates was a feeling that A.A. members were insincere. Sponsorship by an active A.A. member is vital to the organization's techniques; the unsuccessful affiliates reported either that they were unsponsored or that, if sponsored, their relationship with the sponsor was very superficial. Certain A.A. groups may attain such an intense level of interdependence that the acceptance of an outsider is difficult. If the newcomer does not have sponsorship, successful affiliation may be doubtful. A poor sponsorship relation, however, may reflect the newcomer's lack of interactional skills.

The characteristics of an individual's other affiliations when he attempts to affiliate with A.A. are also related to his success. A significant proportion of the unsuccessful affiliates reported that they were still actively engaged in deviant-drinking practices within well defined and tightly organized drinking groups the first time they went to an A.A. meeting. Consequently, the attractiveness of A.A. affiliation was greatly reduced. The unsuccessful affiliates also reported that they received no support in their affiliation attempt from family and friends, this lack of support being in contrast to the successful affiliates. In some cases, however, family groups had reacted to the individual's attempt to affiliate with A.A. in an overprotective manner, thus reducing the possibility of an affiliation success. Apparently, in these cases significant others were reacting negatively to the label of "alcoholic" implied by A.A. membership. Typically, successful affiliates attended A.A. meetings alone for the first few weeks, but were then accompanied by a wife or girl friend at subsequent meetings.

To summarize, despite a policy of no membership selection, A.A. affiliation may be extremely difficult for those with certain personality features and those from lower social statuses. The type of interpersonal skills required for effective interaction, particularly *intense* interaction, may be lacking among those from lower-class statuses. Data on unsuccessful affiliates clearly indicate this kind of personality profile.

Second, as discussed above, an implicit requirement for successful affiliation is some degree of social distance between the deviant underworld and one's normal social status. A person who is in a low social status when he begins his "deviant career" and is at the same status level after he "dries out" may not be able to exemplify the ideals of

A.A. membership. It is assumed that the successful affiliate will be both sober and respectable, and some lower-class statuses are simply not respectable in society's view.

Third, the middle-class assumptions of the A.A. program may prevent the successful affiliation of minority group members whose subcultural backgrounds do not provide them with the skill necessary for this type of participation. Likewise certain minorities may have internalized norms of conduct which forbid such apparent public self-degradation.

Despite these shortcomings, A.A. may be the most suitable agency for referral of employees who are unresponsive to constructive confrontation or who desire help in curbing their drinking. Referrals should be made with care and certainly should not be substituted for use of the confrontation strategy. Given the evidence regarding the necessity of numerous negative alcohol-related experiences for successful affiliation (Trice and Roman, 1970a; Trice and Wahl, 1958), the early-stage deviant drinker revealed through a company-based identification program would likely be a poor A.A. candidate; e.g. he most likely would not see himself as having "hit bottom." On the other hand, the employee with a long series of alcohol-related job disruptions who has lost control of his drinking and is thus unresponsive to constructive confrontation may be ideally suited for the A.A. program.

The voluntarism of the A.A. program is an important consideration in company referral. The employee who is coerced into attendance might not fit with the A.A. program as it has been outlined here. Furthermore, referral of a deviant drinker in control of his drinking might have undesirable labeling effects. Hearing the typical A.A. stories may help him decide he is not as bad off as the A.A. members were before affiliation, and the premature A.A. encounter might encourage further drinking. Thus, constructive confrontation and A.A. referral should be strategically separate from one another, and A.A. referrals should be used only where constructive confrontation fails.

The evidence suggests that the middle- and lower-middle class deviant drinker is a much better candidate than persons from the lower classes. While one need not be concerned with this factor in regard to white-collar workers, the lower level of blue-collar workers who will find A.A. participation difficult is hard to establish. Perhaps the best guide is to take into account the mechanisms of A.A.'s program, asking the question of the similarity between a particular employee's background and the backgrounds of those of the A.A. group. Familiarity with the social-class composition of different A.A. groups in a given locale is thus necessary.

The research reviewed make the personality demands of A.A. quite clear. These demands should be another element in any referral decision. The data, however, do not provide us with a simple objective measure of the "successful affiliate personality," which should be a matter for local judgment.

TREATMENT OF THE DEVIANT DRINKER: OTHER STRATEGIES

Other treatments may be undertaken with individuals who are unresponsive to constructive confrontation and unable to affiliate with A.A. Of the therapies which rely upon dyadic interaction between the patient and a medically trained therapist, the most intense treatment is classical psychoanalysis which assumes that chronic deviant drinking is a symptom of a severe underlying neurosis and that this neurosis must be the primary object of treatment (Knight, 1937). Traditional psychoanalysis hypothesizes that difficult childhood experiences have prevented the adoption of mature adult defense mechanisms; excessive drinking is sometimes seen as fixation at the oral stage of development. This therapy tries to provide the patient with insight into the roots of his deviancy; he then is guided in the development of nonneurotic techniques for managing stress.

A related form of individual therapy is nondirective treatment (Tiebout, 1961; 1965). In this therapy, the patient must realize that alcohol use is beyond his control. Rather than initially confronting the individual with these facts, the therapist allows him to reach this point of surrender at his own speed; it is assumed the patient will retreat from any authoritative behavior by the therapist. The therapist places himself in a nondirective but supportive relation with the patient; and, as the patient moves closer to surrender, the therapist gains increasing control over the situation. In some ways, this treatment resembles a "private A.A." and may involve long-term patient-therapist interaction.

Drug Therapy. Therapies which rely heavily upon the use of drugs have failed when deviant drinkers have stopped using alcohol but have become dependent on drugs. This new addiction typically occurs when physicians inexperienced with alcohol problems prescribe barbiturates or amphetamines. Some tranquilizers such as Librium are, however, extremely valuable in setting the stage for the "talking" types of individual therapy. Thus, most therapists see drugs as adjuncts to therapy rather than as cures for alcohol addiction.

Attention has recently turned to the role of LSD-25 (lysergic acid diethylamide) as a potentially valuable tool in treating alcoholism (Ditman and Whittlesey, 1962; Abramson, 1967). Presumably, the personality changes and insight which accompany certain of these drug experiences reduce the need for alcohol as an alleviator of anxiety. While LSD-users frequently report a long-term reduction in anxiety level, a significant proportion of those who take the drug may have unpleasant experiences which do not help overcome their addiction and may even worsen their personal adjustment. Establishing who might benefit is the nub of the problem. Predictive instruments for preselection have not yet been developed, but appear necessary for any further use of this treatment. Interest in psychedelic therapy waned after an initial surge, and it currently is not widespread.

Conditioned Reflex Therapy. Conditioned-reflex therapy for deviant drinkers usually involves the use of drugs, but in a manner different from that in drug therapy. Conditioned-reflex therapy is based upon Pavlovian principles which hold that an aversion to certain stimuli may be created by associating these stimuli with unpleasant experiences (Voegtlin, 1940; Miller, 1960). Treatment for the deviant drinker attempts to associate an unpleasant experience with the presence of alcohol. Trice describes the procedure as follows:

> In conditioning sessions the patient is first exposed to a maximum of stimuli associated with drinking. Then a nauseant is administered to produce immediate and violent vomiting. Just prior to the onset of the dry heaves (often the subjects do not eat the night before), each patient drinks about four ounces of whiskey of his choice, slowly and one ounce at a time. If the timing is good, the smell, taste, and environmental conditions of the drinking situation will coincide with the extreme discomfort of repeated retchings. Usually the alcoholic is given about eight to ten sessions of approximately thirty to forty-five minutes each. Because individuals vary widely, some persons are conditioned quickly; others do not condition after a dozen sessions. Most, however, leave the experience with a feeling of nausea clearly associated with alcohol. As one patient told the writer, "I couldn't see the beer truck drive down the street without getting the dry heaves." (Trice, 1966:97)

A similar form of treatment involves the drug, Antabuse (Winship, 1957). The patient is required to take a dose of Antabuse regularly. This drug alone causes no reaction, but should the patient take a drink of alcohol he will become violently nauseated and experience difficulty in breathing, headache, rapid heart rate, and severe flushing. The association of these unpleasant effects with alcohol may retard its use and abuse, but the individual must continue to take Antabuse regularly.

It should be noted that both types of conditioned reflex therapy are often used as adjuncts to individual or group therapy; an individual rarely receives these relatively mechanical therapies alone.

Group Therapies. Other than A.A., there are two basic types of group therapy of which the more common is group psychotherapy (Ends and Page, 1957). This therapy emphasizes achieving insight into one's own motivations and shortcomings and learning appropriate skills for effective interpersonal relationships usually through group discussions in which members discuss and criticize each other and themselves. Role-playing techniques, including "psychodramas" in which the individual acts out situations that have been difficult for him, may be employed to improve social effectiveness. These strategies play a prominent role in inpatient treatment.

In a second form of group, the therapeutic community, therapy is similar but much more comprehensive (Jones, 1953; Greenblatt *et al.,* 1957). In this residential setting individuals may live together for all or part of the time. The free flow of communication between patients and staff, patients and patients, and staff and staff is emphasized. As a means of obtaining this communication the typical status and power differences between patients and staff are equalized. This reduction of authority helps the patients to develop more responsibility and to improve their skills in effectively interacting with each other (Milton and Agrin, 1966). Presumably by learning how to live effectively with a group of strangers the individual is prepared for coping more realistically with the problems he encounters in the outside world.

A.A. affiliation is the most effective treatment for deviant drinking and usually allows for job continuity. In addition to having lower success rates and requiring inpatient care, the other treatments we have outlined here (especially individual and group therapy) may assume the same social-class backgrounds and require the same personality skills as A.A. Drug treatments may be less of a problem in this regard, but are usually more costly and disruptive to job continuity. Executive and other high-status deviant drinkers whose status prevents constructive confrontation and who refuse to attempt A.A. affiliation may be employees most suitable for these other strategies.

TREATMENT OF HEROIN ADDICTION:
METHADONE MAINTENANCE

At present professionals concur that addiction to heroin represents the most widespread and serious physiological addiction outside of alcohol. As described previously, the early stage of heroin use may be difficult to detect in an employed population; thus addiction may have already occurred when the deviance is uncovered. In such circumstances constructive confrontation has little chance of effectiveness unless it is used in conjunction with a treatment which aids in withdrawal. Many managements regard prison or mental hospitals as the only appropriate places for heroin addicts. As shown in Chapter Five, however, the degree of role functioning or duration of adequate performance possible while addicted is uncertain. The possibility of functioning addicts remaining in an employee population is a real one, assuming that they have a regular supply of the drug. Addiction among such regular employees calls for more than punitive or rejecting responses; it calls for realistic treatments as outlined below. Until recently, the success rates for drug-addiction treatments were low; however, methadone maintenance and, to a lesser degree, Synanon are treatments which promise job continuity and overall social stability to the heroin addict.

Some evidence does indicate that the heroin habit may be terminated by the addict himself. Data are inadequate on those who "outgrow" their addiction by their mid-thirties (Winick, 1964). Although opinion varies regarding this possibility, at least one study suggests that almost three-quarters may discontinue the use of heroin as they move through adulthood towards middle age (Robins and Murphy, 1967). Another researcher studied six treatment facilities (with 422 male addicts) and found that "many addicts do have long periods of voluntary abstention outside of jails and treatment programs and that the majority during these abstentions make reasonable adjustments to the working world and square life" (Waldorf, 1970:228). Louria (1968) estimates that the voluntary abstinence rate among older addicts at the Lexington Narcotic Rehabilitation Unit may be as high as 25 percent (although almost 95 percent of the people discharged from that institution use heroin again within six months). Although admittedly vague, these data indicate that the idea of permanent addiction might be a myth and might act as a self-fulfilling prophecy among addicts themselves.

The methadone maintenance treatment has become widely known, is currently popular, and has sprung up rapidly throughout the country. A synthetic narcotic, methadone, substitutes for opiates by preventing abstinence distress and thereby eliminating the desire for heroin. The most controversial feature is that the method continues the addiction, with one drug substituted for another. Although methadone is an addictive drug, it is more amenable to medical control than heroin and since its effects last longer, a daily oral dose is usually adequate. Methadone produces few side effects compared to heroin, creating minimal "high" in experienced addicts when taken orally. According to Nyswander and Dole (1967) it acts as a "narcotic blockade" not only obstructing the desire for heroin, but also reducing or eliminating sought-after heroin effects should the patient slip. According to these physicians (an internist and psychiatrist), "The most dramatic effect of this treatment has been the disappearance of narcotic hunger" (Dole and Nyswander, 1965). Nyswander describes the discovery of maintenance doses as an accident which occurred in treating two addicts on extremely high doses of morphine: "We found out that methadone blocked all other narcotics. They couldn't *feel* the effects of another narcotic while they were on methadone. Accordingly there was no craving for heroin" (Hentoff, 1965). Thus developed addicts who are methadone patients can go on working. While intravenous injection of methadone may create a high, oral use greatly reduces impact effect of the drug and other mood effects are usually negligible. There may be as many as 25,000 addicts now on methadone and many of these will seek jobs. Such patients would probably present few employment problems since their addiction would probably be secret and their supply costs amazingly low. Where an addict secures employment through a methadone clinic, his treatment success depends, in large measure, on employer understanding and rejection of the dope-fiend mythology.

Methadone is cheap — a week's supply may cost the addict $2.00 while heroin can run as high as $100.00 a day. Furthermore, it seems to reduce some of the social side effects of heroin. The first group of 22 patients studied by Dole and Nyswander reportedly were able to withstand pressures from addict friends, had stopped dreaming about drugs, and had "even become so indifferent to narcotics as to forget to take a scheduled dose of medication when busy at home" (Nyswander and Dole, 1967). A subsequent report on 128 patients who had undergone methadone treatment for periods of six months to three years indicated seventy percent were "regularly employed or engaged in study. . . . They have abandoned the 'typical addict psyche' and have become responsible persons, able to return safely to their former environment where drug pushers accost them" without the danger of slipping (Gunne, 1966). Nyswander and Dole reported in 1967 that "A three year study involving more than 200 patient-years of medical and behavioral data has shown this procedure to be consistently effective in stopping heroin addiction." Drug use was objectively checked by regular urine tests. The researchers estimated that three-fourths of the patients in treatment at least six months were productively functioning at work or in school. They also reported that the addicts engaged in substantially less crime since they did not need to steal to finance the cost of heroin.

The most recent evaluation data on New York City methadone maintenance contained information on employment, education, crime, patient retention, discharges, medical safety, and mixed drug abuse. The researchers concluded that "82 percent of all patients admitted to the program during 1964–1970 can be considered successes. They have remained in treatment and are no longer addicted to heroin or committing crimes. About two-thirds of the patients who remain in the program are employed, in school, or functioning as homemakers after three months of treatment" (Joseph and Dole, 1970). Fifteen percent were clear failures.

According to Joseph and Dole (1970), criminal convictions dropped from 52 convictions per 100 man-years of addiction (felonies, misdemeanors, and petty offenses) to 5.8 convictions per 100 treatment years, a 90 percent decrease. No undesirable long-term side effects have been revealed. Physical exams and laboratory studies of patients for periods of up to six years have showed normal physiological functioning and autopsies of death from ordinary causes showed no evidence of methadone toxicity. Likewise no significant changes in mood or perception were detected. Babies born to methadone patients showed no adverse effects.

Probably the most objective assessment of the therapy comes from the Methadone Maintenance Evaluation Committee of Rockefeller University (1968:3):

> For those patients selected and treated as described, this program can be considered a success. It does appear that those who remain in the program have on the whole become productive members of society, in contrast to their previous experience and have, to a large extent, become self-supporting and demonstrate less and less anti-social behavior. It should be emphasized that these are volunteers, who are older than the average street addict and may be more highly motivated. Consequently, generalizations of the results of this program in this population to the general addict population probably are not justified.

Eddy (1970:25) also emphasizes that "until recommended control studies have been instituted and evaluated, conclusions cannot be drawn in respect to general application, nor plans formulated for broad extension of the program as an established treatment modality."

The typical methadone maintenance program takes place in three phases. In the first, carefully selected addicts are stabilized with the dosage of methadone necessary to counteract the amount of heroin used. The first week of hospitalization includes a job-placement study and medical and psychiatric consultations, after which the patients are free to move about outside the hospital with mild supervision. During the second phase the addicts become outpatients, but return to the treatment center every day for a dose of methadone and, in some programs, to provide a urine specimen. During these visits help is available in obtaining jobs, housing, and training. Several methadone treatments are being conducted without any supportive service to determine the necessity of ancillary services (Severo, 1970).

In phase three, addicts are encouraged and helped to be self-supporting. The stabilization dosage of methadone used in this phase tends to be around 100 mg. a day, which usually remains constant as a tolerance for methadone does not develop. The goal of phase three is for the patient to have a job, stable residence, a bank account, friends, and plans for the future which need no support from counselors. Einstein (1971) has edited a recent volume describing numerous variations and additions to this basic scheme.

Obviously, this approach generates a primary addiction to methadone itself, despite its goal of rehabilitation. Thus it raises the ideological issue of the undesirability of any addiction. It is argued that methadone addiction is much milder, more easily controlled, and permits normal functioning without stealing to pay for "fixes." It also deprives the beginner of the immediate "peak thrill" (Eddy, 1970) and of the needle ritual that can have such psychological significance. Methadone maintenance is clearly a lesser drug dependency, but nonetheless it is a drug dependency. Some have tried to counter this problem by eventually withdrawing the patient from methadone (Isbell, 1955). Joseph and Dole (1971:44), however, regard this as highly undesirable: "During the past six years, 350 patients have been withdrawn from methadone. . . . In every case, upon completion of withdrawal, a craving for heroin returned regardless of the patient's social or psychological adjustment." Especially relevant is the degree of involvement in an addict subculture. O'Donnell found that index of involvement was significantly associated with the tendency to relapse to drug use (1969).

Although more than 60 methadone centers had applied to the federal government as of July 1970 (Severo, 1970), numerous critics challenge the method's effectiveness. Nyswander and Dole (1967) indicate that the street addict needs help from a therapeutic team that can deal effectively with the social and legal problems he faces. A report by Hicks (1971) and a psychiatric opinion by Kiev (1970) urge this strategy. Rubington (1969:334) points out that "the major social barrier to abstinence is the expectation that persons who attempt to stop drug use will fail." Without substantial contact with treatment-oriented persons and regular monitoring, the drug therapy may not produce the results anticipated. Its long-term physical effects have yet to be determined, although existing studies have detected no unfortunate side effects save constipation.

More specific criticism of the program focuses upon its voluntary nature: "The program is open only to volunteers, and of those who volunteer, approximately 50 percent are rejected. Thus one must be well motivated to begin with, and even such motivation does not guarantee acceptance into the program. . . . It is clear that in its present form it can reach only 20 percent of the addict population at most" (Louria, 1968: 180). Recently, however, some programs have become less selective: "As one treatment program demonstrated its success, and the demand for treatment increased, the criteria were relaxed. The age limit has been lowered to 18, with a minimum two-year addiction history, and the upper limit has been removed. Applicants with major health complications, mixed drug abuse problems, and histories of mental illness are now admitted to treatment" (Joseph and Dole, 1970:43).

Addicts clearly representative of the addict population have not been systematically followed through a methadone maintenance program. Furthermore, Louria (1968:180) insists that the claims of reduction in criminal behavior are exaggerated. He described a program which failed "before it ever got started because well motivated addicts could not be recruited. . .," and a Canadian program in which 321 addicts started with the treatment via methadone, 264 subsequently dropped out, and 57 could legitimately be characterized as successes. It seems quite probable that, as in treatments for alcoholics, there are a certain constellation of factors which make for success and that methadone is clearly not going to work for all addicts. In addition, "Cheating," using heroin or abusing other drugs while "on" methadone, has been reported (Chambers and Taylor, 1970).

Other difficulties with methadone center on the fact that it can provide a high when administered intravenously. Despite precautions, illegal traffic in methadone for such use has developed to an unknown extent. Thus an addiction to methadone is possible among persons not addicted to opiates while the opiate addict may find it an attractive substitute for heroin's high if there are opportunities for injection. Methadone is administered mixed with orange juice to prevent such traffic, has nonetheless developed, according to the Food and Drug Administration (Carey, 1971). Given this drawback in addition to the problem of substitute addiction, it has been recognized that methadone does not represent a final solution to heroin addiction. Extensive research is underway to create drugs which curb physical craving for a much longer period than methadone, in which successful maintenance usually depends on a daily dosage (Carey, 1971). Attempts are likewise being made to develop heroin antagonists which are nonaddictive. Nonetheless, methadone has beyond doubt produced one highly desirable result: It has brought about a reinvolvement of the scientist and the medical profession in the opiate dependency problem; no longer is there solely a legal, punitive approach.

TREATMENT OF HEROIN ADDICTION: SYNANON

A second form of treatment for drug addition resembles A.A. in some ways, but is different in others. Synanon is made up of groups of drug addicts who have devised a live-in, self-help program whereby they hope to stay off drugs (Yablonsky, 1965). It consists of an in-house routine (24 hours a day) in which older members of the Synanon house engage in stringent, abrasive, and often brutal group confrontations with newly accepted members and with each other. Their aim is to break through the mass of accumulated rationalizations and force the individual addict to recognize himself as he really is. The prospective member must be willing to submit to a Synanon group that will deliberately indoctrinate him with a deep hatred for drug addiction and drug addicts. He is first subjected to a series of blunt admission interviews that give a flavor of the process he will encounter once admitted and make him aware of the lack of tolerance for drugs or drug use among members. Upon acceptance as a new member, the addict is constantly reminded of the *intense* singleness of purpose that characterizes the group — their determination to refrain from drugs, alcohol, and crime. Synanon has no recreational program, no vocational education, no "adjustment" goals or related objectives; its only reason for existence is to provide a mechanism for scathing confrontations of one drug addict by another in a mutual effort to stay "clean." It tries to change members' total way of life drastically. The program is different from Alcoholics Anonymous in that it is "a total institution." As in intense indoctrination into military units such as the Marines and into monastic religious orders, older Synanon members insist upon denunciation of one's former associates, in this instance the drug subculture. In group sessions, referred to as "pull-ups," the new member is vigorously downgraded, with the importance of group conformity underscored. For example, Volkman and Cressey (1963:136) describe how the newcomer may well be strongly denounced for "*not* squealing" rather than "squealing."

All members of the group live and work together, with the exception of experienced, long-time members who are "outside." Cohesion is furthered by four or five daily group meetings in which antidrug norms are repeated over and over (Endore, 1968). In addition, daily small-group discussions, called "synanons," involve "attack therapy" on the outside drug use of members by others in the group. New members are special targets for the "haircut" in which they are "taken apart," but emotional support is readily extended to those who show signs of accepting the reality of addiction. An example of this combination of intense confrontation surrounded by group emotional support is the newcomer who is going through withdrawal distress: He is not segregated from the other members and sees right before him, during his most agonizing period of withdrawal distress, that other addicts have "made it" (Volkman and Cressey, 1963).

The Synanon career is "a rational and attainable opportunity structure," a series of stages that represent assuming nonaddict behavior and beliefs (Yablonsky, 1962:50–51). The first stage is made up of newcomers who are sick and "kicking," nonworkers who are treated like infants and closely supervised while in withdrawal distress. Soon the addict begins to "grow up" and is assigned to some kind of work. This stage also contains the "adolescent" period in which he begins to participate in group meetings, is urged to help supervise newcomers, and generally acts the role of apprentice. In the "young adult" stage he begins to make choices: attending school, going to work, or acting in some instrumental capacity within the Synanon house, such as office manager, senior coordinator, assistant director, business manager, or department chief. Finally, there is the "adult" stage when the member moves into a position on the policy-making board of directors or moves out of the Synanon house entirely, returning frequently with family and friends. During this period the member acts as an ordinary member of the community: he may, for example, marry or divorce or change jobs, but is expected never to sever his ties with his Synanon "family." He is expected to return often to display himself to newcomers as a successful example (Volkman and Cressey, 1963).

Compared with Alcoholics Anonymous (which is an outpatient, self-help group), Synanon "extends maximal social and technical support to its residents while it also puts maximal social and technical pressures upon them" (Rubington, 1969:135). One of the criticisms against Synanon is for its consistent refusal to provide data on its failure rate or to permit systematic evaluation. The program allows addicts to leave at any time; thus the total breadth of addict exposure is unknown. Louria

(1968:183) estimates that over a decade "an average of no more than twenty persons per year has been returned to the community drug-free, and even for these the follow-up data are currently inadequate." Like other observers, he believes Synanon is of great value to a small number of the total addicts exposed to the program and, as such, is a valuable addiction treatment. It offers, however, little hope from the public health standpoint; in 1968 there were apparently only five groups on the West Coast and one in New York City.

It should be noted that similar but less known programs have also shown results. For example, two "Daytop Villages" on Staten Island have a program structured somewhat like Synanon but will accept involuntary as well as voluntary addicts. They are mainly operated by Synanon residents but unlike Synanon have a medical director and local and federal funds. Daytop has added a form of marathon group therapy. Here, for 30 to 36 hours, a "gut" discussion among 10 to 15 addicts continues relentlessly, and at times savagely, in an effort to penetrate the addict's extensive defense mechanisms.

In sum, what is essential is that group treatments be tried even though they vary widely in strategy. Studies must be made to determine the physiological, psychological, and sociological factors that characterize those who respond to different types of therapies. Then it will be possible to assign a given addict more confidentally to a particular type of therapeutic effort with a greater likelihood of favorable response (Trice, et al., 1969).

TREATMENT OF OTHER DRUG DEPENDENCIES

Other than the methadone treatment and Synanon, only a few scattered discrete treatment modalities are employed with narcotic users or addicts. Narcotics Anonymous has appeared (Patrick, 1965), but its extent and effectiveness seems to be limited. Obviously, as with alcohol, the individual is controlling his own deviant behavior unless physiologically addicted; thus the "treatment" of marihuana users and most amphetamine or barbiturate users is irrelevant. The constructive confrontation strategy is directly relevant with such deviants.

Addiction to the amphetamines or barbiturates, however, is possible and calls for treatment by medical specialists. The type of amphetamine or barbiturate use which leads to addiction, as well as the preaddictive role impairments, could escape notice in only the most unsupervised and casual work settings. Thus referral of such addicts for treatment should be very infrequent in most work organizations.

Successful treatment for amphetamine addiction has not been established (Cox and Smart, 1970). Amphetamine-dependent persons' extraordinary ability to conceal their addiction poses a formidable barrier to diagnosis (Bell and Trethowan, 1961:494). Even if "careful" history indicates amphetamine dependency and some form of therapy is administered, "poor prognosis and high relapse rate" seem likely. Efforts at maintenance treatment similar to the methadone strategy failed in Sweden (Louria, 1968). Generally speaking, the amphetamine addict is referred to general medical treatment which, as with any drug, is initially oriented to detoxification. Various types of sedation or restraint may be necessary during this withdrawal period. Following detoxification, many strategies are possible: direct return to the community, counseling, referral to group therapy, individual therapy, institutionalization. There is no set pattern here and individual strategies have not been evaluated. Any such treatment relies heavily on the addict's willpower; and, without physiological or social support, the pressures of addiction may predominate. Both methadone and Synanon supplement willpower, and this is the cornerstone of whatever success might be claimed for either approach. Combined treatments for various drug dependencies may emerge as a viable alternative (Ottenberg and Rosen, 1971).

The stigma of alcohol or drug abuse may tempt significant others, whether in the family, friendship group, or work organization, to secrecy and to referral to various private treatments, the success of which may be dubious. With a detailed account of methods where the individual is provided support, we hope to have illustrated the long-term risks of trying to "go it alone" with an alcohol or drug addict or commending him to the hands of the well meaning but inexperienced private physician.

References

Abramson, Harold, ed.
   1967   *The use of LSD in psychotherapy and alcoholism.* Indianapolis: Bobbs-Merrill.

Addiction Research Foundation of Ontario
   1969   A preliminary report on attitudes and behavior of Toronto students in relation to drugs. Mimeographed. Toronto: Addiction Research Foundation of Ontario, January.

Alcoholics Anonymous
   1939   *Alcoholics Anonymous: The Story of how more than one hundred men and women have recovered from alcoholism.* New York: Works Publishing Company.

American Medical Association, Committee on Alcoholism and Drug Dependency
   1967   Dependence on cannabis. *Journal of the American Medical Association* 201:369–371.

Andrus, Ray
   1971   Personal correspondence, May 10.

Angle, M.
   1971   Truckers 'driven' to use pep pills. *New Orleans States-Item,* October 15.

Archibald, David, Robert E. Popham, and Harold Kalant
   1969   *Preliminary brief to the Commission of Inquiry into Nonmedical Use of Drugs.* Toronto: Addiction Research Foundation of Ontario.

Armstrong, John D.
   1958   The search for the alcoholic personality. *Annals of the American Academy of Political and Social Science* 315:40–47.

Ausubel, David
   1960   Controversial issues in the management of drug addiction: Legalization, ambulatory treatment and the British system. *Mental Hygiene* 44:535–544.

Babbitt, H.
   1967   What does it cost to be an alcoholic? In *Alcoholism,* ed. David J. Pittman, pp. 45–52. New York: Harper and Row.

Bacon, Selden D.
   1962   Alcohol and complex society. In *Society, culture, and drinking patterns,* eds. David J. Pittman and Charles R. Snyder, pp. 78–84. New York: John Wiley.
   1967   The classic temperance movement of the U.S.A.: Impact today on attitudes, action, and research. *British Journal of Addictions* 62:5–18.

Bales, Robert F.
   1946   Cultural differences in rates of alcoholism. *Quarterly Journal of Studies on Alcohol* 6:480–499.

Ball, John C.
   1970   Two patterns of opiate addiction. In *Epidemiology of opiate addiction in the United States*, eds. John Ball and Carl Chambers, pp. 81–94. Springfield, Ill.: Charles C. Thomas.

Ball, John and Carl Chambers
   1970   Overview of the problem. In *Epidemiology of opiate addiction in the United States*, eds. John Ball and Carl Chambers, pp. 5–21. Springfield, Ill.: Charles C. Thomas.

Bailey, Margaret B. and Barry Leach
   1965   *Alcoholics Anonymous: Pathway to recovery*. New York: National Council on Alcoholism.

Barber, Bernard
   1967   *Drugs and society*. New York: Russell Sage Foundation.

Barnett, M.
   1955   Alcoholism in the Cantonese of New York City: An anthropological study. In *Etiology of chronic alcoholism,* ed. Oskar Diethelm, pp. 179–227. Springfield, Ill.: Charles C. Thomas.

Bazell, Robert J.
   1971   The Berkeley scene 1971: Patching up the ivory tower. *Science* 173: 1006–1009.

Becker, Howard S.
   1953   Becoming a marihuana user. *American Journal of Sociology* 59: 236–242.
   1963   *Outsiders: Studies in the sociology of deviance.* Glencoe, Ill.: The Free Press.
   1967   History, culture, and subjective experience: An exploration of the social bases of drug-induced experiences. *Journal of Health and Social Behavior* 8:163–176.
   1968   Ending campus drug incidents. *Trans-Action* 5:4–8.

Becker, Howard S. and Anselm L. Strauss
   1968   Careers, personalities, and adult socialization. In *Organizational careers: A source book for theory,* ed. Barney G. Glaser, pp. 21–34. Chicago: Aldine.

Belasco, James A.
   1966   A new look at salesmen selection. *Personnel* 43:23–28.

Belasco, James A. and Harrison M. Trice
   1969   *The assessment of change in training and therapy.* New York: McGraw-Hill.

Belasco, James A., Harrison M. Trice, and George Ritzer
   1969   Role of unions in industrial alcoholism programs. *Addictions* 16:13–30.

Bell, D. S. and W. H. Trethowan
   1961   Amphetamine addiction. *Journal of Nervous and Mental Disease* 133: 489–496.

REFERENCES

Bell, R. G.
 1958 The problem within industry. *American Journal of Public Health* 48: 585–589.

Bensman, J.
 1967 *Dollars and sense: Ideology, ethics, and the meaning of work in profit and non-profit organizations.* New York: The MacMillan Company.

Berg, Dorothy
 1970 The non-medical use of dangerous drugs in the U.S. *International Journal of the Addictions* 5:777–834.

Blane, Howard T.
 1966 Attitudes, treatment, and prevention. In *Alcoholism,* ed. Jack H. Mendelson, pp. 103–126. Boston: Little, Brown and Company.
 1968 *The personality of the alcoholic: Guises of dependency.* New York: Harper and Row.

Blane, Howard T., Willis Overton, and Morris Chafetz
 1963 Social factors in the diagnosis of alcoholism: I. Characteristics of the patient. *Quarterly Journal of Studies on Alcohol* 24:640–663.

Blau, Peter
 1955 *Dynamics of bureaucracy.* Chicago: University of Chicago Press.

Blau, Peter and W. Richard Scott
 1962 *Formal organizations.* San Francisco: Chandler Publishing Company.

Blauner, Robert
 1964 *Alienation and freedom: The factory worker and his industry.* Chicago: University of Chicago Press.

Blum, Richard H. and associates
 1969a *Society and drugs: Social and cultural observations.* San Francisco: Jossey-Bass, Inc.
 1969b *Students and drugs: College and high school observations.* San Francisco: Jossey-Bass, Inc.

Blumer, Herbert
 1967 The world of youthful drug use. Mimeographed. Berkeley: School of Criminology, University of California.

Bordua, D. J.
 1967 Recent trends: Deviant behavior and social control. *Annals of the American Academy of Political and Social Science* 369:149–163.

Brenner, Joseph H., Robert Coles, and Dermot Meagher
 1970 *Drugs and youth: Medical, psychiatric and legal facts.* New York: Liveright Corporation.

Brenner, Berthold
 1967 Alcoholism and fatal accidents. *Quarterly Journal of Studies on Alcohol* 28:517–527.

Brim, Orville G. and Stanton Wheeler
 1966 *Socialization after childhood: Two essays.* New York: John Wiley.

Brown, Michael E.
 1969 The condemnation and persecution of hippies. *Trans-Action* 6: 33–46.

Bruner, J. S., J. J. Goodenough, and G. A. Austin
   1956 *A study of thinking.* New York: John Wiley.

Bureau of National Affairs
   1954 *Computing absenteeism rates.* Washington: Bureau of National Affairs, Personnel Policies Survey No. 27, October.

Business Week
   1971 Where cigarette makers spend ad dollars now. *Business Week* December 25:56–57.

Cahalan, Don
   1970 *Problem drinkers: A national survey.* San Francisco: Jossey-Bass.

Cahalan, Don, Ira H. Cisin, and Helen Crossley
   1969 *American drinking practices. A national study of drinking behavior and attitudes.* New Haven: College and University Press.

Caplan, G.
   1964 *Principles of preventive psychiatry.* New York: Basic Books.

Carey, Frank
   1971 Methadone substitutes aim of drug war researchers. *New Orleans Times-Picayune,* November 7.

Carey, James T. and Jerry Mandel
   1968 A San Francisco Bay Area "speed scene." *Journal of Health and Social Behavior* 9:164–174.

Cavalie, B.
   1956 Influence de l'ethylisme chronique sur la morbidite et les accidents du travail. *Arch. Mal. Prob.* 17:98.

Chafetz, M. E.
   1967 Alcoholism prevention and reality. *Quarterly Journal of Studies on Alcohol* 28:345–348.

Chafetz, M. E. and H. Demone
   1962 *Alcoholism and society.* New York: Oxford University Press.

Chambers, Carl D. and W. Russell Taylor
   1970 Patterns of cheating among methadone maintenance patients. Paper presented to Eastern Psychiatric Research Association, November 7-8, New York, New York.

Chapin, F. S.
   1947 *Experimental designs in sociological research.* New York: Harper.

Chein, Isidor, Donald Gerard, and Robert Lee
   1964 *The road to H: Narcotics, delinquency, and social policy.* New York: Basic Books.

Chodorkoff, Bernard, Henry Krystal, and James Nunn
   1961 Employment characteristics of hospitalized alcoholics. *Quarterly Journal of Studies on Alcohol* 22:106–110.

Clausen, John A.
   1961 Drug addiction. In *Contemporary social problems,* eds. Robert K. Merton and Robert A. Nisbet, pp. 181–221. New York: Harcourt, Brace, and World.

REFERENCES

Clinard, Marshall B.
1962   The public drinking house and society. In *Society, culture and drinking patterns,* eds. David J. Pittman and Charles R. Snyder, pp. 270–292. New York: John Wiley.

Cohen, Albert K.
1959   The study of social disorganization and deviant behavior. In *Sociology today,* eds. Robert K. Merton, Leonard Brown, Leonard S. Cottrell, pp. 461–474. New York: Basic Books.
1965   The sociology of the deviant act: Anomie theory and beyond. *American Sociological Review* 30:5–14.

Cohen, S.
1967   The beyond within: Hallucinogens at work and play. In *Drugs on the campus: An assessment,* the Sarasota Springs Conference of Colleges and Universities of New York State, Oct. 25–27. Mimeographed. Albany: New York State Narcotics Addiction Control Commission.

Colbach, E.
1971   Marihuana use by G.I.'s in Vietnam. *American Journal of Psychiatry* 128:204–207.

Comptroller General of the United States
1970   *Report to the special sub-committee on labor and public welfare, United States Senate: Substantial cost savings from establishment of alcoholism program for federal civilian employees.* Washington: Government Printing Office.
1971   *Alcoholism among military personnel: Report to the sub-committee on alcoholism and narcotics, Committee on Labor and Public Welfare, United States Senate.* Washington: U.S. General Accounting Office.

Connor, Ralph G.
1962   The self-concepts of alcoholics. In *Society, culture, and drinking patterns,* eds. David J. Pittman and Charles R. Snyder, pp. 455–467. New York: John Wiley.

Coser, Lewis
1956   *The functions of social conflict.* New York: The Free Press.

Court, A. T.
1943   Absenteeism in industrial workers. *Journal of Michigan Medical Society* 42:707–714.

Covner, Bernard
1950   Management factors affecting absenteeism. *Harvard Business Review* 28:42–47.

Cox, Carole and Reginald Smart
1970   The nature and extent of speed use in North America. *Canadian Medical Association Journal* 102:72–729.

Cressey, Donald
1969   *Theft of the nation.* New York: Harper and Row.

Cumming, E.
   1963   Pathways to prevention. In *Key issues in the prevention of alcoholism,*
           pp. 11–25. Harrisburg, Pa.: State Department of Health.
   1969   Addiction, or the human condition. Mimeographed. Albany: New York
           State Department of Mental Hygiene, Mental Health Research Unit,
           pp. 1–9.

Dalton, Melville
   1959   *Men who manage.* New York: John Wiley.

Darnton, John
   1971   Many on campus shifting to softer drugs and alcohol. *New York Times,*
           January 17.

Derber, Milton, W. E. Chalmers, and Milton Edelman
   1961   Union participation in plant decision making. *Industrial and Labor
           Relations Review* 15:83–101.

Devenyi, Paul
   1970   Barbiturate abuse in young people. *Addictions* 17:19–25.

Devenyi, Paul and Mary Wilson
   1971a Barbiturate abuse and addiction in their relationship to alcohol and
           alcoholism. *Canadian Medical Association Journal* 104:215–218.
   1971b Abuse of barbiturates in an alcoholic population. *Canadian Medical
           Association Journal* 102:219–222.

Ditman, K. S. and Mayman M. Whittlesey
   1962   Nature and frequency of claims following LSD. *Journal of Nervous and
           Mental Disease* 134:346–352.

Dock, William
   1963   The clinical value of alcohol. In *Alcohol and civilization,* ed. S. Lucia,
           pp. 75–86. New York: McGraw-Hill.

Dole, Vincent and Marie Nyswander
   1965   A medical treatment for diacetylmorphine (heroin) addiction. *Journal
           of the American Medical Association* 193:646–650.

Douglas, Jack, ed.
   1970   *Observations of deviance.* New York: Random House.

Eddy, Nathan B.
   1970   Methadone maintenance for the management of persons with drug
           dependance of the morphine type. *Drug Dependence* 3:17–27.

Edgerton, Robert
   1967   *The cloak of competence: Stigma in the lives of the mentally retarded.*
           Berkeley: University of California Press.

Eels, Kenneth
   1968   Marihuana and LSD: A survey of one college campus. *Journal of
           Counseling Psychology* 15:459–467.

Einstein, Stanley
   1971   *Methadone maintenance.* New York: Marcel Dekker.

Endore, Guy
   1968   *Synanon.* Garden City: Doubleday and Company.

REFERENCES

Ends, Earl J., and Curtis W. Page
 1957 A study of three types of group therapy with hospitalized male inebriates. *Quarterly Journal of Studies on Alcohol* 18:263–277.

Enterline, P.
 1968 Recent developments in sick absence statistics. In *Proceedings of the 33rd annual meeting of the Industrial Hygiene Foundation,* pp. 31–40. Pittsburgh: Industrial Hygiene Foundation.

Erikson, Erik H.
 1968 *Identity: Youth and crisis.* New York: W. W. Norton and Company.

Erikson, Kai
 1962 Notes on the sociology of deviance. *Social Problems* 9:307–314.

Erskine, Hazel G.
 1966 The polls: morality. *The Public Opinion Quarterly* 30:669–680.
 1967 The polls: more on morality and sex. *The Public Opinion Quarterly* 31:116–128.

Essig, Carl
 1970 Drug dependence of the barbiturate type. *Drug Dependence* issue no. 5:24–28.

Falkey, Bruce and S. Schneyer
 1957 Characteristics of male alcoholics admitted to a medical ward of a general hospital. *Quarterly Journal of Studies on Alcohol* 18:67–97.

Farber, Leslie H.
 1970 Ours is the addicted society. In *Youth and drugs,* eds. John H. McGrath and Frank R. Scarpitti, pp. 57-66. Glenview, Ill.: Scott Foresman.

Feinberg, Mortimer
 1971 Making the generation gap work for you. *Sales Management* 107:113–122.

Fejer, Dianne, Reginald Smart, Paul Whitehead, and Lucien LaForest
 1971 Sources of information about drugs among high school students. *The Public Opinion Quarterly* 35:235–241.

Feuer, Lewis S.
 1969 *The conflict of generations: The character and significance of student movements.* New York: Basic Books.

Fiddle, Seymour
 1968 Circles beyond the circumference: Some hunches about amphetamine abuse. In *Amphetamine abuse,* ed. J. Russo, pp. 66–87. Springfield, Ill.: Charles C. Thomas.

Fielden, John S.
 1970 Today the campuses, tomorrow the corporations. *Business Horizons* 13:13–20.

Fischman, V. S.
 1968 Stimulant users in the California Rehabilitation Center. *International Journal of the Addictions* 3:113–130.

Fort, Joel
 1970 Social problems of drug use and drug policies. *International Journal of the Addictions* 5:321–333.

Fox, Ruth
  1958   Treatment of chronic alcoholism. *The Medical Clinics of North America* 42:804–814.

Franco, S. Charles
  1954   Problem drinking and industry: Policies and procedures. *Quarterly Journal of Studies on Alcohol* 15:443–459.
  1960   A company program for problem drinking: Ten years followup. *Journal of Occupational Medicine* 2:157–162.
  1965   Alcoholism in industry. Speech presented to the Maryland Industrial Physicians Association, Baltimore, Maryland, February 25, pp. 1–15.

Freeman, H. and W. Jones
  1970   *Social problems.* Chicago: Rand McNally.

Freud, Anna
  1965   *Normality and pathology in childhood.* New York: International Universities Press.

Fuchs, Victor
  1968   *The Service Economy.* New York: National Bureau of Economic Research, Columbia University Press.

Gallese, Liz R.
  1971   College students find a new kick that is replacing drugs: Beer. *The Wall Street Journal,* Wednesday, May 26.

Game, Sherrell and Paul Devenyi
  1971   Cigarette smoking and its effects. *Addictions* 18:30–35.

Gellman, Irving P.
  1964   *The sober alcoholic: An organizational analysis of alcoholics anonymous.* New Haven: College and University Press.

George, William
  1971   Some of labor's updated views on alcoholism. *Labor-Management Alcoholism Newsletter* 1:1–5.

Gerard, Donald
  1962   The abstinent alcoholic. *Archives of General Psychiatry* 6:99–111.

Glad, Donald D.
  1947   Attitudes and experiences of American-Jewish and American-Irish male youth as related to differences in adult roles of inebriety. *Quarterly Journal of Studies on Alcohol* 8:406–472.

Glaser, Frederick and John C. Ball
  1970   Death due to withdrawal from narcotics. In *The epidemiology of opiate addiction in the United States,* eds. John C. Ball and Carl Chambers, pp. 263–287. Springfield, Ill.: Charles C. Thomas.

Godeau, L. and R. Quaetel
  1958   L'alcoolisme dane les arnsenaux. *Rev. Med. Nav.* 13:75–78.

Goeke, Joseph
  1971   America's future as reflected in public opinion trends. *The Futurist* 5:79–84.

REFERENCES

Goffman, Erving
1961 *Asylums.* Garden City: Anchor Books.
1963 *Stigma: Notes on the management of spoiled identity.* Englewood Cliffs, N.J.: Prentice Hall.

Goldberg, L.
1968 Drug abuse in Sweden. *Bulletin on Narcotics* 20:1–29.

Goldner, Fred H.
1965 Demotion in industrial management. *American Sociological Review* 30:714–724.

Goode, Erich
1969a *Marihuana* [ed.] New York: Atherton Press.
1969b Marihuana and the politics of reality. *Journal of Health and Social Behavior* 10:83–94.
1969c Multiple drug use among marihuana smokers. *Social Problems* 17:48–64.
1970a How the American marihuana market works. *New Society* 15:992-994.
1970b *The marihuana smokers.* New York: Basic Books.
1971 Cigarette smoking and drug use on a college campus. *International Journal of Addictions* [forthcoming].

Gouldner, Alvin W.
1960 The norm of reciprocity: A preliminary statement. *American Sociological Review* 25:161–178.
1970 *The coming crisis in western sociology.* New York: Basic Books.

Greathouse, Pat
1969 The union and the problem drinker. In *Proceedings of the 28th International Congress on Alcohol and Alcoholism,* eds. Mark Keller and Timothy G. Coffey, pp. 140–144, vol. 2. Highland Park, N.J.: Hillhouse Press.

Greenblatt, Milton, Daniel Levinson, and Richard Williams
1957 *The patient and the mental hospital: Contributions of research in the science of behavior.* Glencoe, Ill.: The Free Press.

Griffith, J.
1968 Psychiatric implication of amphetamine abuse. In *Amphetamine abuse,* ed. J. Russo, pp. 15–32. Springfield, Ill.: Charles C. Thomas.

Gunne, Lars-M.
1966 Treatment of drug addiction with narcotic blocking medication. *Lakartidningen* [Stockholm] 63:4060–4064.

Gusfield, Joseph R.
1962 Status conflicts and the changing ideologies of the American temperance movement. In *Society, culture, and drinking patterns,* eds. David J. Pittman and Charles R. Snyder, pp. 101–120. New York: John Wiley.
1963 *Symbolic crusade.* Urbana: University of Illinois Press.

Haberman, Paul W. and Jill Sheinberg
1969 Public attitudes toward alcoholism as an illness. *American Journal of Public Health* 59:1209–1216.

Harris Survey
    1968   Parents draw line on teenagers using drugs, *Philadelphia Inquirer*, March 4.

Henderson, R. M. and S. D. Bacon
    1953   Problem drinking: The Yale plan for business and industry. *Quarterly Journal of Studies on Alcohol* 14:247–262.

Hentoff, Nat
    1965   Profiles: The treatment of patients, II. *New Yorker,* July 3:32–57.

Hicks, Nancy
    1971   Methadone case brings warning. *New York Times,* December 7.

Hoff, E. C.
    1968   The alcoholisms. In *Proceedings of the 28th International Congress on Alcohol and Alcoholism,* eds. Mark Keller and Timothy G. Coffey, pp. 84–90. Highland Park, N.J.: Hillhouse Press.

Hollister, Leo
    1971   Marihuana in man: Three years later. *Science* 172:21–29.

Holmes, Douglas
    1963   Report of New York City alcoholism project. Mimeographed. New York: National Council on Alcoholism.

Holmes, S. J.
    1963   Barbiturates: Friend or foe? *Addictions* 10:3–12.

Horn, Daniel
    1968   The health consequences of smoking. In *Smoking, health and behavior,* eds. Edgar F. Borgatta and Robert Evans, pp. 52–80. Chicago: Aldine.

Imperi, Lillian L., H. Klever, and J. Davie
    1968   Use of hallucinogenic drugs on campus. *Journal of the American Medical Association* 204:1021–1024.

Industrial Bulletin
    1971   Labor council wars on drug abuse. 50:16–20.

Inkeles, Alex
    1968   Society, social structure, and child socialization. In *Socialization and society,* ed. John Clausen, pp. 75–129. Boston: Little, Brown and Company.

Irwin, Samuel
    1971   Drugs of abuse: An introduction to their actions and potential hazards. *Journal of Psychedelic Drugs* 3:5–15.

Isbell, Harris
    1955   Medical aspects of opiate addiction. *Bulletin of the New York Academy of Medicine* 31:886–901.

Jackson, B.
    1970   White collar pill party. In *Observations of deviance,* ed. Jack D. Douglas, pp. 255–265. New York: Random House.

Jacobsen, E.
    1961   Alcohol and other addicting drugs affect both individual and state. *Addictions* 8:1–10.

REFERENCES

Jaffee, Jerome
1965 Cannabis (marihuana): Drug addiction and drug abuse. In *The pharmacological basis of therapeutics,* eds. Louis S. Goodman and Alfred Gilman, pp. 299–301. New York: Macmillan.

Jahoda, Marie
1958 *Current concepts of positive mental health.* New York: Basic Books.

Jaques, Elliott
1956 *Measurement of responsibility.* Cambridge, Mass.: Harvard University Press.

Jellinek, E. M.
1947 What shall we do about alcoholism? *Vital Speeches* 13:252–254.
1960 *The disease concept of alcoholism.* New Haven, Conn.: Hillhouse Press.

Jennings, Eugene E.
1971 The co-worldly executive. *Management of Personnel Quarterly* 10:4–8.

Johnson, Bruce
1971 Social determinants of the use of dangerous drugs by college students. Ph.D. thesis, Columbia University.

Jones, Charles
1967 Narcotic addiction of physicians. *Northwest Medicine* 66:559–564.

Jones, Maxwell
1953 *Therapeutic community: A new treatment method in psychiatry.* New York: Basic Books.

Joseph, Herman and Vincent P. Dole
1970 Methadone patients on probation and parole. *Federal Probation* 34:42–49.

Kadushin, Charles
1969 *Why people go to psychiatrists.* New York: Atherton Press.

Kahn, Robert L., Donald Wolfe, Robert Quinn, and J. Diedrick Snoek
1964 *Organizational stress: Studies in role conflict and ambiguity.* New York: John Wiley.

Kaim, Samuel C.
1971 Press release of address on federal resources for alcoholism, North American Association of Alcoholism Programs, August 9, Denver Hilton Hotel, Denver, Colorado.

Kalant, Oriana J.
1966 *The amphetamines: Toxicity and addiction.* Springfield, Ill.: Charles C. Thomas.

Kalant, O. and H. Kalant
1968 Marihuana and its effects: An assessment of current knowledge. *Addictions* 15:1–7.

Kandel, Denise and Richard H. Williams
1964 *Psychiatric rehabilitation: Some problems of research.* New York: Atherton Press.

Kaplan, John
1970   *Marihuana: The new prohibition.* Cleveland: World Publishing Company.

Karvinen, Esko, Matti Miettinen, and Kaj Ahlman
1962   Physical performance during hangover. *Quarterly Journal of Studies on Alcohol* 23:208–214.

Kellam, S. G. and S. K. Schiff
1967   Adaptation and mental illness of first grade classrooms of an urban community. In *Poverty and mental health,* eds. M. Greenblatt, P. Emery, and B. C. Glueck, pp. 79–91. Washington, D.C.: American Psychiatric Association.

Keller, Mark
1962   The definition of alcoholism and the estimation of its prevalence. In *Society, culture, and drinking patterns,* eds. David J. Pittman and Charles R. Snyder, pp. 310–329. New York: John Wiley.

Kelly, Norbert
1964   Social and legal problems of control in the United States. In *Alcohol education for classroom and community,* ed. Raymond McCarthy, pp 11–31. New York: McGraw Hill.

Keniston, Kenneth
1969   Introduction. In *Drugs on the college campus,* ed. H. Nowlis, pp. x–xvi. Garden City, N.J.: Anchor Books.

Kennedy, Robert F.
1967   Setting the theme. In *World conference on smoking and health,* ed. Luther Terry, pp. 4–6. New York: National Interagency Council on Smoking and Health and American Cancer Society.

Keup, Wolfram
1971   The vocabulary of the drug user and alcoholic: A glossary. *International Journal of the Addictions* 6:347–373.

Kew, M. C., I. Bersohn, and S. Siew
1969   Possible hepatotoxicity of cannabis. *Lancet* 7594:578–579.

Kiev, Ari
1970   An eight point drug abuse plan for business organizations. Mimeographed. Paper presented at American Medical Association headquarters, New York City, briefing session no. 8302-01.

Kinsey, Barry A.
1966   *The female alcoholic.* Springfield, Ill.: Charles C. Thomas.

Kisker, George W.
1964   *The disorganized personality.* New York: McGraw-Hill.

Klein, Julius and Derek L. Phillips
1968   From hard to soft drugs: Temporal and substantive changes in drug use among gangs in a working class community. *Journal of Health and Social Behavior* 9:139–145.

REFERENCES

Klerman, Gerald L.
  1970   Drugs and social values. *International Journal of the Addictions* 5:313–319.

Knight, R. P.
  1937   The dynamics and treatment of chronic alcohol addictions. *Bulletin of the Menninger Clinic* 1:233–250.

Kogon, Eugene
  1950   *The theory and practice of hell.* New York: Farrar, Straus.

Kolansky, Harold, and William Moore
  1971   Effects of marihuana on adolescents and young adults. *Journal of American Medical Association* 216:486–492.

Koprowski, Eugene
  1969   The generation gap from both sides now. *Management of Personnel Quarterly* 8:2–7.

Kramer, John C., V. S. Fischmann, and D. C. Littlefield
  1967   Amphetamine abuse. *Journal of the American Medical Association* 201:305–310.

Kuhn, Arnold J.
  1961   Industry programs succeed, national survey shows. *Signposts* 2:2–4.

Kuhn, James W.
  1961   *Bargaining in grievance settlements: The power of industrial work groups.* New York: Columbia University Press.

Kurtis, Carol
  1970   *Drug abuse as a business problem.* New York: New York Chamber of Commerce.

Lancet
  1968   Drug dependence: A symptom. 7547:853–857.

Landsberger, Henry A.
  1958   *Hawthorne revisited.* Ithaca: New York State School of Industrial and Labor Relations, Cornell University.

Laurie, Peter
  1969   *Drugs: Medical, psychological and social facts.* Baltimore, Md.: Penguin Books.

Leavy, S. A. and L. Z. Freedman
  1956   Psychoneurosis and economic life. *Social Problems* 4:55–61.

Lemere, Frederick
  1958   Motivation and treatment of alcoholism. *Quarterly Journal of Studies on Alcohol* 19:428–432.

Lemert, Edwin
  1951   *Social pathology.* New York: McGraw-Hill.
  1967   *Human deviance, social problems, and social control.* Englewood Cliffs, N. J.: Prentice Hall.

Lennard, Henry L., Leon Epstein, Arnold Bernstein, and Donald Ransom
  1971   *Mystification and drug misuse.* San Francisco: Jossey-Bass, Inc.

249

Levinson, Harry
  1963   Who killed Bob Lyons? *Harvard Business Review* 41:127–143.
  1965   Reciprocation: the relationship between man and organization. *Administrative Science Quarterly* 9:370–390.

Lieberman, Seymour
  1956   The effects of changes in role on the attitudes of role occupants. *Human Relations* 9:385–402.

Liebow, E.
  1967   *Tally's corner.* Boston: Little, Brown and Company.

Lindesmith, Alfred R.
  1947   *Opiate addiction.* Bloomington, Ind.: Principia Press.
  1967   *The addict and the law.* New York: Vintage Books.
  1968   *Addiction and opiates.* Chicago: Aldine.
  1971   Personal correspondence, November 15.

Lindesmith, Alfred R. and John H. Gagnon
  1964   Anomie and drug addiction. In *Anomie and deviant behavior: A discussion and a critique,* ed. Marshall B. Clinard, pp. 158–188. New York: The Free Press.

Lingren, G. M.
  1957   Alkohol och arbete. *Svenska Lakartidn* 54:3613–3620.

Litman, Robert E.
  1970   Suicide as acting out. In *The psychology of suicide,* eds. Edwin Schneidman, Norman Farberow, and Robert Litman, pp. 293–304. New York: Science House.

Lofland, John
  1969   *Deviance and identity.* Englewood Cliffs, N. J.: Prentice Hall.

Lolli, G., E. Serianni, G. M. Golder, and P. Luzzatto-Fegiz
  1958   *Alcohol in Italian culture.* New Brunswick, N. J.: Rutgers Center of Alcohol Studies.

Louria, Donald B.
  1968   *The drug scene.* New York: McGraw-Hill.

MacAndrew, Craig and Robert B. Edgerton
  1969   *Drunken comportment: A social explanation.* Chicago: Aldine.

MacAndrew, Craig and Harold Garfinkel
  1962   A consideration of changes attributed to intoxication as common-sense reasons for getting drunk. *Quarterly Journal of Studies on Alcohol* 23:252–266.

McClelland, David C.
  1971   The power of positive drinking. *New Society,* May 13:933–937.

McCord, William, and Joan McCord
  1962   A longitudinal study of the personality of alcoholics. In *Society, culture, and drinking patterns,* eds. David J. Pittman and Charles R. Snyder, pp. 413–430. New York: John Wiley.

McGavran, E.
  1963   Facing reality in public health. In *Key issues in the prevention of alcoholism,* pp. 55–61. Harrisburg, Pa.: State Department of Health.

REFERENCES

McGee, L. C. and J. D. Cregor
   1942   Gastro-intestinal disease among industrial workers. *Journal of the American Medical Association* 120:1367–1372.

McGlothlin, William H.
   1966   Cannabis: A reference. In *The marihuana papers,* ed. David Solomon, pp. 455–471. New York: Signet Books.

McKinney, John C.
   1966   *Constructive typology and social theory.* New York: Appleton-Century-Crofts.

McLean, Alan A., ed.
   1970   *Mental health and work organizations.* Chicago: Rand McNally.

McNeil, John S. and Martin B. Giffen
   1967   Military retirement: The retirement syndrome. *American Journal of Psychiatry* 123:848–854.

Maddox, George L. and Bevode C. McCall
   1964   *Drinking among teenagers.* New Haven: College and University Press.

Malcolm, Andrew J.
   1970   Drugs in modern sports. *Addictions* 17:1–10.
   1971   *The pursuit of intoxication.* Toronto: Thorn Press.

Maloney, Ralph
   1962   *The twenty-four hour drink book: A guide to executive survival.* New York: Ivan Obolensky, Inc.

Manheimer, Dean I., G. Mellinger, and M. Balter
   1969   Marihuana use among urban adults. *Science* 166:1544–1545.

Mann, Floyd
   1952   *Absences and employee attitudes in an electric power company.* Human Relations Program, series no. 1, report no. 2. Ann Arbor: University of Michigan, Survey Research Center.

Mauss, Armand L.
   1969   Anticipatory socialization toward college as a factor in adolescent marihuana use. *Social Problems* 16:357–364.

Maxwell, Milton
   1960   Early identification of problem drinkers in industry. *Quarterly Journal of Studies on Alcohol* 21:655–678.

Maxwell, Milton, and J. Wasson
   1963   Social variables and early identification of alcoholism on the job. Unpublished manuscript.

Mayor's Committee on Marihuana
   1944   *The marihuana problem in the City of New York: Sociological, medical, psychological and pharmacological studies* [LaGuardia Report]. Lancaster, Pa.: Jacques Cattell Press.

Mead, Margaret
   1970   *Culture and commitment: A study of the generation gap.* Garden City: Natural History Press, Doubleday and Company.

Menninger, Karl A.
  1938   *Man against himself.* New York: Harcourt, Brace.
Merton, Robert K.
  1957   *Social theory and social structure.* Glencoe, Ill.: The Free Press.
Methadone Maintenance Evaluation Committee
  1968   *First national conference on methadone treatment.* New York: Rockefeller University Press.
Mikuriya, Tod
  1968   Physical, mental, and moral effects of marihuana: The Indian Hemp Drugs Commission Report. *The International Journal of the Addictions* 3:253:271.
Miller, Dorothy
  1965   *Worlds that fail.* Sacramento: California Department of Mental Hygiene.
Miller, Ernest C., Anthony Dvorak, and Don Turner
  1960   A method of creating aversion to alcohol by reflex conditioning in a group setting. *Quarterly Journal of Studies on Alcohol* 21:424–431.
Miller, S. Michael and Frank Riessman
  1961   The working class subculture. *Social Problems* 9:86–97.
Miller, Glen and Ned Rosen
  1957   Member attitudes toward the shop steward. *Industrial and Labor Relations Review* 10:516–631.
Milton, Rod and Alfred A. Agrin
  1966   Resolution of a crisis in a therapeutic community for alcoholics. *Quarterly Journal of Studies on Alcohol* 27:517–524.
Modlin, H. and Alberto Montes
  1964   Narcotic addiction in physicians. *American Journal of Psychiatry* 121:358–365.
More, Douglas M.
  1962   Demotion. *Social Problems* 9:213–221.
Mulford, Harold
  1970   *Meeting the problems of alcohol abuse.* Cedar Rapids, Iowa: Iowa Alcoholism Foundation.
Mulford, Harold A. and Donald E. Miller
  1960   Drinking in Iowa. II. The extent of drinking and selected sociocultural categories. *Quarterly Journal of Studies on Alcohol* 21:26–39.
  1961   Public definitions of the alcoholic. *Quarterly Journal of Studies on Alcohol* 22:312–320.
  1964a Measuring public acceptance of the alcoholic as a sick person. *Quarterly Journal of Studies on Alcohol* 25:314–322.
  1964b Iowa's drinking driver, 1961: With a method for identifying drinking drivers in a survey sample. *Social Problems* 12:196–211.
Murphy, H.
  1966   The cannabis habit: A review of recent psychiatric literature. *Addictions* 13:1–23.
Murray, Thomas J.
  1971   It's hell in personnel. *Dun's Review* 97:40–44.

REFERENCES

Myerson, David J.
1956   The skid row problem. *New England Journal of Medicine* 254:1168–1173.

National Institute of Mental Health
1968   *Alcohol and alcoholism.* Washington, D.C.: Government Printing Office.

Newsweek
1971   The G.I.'s other enemy: Heroin. May 24:26–28.

Nowlis, Helen
1969   *Drugs on the college campus.* Garden City, N. J.: Anchor Books.

Nunnally, J. C.
1961   *Popular conceptions of mental health.* New York: Holt, Rinehart, and Winston.

Nyswander, Marie and Vincent Dole
1967   The present status of methadone blockage treatment. *American Journal of Psychiatry* 123:1441–1442.

O'Brien, Cyril
1949   Alcoholism among disciplinary cases in industry. *Quarterly Journal of Studies on Alcohol* 10:268–273.

Observer and Milton Maxwell
1959   A study of absenteeism, accidents, and sickness payments in problem drinkers in one industry. *Quarterly Journal of Studies on Alcohol* 20:302–312.

O'Donnell, John A.
1969   *Narcotic addicts in Kentucky: A National Institute of Mental Health study.* Lexington: Department of Health, Education, and Welfare.

O'Donnell, John A. and John C. Ball, eds.
1969   *Narcotic addiction.* New York: Harper and Row.

Offer, Daniel and Melvin Sabshin
1966   *Normality: Clinical and theoretical concepts of mental health.* New York: Harper and Row.

Osgood, Charles, George Suci, and Percy Tannenbaum
1965   *The measurement of meaning.* Urbana, Ill.: University of Illinois Press.

Ottenberg, D. J. and A. Rosen
1971   Merging the treatment of drug addicts into an existing program for alcoholics. *Quarterly Journal of Studies on Alcohol* 32:94–103.

Parrish, Bernie
1971   *They call it a game.* New York: Dial Press.

Parsons, Talcott
1951   *The social systems.* Glencoe, Ill.: The Free Press.

Partenen, J.
1966   *Inheritance of drinking behavior.* Helsinki: Finnish Foundation for Alcohol Studies.

Patrick, Sherman
1965   Our way of life: A short history of Narcotics Anonymous. In *Drug addiction in youth,* ed. Ernest Harms, pp. 148–157. New York: Pergamon Press.

Pearlman, Samuel
    1968   Drug use and experience in an urban college population. *American Journal of Orthopsychiatry* 38:503–514.

Pelz, Donald C. and Frank M. Andrews
    1966   *Scientists in organizations: Productive climate for research and development.* New York: John Wiley.

Perlis, Leo
    1958   Labor's viewpoint of alcoholism in industry. *Industrial Medicine and Surgery* 27:535–537.
    1970   Drug abuse among union members. Mimeographed. Washington, D.C.: AFL-CIO Department of Community Services.
    1971   *Labor-Management Alcoholism Newsletter* 1:1–2.

Perrucci, Robert and Robert A. Rothman
    1969   Obsolescence of knowledge and the professional career. In *The engineers and the social system,* eds. Robert Perrucci and Joel Gerstl, pp. 247–277. New York: John Wiley.

Pescor, M. J.
    1942   Physician drug addicts. *Diseases of the Nervous System* 3:2–3.

Pfeffer, Arnold and Daniel Feldman.
    1956   A treatment program for the alcoholic in industry. *Journal of the American Medical Association* 161:827–836.

Pittman, David J.
    1967   The rush to combine: Sociological dissimilarities of alcoholism and drug abuse. *British Journal of Addictions* 62:337–343.

Pittman, David J. and Charles R. Snyder, eds.
    1962   *Society, culture, and drinking patterns.* New York: John Wiley.

Plaut, Thomas F. A.
    1963   Translating concepts into action. In *Key issues in the prevention of alcoholism,* pp. 62–72. Harrisburg, Pa.: State Department of Health.
    1967   *Alcohol problems: A report to the nation.* New York: Oxford University Press.

Plunkett, Richard J. and John E. Gordon
    1960   *Epidemiology and mental illness: A report to the staff director, Jack R. Ewalt,* 1960. New York: Basic Books.

Presnall, Lewis
    1967   Folklore and facts about employees with alcoholism. *Journal of Occupational Medicine* 9:187–192.

Pritchett, S. T.
    1967   A study of some measurable consequences of the problem drinker. Master's thesis, School of Business, Virginia Polytechnic Institute.

Purcell, Theodore D.
    1953   *The worker speaks his mind on company and union.* Cambridge: Harvard University Press.

Quarterly Journal of Studies on Alcohol
    1942   Alcohol and industrial efficiency *Quarterly Journal of Studies on Alcohol,* Lay Supplement no. 3.

REFERENCES

Rawlings, John W.
1968 Street level abuse of amphetamines. In *Amphetamine abuse,* ed. J. Russo, pp. 51–66. Springfield, Ill.: Charles C. Thomas.

Recovery
1971 Nicotine found contributor to alcohol effect. 5:1–2.

Reinert, R. E.
1968 The concept of alcoholism as a bad habit. *Bulletin of the Menninger Clinic* 32:25–36.

Ritzer, G. and H. Trice
1969 *An occupation in conflict: The personnel manager.* Ithaca: New York State School of Industrial and Labor Relations, Cornell University.

Robbins, Thomas
1970 Characteristics of amphetamine addicts. *International Journal of the Addictions* 5:183–193.

Roberts, J. I. and E. A. Russo
1955 The alcoholic in industry and his rehabilitation. *Industrial Medicine and Surgery* 24:270–276.

Robins, Lee N., William Bates and Patricia O'Neal
1962 Adult drinking patterns of former problem children. In *Society, culture, and drinking patterns,* eds. David J. Pittman and Charles R. Snyder, pp. 395–412. New York: John Wiley.

Robins, Lee N. and George E. Murphy
1967 Drug use in a normal population of young Negro men. *American Journal of Public Health* 57:1580–1596.

Robins, Lee N., Harriet Darvish, and George Murphy
1970 The long-term outcome for adolescent drug users: A follow-up study of 76 users and 146 nonusers. In *The psychopathology of adolescence,* eds. Joseph Zubin and Alfred M. Freedman, pp. 159–176. New York: Grune and Stratton.

Roethlisberger, F. J. and William J. Dickson
1946 *Management and the worker.* Cambridge: Harvard University Press.

Roffman, Roger and Ely Sapol
1970 Marihuana in Vietnam: A survey of use among Army enlisted men in two southern corps. *International Journal of the Addictions* 5:1–42.

Rokeach, Milton
1960 *The open and closed mind.* New York: Basic Books.

Roman, Paul M.
1968 Constructive coercion and the alcoholic: A critique of assumptions. Paper presented at the 28th International Congress on Alcohol and Alcoholism, September 17, Shoreham Hotel, Washington, D.C.
1970 The future professor: Functions and patterns of drinking among graduate students. In *The domesticated drug: Drinking among collegians,* ed. George L. Maddox, pp. 204–218. New Haven: College and University Press.

Roman, Paul M. and Harrison M. Trice
1967   *Schizophrenia and the poor*. Ithaca: New York State School of Industrial and Labor Relations, Cornell University.
1968   The sick role, labeling theory and the deviant drinker. *International Journal of Social Psychiatry* 14:245–251.
1971a   Mental health and white-collar urbanites: Psychiatric impairment among New York City clerical workers. Paper presented to the Southern Sociological Society, April 14, Miami Beach, Florida.
1971b   Normalization: A neglected complement to labeling theory. Paper presented to the American Sociological Association, August 31. Denver, Colorado.

Rose, Arnold
1952   *Union solidarity*. Minneapolis: University of Minnesota Press.

Roszak, Theodore
1969   *The making of a counter-culture*. New York: Doubleday and Company.

Roth, Julius A. and Elizabeth M. Eddy
1967   *Rehabilitation of the unwanted*. New York: Atherton Press.

Rubington, Earl
1962   'Failure' as a heavy drinker: The case of the chronic-drunkenness offender on Skid Row. In *Society, culture, and drinking patterns*, eds. David J. Pittman and Charles R. Snyder, pp. 146–153. New York: John Wiley.
1967   Drug addiction as a deviant career. *International Journal of the Addictions* 2:3–30.
1969   Drug culture and treatment outcome. *International Journal of the Addictions* 4:331–349.
1971   The language of drunks. *Quarterly Journal of Studies on Alcohol* 32: 721–740.

Rush, Harold and James Brown
1971   The drug problem in business: A survey of business opinion and experience. *The Conference Board Record* 8:6–15.

Sagarin, Edward
1969   *Odd man in: Societies of deviants in America*. Chicago: Quadrangle Press.
1971   *The other minorities*. Boston: D.C. Heath.

Salpukas, Agis
1971   Workers' use of drugs widespread in nation. *New York Times,* June 21.

Sayles, Leonard and George Strauss
1967   *The local union*. New York: Harcourt, Brace and World.

Schaps, Eric and Clinton R. Sanders
1970   Purposes, patterns, and protection in a campus drug using community. *Journal of Health and Social Behavior* 11:135–145.

Scheff, Thomas J.
1966   *Being mentally ill: A sociological theory*. Chicago: Aldine.

Schoenfeld, Dudley
1966   The sociological study. In *The marihuana papers,* ed. David Solomon, pp. 284–308. New York: Signet Books.

REFERENCES

Schur, Edwin M.
1971 *Labeling deviant behavior: Its sociological consequences.* New York: Harper and Row.

Scott, Peter D.
1964 Amphetamine and delinquency. *Lancet* 7357:452.

Scott, Jack
1971 It's not how you play the game, but what pill you take. *The New York Times Magazine,* October 17.

Seevers, M.
1968 Classifications of amphetamine and amphetamine-like drugs. In *Amphetamine abuse,* ed. J. Russo, pp. 116–120. Springfield, Ill.: Charles C. Thomas.
1968 Use, misuse, and abuse of amphetamine-type drugs from the medical viewpoint. In *Amphetamine abuse,* ed. J. Russo, pp. 7–15. Springfield, Ill.: Charles C. Thomas.

Severo, Richard
1970 Methadone: Only program undergoing crucial tests. *New York Times,* July 26.

Sheppard, Charles, George Gay, and David Smith
1971 The changing patterns of heroin addiction in the Haight-Asbury subculture. *Journal of Psychedelic Drugs* 3:22–30.

Sherlock, Basil J.
1967 Career problems and narcotics addiction in health professions: an exploratory study. *International Journal of the Addictions* 2:191–206.

Silverman, Charlotte
1968 *The epidemiology of depression.* Baltimore: Johns Hopkins University Press.

Simmel, Georg
1950 *The sociology of Georg Simmel.* Translated by Kurt Wolff. Glencoe, Ill.: The Free Press.

Simmons, Jerry L.
1969 *Deviants.* Berkeley, Calif.: Glendessary Press.

Simmons, Jerry L. and Barry Winograd
1967 *It's happening: A portrait of the youth scene today.* Santa Barbara, Calif.: Marc-Laird Publications.

Simon, Warner and Gayle K. Lumry
1969 Alcoholism and drug addiction among physicians: Chronic self destruction? *Drug Dependence,* Issue no. 1:11–14.

Sinclair, A.
1962 *Prohibition: The era of excess.* Boston: Little, Brown and Co.

Slight, David
1948 Alcoholism and alcohol addiction. In *Proceedings of the first Industrial Conference on Alcoholism.* Chicago, Ill.: privately printed.

257

Smart, Reginald G.
　　1970　Some current studies of psychoactive and hallucinogenic drug use. *Canadian Journal of Behavioral Science* 2:232–245.

Smart, Reginald, Dianne Fejer, and Jim White
　　1971　The extent of drug use in metropolitan Toronto schools: A study of changes from 1968 to 1970. *Addictions* 18:1–17.

Smart, Reginald G. *et al.*
　　1969　Psychoactive drugs and traffic accidents. *Journal of Safety Research* 1:67–72.

Smith, David E. and Clark Sturges
　　1969　The semantics of the San Francisco drug scene. *Etc.: A Review of General Semantics* 26:168–175.

Smith, David E. and Donald R. Wesson
　　1970　A new method for treatment of barbiturate dependence. *Journal of the American Medical Association* 213:294–296.

Smith, David E., Donald R. Wesson, and Richard Lannon
　　1970　New developments in barbiturate abuse. *Clinical Toxicology* 3:57–65.

Smith, Stanley N. and Paul H. Blachly
　　1966　Amphetamine usage by medical students. *Journal of Medical Education* 41:167–170.

Smithers Foundation
　　1969　*Alcoholism and industry: Modern procedures.* 3rd. pr. rev. New York: Christopher D. Smithers Foundation.
　　1970　*The key role of labor in employee alcoholism programs.* New York: Christopher D. Smithers Foundation.

Snyder, Charles R.
　　1958　*Alcohol and the Jews.* Glencoe, Ill.: The Free Press.
　　1964　Inebriety, alcoholism, and anomie. In *Anomie and deviant behavior,* ed. Marshall B. Clinard, pp. 189–213. New York: The Free Press.

Snyder, Solomon
　　1971　*Uses of marihuana.* New York: Oxford University Press.

Sohn, David
　　1970　Screening for drug addiction. *Personnel* 47:22–30.

Solomon, Richard
　　1949　An extension of control group design. *Psychological Bulletin* 46:137–150.

Spivak, Jonathan
　　1971　FDA evaluating weight-reducing drugs for effectiveness and potential dangers. *Wall Street Journal,* December 22.

Stagner, Ross
　　1956　*Psychology of industrial conflict.* New York: John Wiley.

Stamps, Roland
　　1965　Alcoholic employees and problem concealment. Masters thesis, Washington State University.

Stanton, A. H. and M. S. Schwartz
　　1954　*The mental hospital.* New York: Basic Books.

REFERENCES

Stevenson, R. W.
  1942   Absenteeism in an industrial plant due to alcoholism. *Quarterly Journal of Studies on Alcohol* 2:661–667.

Straus, Robert
  1970   Drinking in college in the perspective of social change. In *The domesticated drug: Drinking among collegians,* ed. George L. Maddox, pp. 27–44. New Haven: College and University Press.
  1971   Alcohol and alcoholism. In *Contemporary social problems,* eds. Robert Merton and Robert Nisbet, pp. 227–270. 3rd ed. New York: Harcourt, Brace, Jovanovich.

Straus, Robert and Seldon Bacon
  1951   Alcoholism and social stability: A study of occupational integration in 2,023 male clinic patients. *Quarterly Journal of Studies on Alcohol* 12:231:260.

Strauss, George and Leonard R. Sayles
  1967   *Personnel: The human problems of management.* Englewood Cliffs, N.J.: Prentice Hall.

Strayer, Robert
  1957   A study of employment adjustment of 80 male alcoholics. *Quarterly Journal of Studies on Alcohol* 18:278–287.

Suchman, Edward A.
  1968   The 'hang-loose' ethic and the spirit of drug use. *Journal of Health and Social Behavior* 9:146–156.

Sussman, Arthur M.
  1964   Work discipline versus private life: An analysis of arbitration cases. *I.L.R. Research* 10:3–13.

Sussman, Marvin B., ed.
  1966   *Sociology and rehabilitation.* Washington: American Sociological Association.

Szasz, Thomas
  1972   Scapegoating military addicts: The helping hand strikes again. *Trans-Action* 9:4–6.

Takala, Martti, Eljas Siro, and Yrjö Toivainen
  1958   Intellectual functions and dexterity during hangover. *Quarterly Journal of Studies on Alcohol* 19:1–13.

Talbott, John A. and James W. Teague
  1969   Marihuana psychosis. *Journal of the American Medical Association* 210: 299–302.

Tannenbaum, Arnold S.
  1965   Unions. In *Handbook of organizations,* ed. James G. March, pp. 710–764. Chicago: Rand McNally & Co.

Tannenbaum, Jeffrey
  1971   Christmas is coming, so be of good cheer and keep your guard up. *Wall Street Journal,* December 10.

Teele, James E.
1970   Social pathology and stress. In *Social Stress,* eds. Sol Levine and Norman A. Scotch, pp. 228–258. Chicago: Aldine.

Thorpe, J. J. and J. T. Perrey
1959   Problem drinking: A follow-up study. *Archives of Industrial Health* 19:24–29.

Tiebout, Harry M.
1949   The act of surrender in the therapeutic process with special reference to alcoholism. *Quarterly Journal of Studies on Alcohol* 10:48–58.
1965   Crisis and surrender in treating alcoholism. *Quarterly Journal of Studies on Alcohol* 26:496–497.

Toynbee, Arnold
1969   The whole iceberg. In *Natural enemies: Youth and the clash of generations,* ed. Alexander Klein, pp. 333–335. New York: Lippincott Company.

Trice, Harrison M.
1957a Identifying the problem drinker on the job. *Personnel* 34:527–533.
1957b A study of the process of affiliation with Alcoholics Anonymous. *Quarterly Journal of Studies on Alcohol* 18:34–47.
1958   Alcoholics Anonymous. *The Annals of the American Academy of Political and Social Science* 315:108–117.
1959   The affiliation motive and readiness to join Alcoholics Anonymous. *Quarterly Journal of Studies on Alcohol* 20:313–320.
1962   The job behavior of problem drinkers. In *Society, culture, and drinking patterns,* eds. David J. Pittman and Charles R. Snyder, pp. 493–510. New York: John Wiley.
1964   New light on identifying the alcoholic employee. *Personnel* 41:1–8.
1965a Reaction of supervisors to emotionally disturbed employees. *Journal of Occupational Medicine* 7:177–188.
1965b Alcoholic employees: A comparison of psychotic, neurotic, and 'normal' personnel. *Journal of Occupational Medicine* 7:94–99.
1966   *Alcoholism in America.* New York: McGraw-Hill.

Trice, Harrison M. and James A. Belasco
1965   Identifying and confronting the alcoholic employee: Role of the industrial nurse. *Industrial Nurses' Journal* 13:7–12.
1966a *Emotional health and employer responsibility.* Bulletin 57. Ithaca: New York State School of Industrial and Labor Relations, Cornell University.
1966b The alcoholic and his steward: A union problem. *Journal of Occupational Medicine,* 12:481–487.
1967   Job absenteeism and drinking behavior. *Management of Personnel Quarterly* 6:7–13.
1968   Supervisory training about alcoholic and other problem employees. *Quarterly Journal of Studies on Alcohol* 29:382–398.
1970   The aging collegian: Drinking pathologies among executive and professional alumni. In *The domesticated drug: Drinking among collegians,* ed. George L. Maddox, pp. 218–234. New Haven: College and University Press.

REFERENCES

Trice, Harrison M. and Paul M. Roman
  1970a Sociopsychological predictors of affiliation with Alcoholics Anonymous: A longitudinal study of treatment success. *Social Psychiatry* 5:51–59.
  1970b Delabeling, relabeling and Alcoholics Anonymous. *Social Problems* 17: 468–480.
  1971 Occupational risk factors in mental health and the impact of role change experience. In *Compensation factors in psychiatric disability and rehabilitation,* ed. Jack J. Leedy, pp. 145–205. Springfield, Ill.: Charles C. Thomas.

Trice, Harrison M., Paul M. Roman, and James A. Belasco
  1969 Selection for treatment: A predictive evaluation of an alcoholism treatment regimen. *International Journal of the Addictions* 4:303–317.

Trice, Harrison M. and J. Richard Wahl
  1958 A rank-order analysis of the symptoms of alcoholism. *Quarterly Journal of Studies on Alcohol* 19:636–648.

Turfboer, Robert
  1959 The effects of in-plant rehabilitation on alcoholics. *The Medical Bulletin of the Standard Oil Company* 19:108–111.

Ullman, A.
  1960 *To know the difference.* New York: St. Martin's Press.

U.S. Congress. House Select Committee on Crime
  1971 *Amphetamines: Fourth report.* House Report no. 91–1807. Washington: Government Printing Office.

U.S. Department of Health, Education and Welfare, National Clearinghouse for Mental Health Information
  1965 *Occupational mental health: A selected bibliography.* Public Health Service Publication no. 1338. Washington, D.C.: Government Printing Office.

U.S. Department of Labor
  1970 *Statistics on manpower: A reprint from the 1970 Manpower Report of the President.* Washington: Government Printing Office.

Visotsky, H.
  1967 Primary prevention. In *Comprehensive textbook of psychiatry,* eds. Alfred M. Freedman and Harold I. Kaplan, pp. 1537–1541. Baltimore: Williams and Wilkins.

Voegtlin, Walter L.
  1940 The treatment of alcoholism by establishing a conditioned reflex. *American Journal of the Medical Sciences* 199:802–810.

Volkman, Rita and Donald R. Cressey
  1963 Differential association and the rehabilitation of drug addicts. *American Journal of Sociology* 69:129–142.

Vollmer, H. and D. Mills
  1966 *Professionalization.* Englewood Cliffs, N.J.: Prentice Hall.

Waldorf, Dan
  1970 Life without heroin: Some social adjustments during long-term periods of voluntary abstentions. *Social Problems* 18:228–243.

Walsh, J.
1964 Psychotoxic drugs: Dodd bill passes Senate, comes to rest in House; critics are sharpening their knives. *Science* 145:1418–1420.

Walton, Richard and Robert McKersie
1965 *A behavioral theory of labor negotiations.* New York: McGraw-Hill.

Warkov, Seymour, Seldon Bacon, and A. Hawkins
1965 Social correlates of industrial problem drinking. *Quarterly Journal of Studies on Alcohol* 26:58–71.

Wechsler, H.
1960 The self-help organization in the mental health field: Recovery, Inc. *Journal of Nervous and Mental Disease* 130:297–314.

Weil, Andrew T., Norman Zinberg and Judith Nelsen
1968 Clinical and psychological effects of marihuana in man. *Science* 162:1234–1242.

Weiner, Hyman
1966 Quoted in *Occupational Mental Health Notes* (September).
1967 Labor-management relations and mental health. In *To work is human,* ed. Alan McLean, pp. 193–202. New York: Macmillan.

Weinstein, Edwin A.
1967 Denial of presidential disability: A study of Woodrow Wilson. *Psychiatry* 30:376–391.

Wellman, W. M., Milton Maxwell, and Pat O'Hollaren
1957 Private hospital alcoholic patients and the changing conception of the typical alcoholic. *Quarterly Journal of Studies on Alcohol* 18:388–408.

Westermeyer, Joseph
1971 Use of alcohol and opium by the Meos of Laos. *American Journal of Psychiatry* 127:1019–1023.

Whyte, William F.
1961 *Men at work.* Homewood, Ill.: Dorsey-Irwin Press.
1969 *Organizational behavior: theory and application.* Homewood, Ill.: Richard Irwin, Inc.

Wiley, Ruth C.
1961 *The self concept.* Lincoln: University of Nebraska Press.

Williams, A. F., L. M. DiCicco, and H. Unterberger
1968 Philosophy and evaluation of an alcohol education program. *Quarterly Journal of Studies on Alcohol* 29:685–702.

Williams, Robin M.
1970 *American society.* 3rd ed. New York: Alfred A. Knopf.

Williams, Roger J.
1959 *Alcoholism: The nutritional approach.* Austin: University of Texas Press.

Willig, Sidney
1971 *Legal considerations: Drug abuse in industry and business.* North Miami, Fla.: Symposium Enterprises.

Wilner, Daniel and Gene Kassebaum
1965 *Narcotics.* New York: McGraw-Hill.

REFERENCES

Winick, Charles
  1960 The use of drugs by jazz musicians. *Social Problems* 7:240–248.
  1961 Physician narcotic addicts. *Social Problems* 9:174–186.
  1964 The cycle of the narcotic addict and of addiction. *United Nations Bulletin of Narcotics* 16:1–11.

Winship, G. M.
  1957 Disulfiram as an aid to psychotherapy in the case of an impulsive drinker. *Quarterly Journal of Studies on Alcohol* 18:666–672.

Winslow, Walter W., Kaney Hayes, Leslie Prentice, William Powles, and W. Donald Ross
  1966 Some economic estimates of job disruption from an industrial mental health project. *Archives of Environmental Health* 13:13–24.

Witkin, Herman, R. Dyk, H. Faterson, D. Goodenough, and S. Karp
  1962 *Psychological differentiation.* New York: John Wiley.

Witkin, Herman A., Stephan A. Karp, and Donald Goodenough
  1959 Dependence in alcoholics. *Quarterly Journal of Studies on Alcohol* 20:493–504.

World Health Organization
  1964 *Report of Expert Committee on Addiction-Producing Drugs.* W.H.O. Technical Report Series no. 273. Geneva: World Health Organization.
  1965 *Report of Expert Committee on Dependence-Producing Drugs.* W.H.O. Technical Report Series no. 312. Geneva: World Health Organization.

Yablonsky, Lewis
  1962 The anti-criminal society: Synanon. *Federal Probation* 26:50–57.
  1965 *The tunnel back: Synanon.* New York: Macmillan.
  1968 *The hippie trip.* New York: Pegasus.

Yolles, S.
  1968 Recent research on LSD, marihuana, and other dangerous drugs. Statement read before the Subcommittee on Juvenile Delinquency of the Committee on the Judiciary, U.S. Senate, March 6.

Zimmerman, Paul
  1971 *A thinking man's guide to pro football.* rev. ed. New York: E. P. Dutton.

Zinberg, N. E. and A. T. Weil
  1969 The effects of marihuana on human beings. *Addictions* 16:26–43.

Index

91